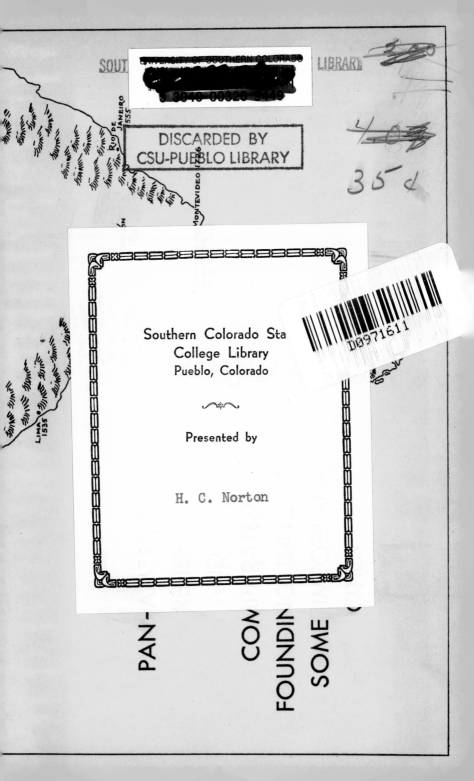

THE ALL-AMERICAN FRONT

Books by
DUNCAN AIKMAN

THE ALL-AMERICAN FRONT

CALAMITY JANE AND THE LADY WILDCATS

THE HOME-TOWN MIND

AMERICA'S CHANCE OF PEACE
(With Blair Bolles)

DUNCAN AIKMAN

THE
ALL-AMERICAN
FRONT

DOUBLEDAY, DORAN & COMPANY, INC.

NEW YORK   1941

PRINTED AT THE *Country Life Press*, GARDEN CITY, N. Y. U. S. A.

To lighten the burro's burden, the gringo eats his hay.

☆

Old customs are breached oftenest.

☆

Lies are the perfumes of dictators.

☆

Only a tailor can consecrate a priest or commission a general.

☆

Nameless men might exist without politics.

☆

*Nature, ashamed that the Andes did not hide the sun,
made the foolishness of man.*

☆

In the brothels of Sorrow, Love is chief procuress.

☆

Even the devil is swindled by hypocrites.

—LATIN-AMERICAN PROVERBS.

Contents

CHAPTER I

Twenty-one Republics among the "Prescriptioneers"

IF YOU HAVE BEEN in touch with Latin America or traveling there recently, your friends and acquaintances, including people who become acquaintances by introducing themselves in public places, have these days an overall consuming question to ask you.

They ask it in tones ranging from suspicion and disgust to acute consternation but rarely any more in tones of purely casual curiosity. Some, including many who are close to the Washington government's defense problems, ask it with hardly less symptoms of mental and glandular tension than patriotic Frenchmen must have suffered in asking, as desperate May sank into despairing June 1940: Will the Maginot line hold?

Freed from superficial exclamations and tangential curiosities, however, America's Question No. 1 about Latin America is this:

"If we get into trouble with the Nazis, will those people down there be with us or against us?"

Suddenly it has become clear, like new perils of the night seen by the light of burning cities, that the twenty republics and 120,000,000 people from the Rio Grande to Cape Horn hold in their hands the key to the future of the United States and to the safety of the Western Hemisphere. Over the awakened groups in our population has come something of the mood—and the dread—of President Jefferson when he announced that he must buy Louisiana because the United States could never be free or secure while a foreign power controlled the mouth of the Mississippi.

Overnight in this year of debacle it has broken in upon the

millions who read their war news and their peace prognoses with horse sense and realism that occupation or domination of any considerable Latin-American area by the totalitarian powers, or even a simple alliance between them and any Latin state, brings the threat of Blitzkrieg to the American land mass; that after that neither the life nor the institutions nor the liberties of the United States can ever be the same.

The frontiers, which *were,* perhaps, on the Rhine after all, must from now on be defended wherever the ruthless power and will-to-conquest of the totalitarian states choose to strike: On the Galapagos, in the tangled politics of Mexico, on the far eastern, Africa-seeking capes of Brazil, in the Panama-commanding valleys of Colombia, along the La Plata estuary. And not defended by arms alone; but by the tact, the will to fair co-operation and the friendliness which, among nations as among individuals, wins friends and keeps them.

For the problem of defending the Western Hemisphere is not to be solved without the help of those near and far neighbors, the peoples of the twenty Latin republics. And whether that help is to be forthcoming now, or in a lasting future, is no question to be simply answered—the more so since it is posed in the midst of today's high-pressure winds of immense wishfulness.

Nothing is simple about Latin America, in fact, and nothing about Latin America is less simple than its complex of feelings toward the United States.

Nor are all the complexes on the below-the-Rio-Grande side. The roots of difficulty in the relationship are tangled as much in North American misunderstanding of Latin values and conventions, in North American indifference to Latin America's vital economic needs, as in Latin misconceptions of North American motives.

How can the United States prepare itself, then, to win from Latin America confidence, support in world policies and hemisphere defense measures, vital economic co-operation, in the eye wink of time there may still be left before we desperately need them?

How ready are the Latin Americans to provide these things?

The answers to these complexities have been unfortunately complicated still further by the incessant labors of ready rationalizers who honestly believe that simplifications *are* answers. During the whole 117 years of the Monroe Doctrine's lifetime, Latin America —doubtless for Washington's diplomatic sins—has been the happy hunting ground of the policy prescriptioneers.

Among the ranking Latin-American experts, for example, Mr Carleton Beals is possibly the liveliest reporter and certainly the nearest thing to a one-man assembly line as a fact collector. But Mr Beals has maintained in his annual rush of persuasive volumes that little more is involved in bettering our understandings with Latin America than having the State Department follow a consistent policy of supporting only liberal and constructively leftist regimes in the "neighbor" republics. The prescription, however, omits a consideration in which complications burgeon like seeds in a weed patch: the fact that championship of "left vs. rightward" ideologies beyond our boundaries would involve us perpetually in Latin America's twenty brands of domestic politics; to say nothing of the embarrassments which sometimes have arisen quite factually in the record when Latin reform statesmen, promoted to presidencies by Washington's favor, have failed to stay put as liberals.

On a slightly higher plane, Mr Waldo Frank—whose several hundred thousand words on the subject are insistently cadenced to leap with Latin-American "life rhythms"—recommends that nothing is so important to hemisphere concord as getting the more or less mystical oversouls of Latin and Northern Americans tuned in together. Quite apart from the obstacles to close esthetic comradeship between masses of people of highly diverse cultural traditions, the difficulty here is that comparatively few social groups in the United States are conscious of having any oversoul to do their chiming with.

On an opposite tangent of perfectionism, I find such clippings as this from the 1939 New York *Times,* in which a certain Colonel H. Murray Jacoby announces, apparently on behalf of certain investment interests, that the kinks in our Latin-American relations can be straightened out by the simple process of putting "radical and experimental" regimes like Mexico's and Chile's in their places, and throwing our diplomatic support to "strong, property-respecting" regimes. Besides involving us in the Latin-American domestic scene almost as gynecologically as Mr Beals' prescription, the Jacoby nostrum would also have the effect of earning us the chronic ill will of the very elements working in the twenty republics to increase the mass purchasing power which Colonel Jacoby's clients presumably would like to thrive on.

One could go on to write an exceptionally enlivening book and do nothing but list the prescriptions. Not all of them come from our side of the Rio Grande. My friends among the Mexican publicists often assert with burning emphasis that all will be well if the New Deal—and its successors—will only restrain "economic imperialists" in their southward ventures and thus relieve the republics of their status as "semi-colonials" of Wall Street. On the other hand, in a recent journey to nineteen of the twenty Latin nations, I seldom in any capital failed to receive persuasive hospitality from financial and political groups who reasoned that a kind of millennium in hemispheric understanding could be achieved if only the Good Neighbor policy were converted into a no-limit—and practically no-collateral—loan policy.

Again, some of the prescriptions have been applied. The Pan-American Union in Washington, for instance, has for decades conducted a publicity campaign to vitalize the twenty-one republics' communities of interest: mainly by representing the neighboring civilizations as being utterly charming and wishfully well disposed toward intrahemispheric tenderness, and free from all evils, social, medical or political, except such as are in the process of hasty cure by miracle-working experts.

More recently, it is only fair to set forth, the Union has risked a bolder—not to say more realistic—venture. As the result of more than three years of effort from two Washington experts in labor problems, Gardner Jackson, of Labor's Non-Partisan League, and Ernest Galarza, it has established, for the collection of factual information on labor relations and mass living standards throughout the hemisphere, a Labor Division of its own, under Mr Galarza's directorship. Director Galarza's scholarly qualities and long specialization in this field are sufficient indication that the fact-gathering phase of the job will be done with extraordinary competence. But the question still remains as to whether the tender-minded urbanity of the Pan-American Union will permit the facts to be presented in their true framework of realism: whether a Labor Division in a "glittering soiree" resort for diplomats will, in the long run, prove more effective than the establishment of a Class Struggle Lodge in the New York Yale Club.

Prescriptioneering is, indeed, the liveliest, if not the best-paid, branch of typewriter and shovel work in the whole field of Latin-American "expertness." And on this point a solemn confession should be made. With my best traveler's virtuosity, I have argued in print for as many different methods of controlling dictators and refining the approach of North American business to the Latin markets as the next "expert." Doubtless even before this chapter is over, I shall be caught prescriptioneering again.

But this does not alter a fundamental confusing factor in the whole scheme of hemisphere politics: nothing is so poisonous to our prospects of an eventual working adjustment to Latin America as—bunk about Latin America.

☆   ☆   ☆

Over against these happy plans for creating beautiful friendships by the twist of a rationalization, we must—if we are to get anywhere in Latin America—place certain realities.

Of the 120,000,000 people in the twenty republics, more than half, certainly, live in a poverty so abject that it makes the standards of living in lower brackets of WPA workers look like the life of Riley. Millions of them do not even know how to want—and this is a point to consider when the prescriptioneers begin talking about the "interplay of mass sympathies"—the leftovers from the national economic table which the WPA workers complain about.

Close to half—more than 90 per cent in at least one republic—are illiterate. An uncounted proportion of them, but certainly a vastly larger proportion than is true of the United States, are chronically sick with debilitating tropical—and tropical slum—diseases.

The 120,000,000 have a basic economy almost as different from ours as ours is different from that of the ancient Roman latifundia: a kind of a master-and-serf relationship, softened here and there by personal courtesy and kindliness, yet hardened, as Southern share-cropper economy has never hardened, by centuries of use and acceptance.

The Latin peoples have come out of a strikingly different set of historical experiences (history textbooks often spread a special brand of pedagogical silliness by emphasizing the chance resemblances!) with a startlingly different set of objectives in life and politics, and of methods in attaining them.

Out of different racial stocks, different educational mills and different religious orientations, they have emerged with a culture so distinct from ours that it sometimes has difficulty in understanding what our culture is talking about.

And even if all the experiences of the republics exactly had duplicated ours, and the 120,000,000 were swept by some sudden uncontrollable impulse to make themselves exactly "like us," their geography and their climate would not allow it.

There is nothing in all these sharp differentiations, however, for the citizens of the United States, awash in their natural and fiscal and educational bounties, to feel superior and smug about. We took, by luck rather than prevision, the better part of the Western land mass; and, coming from a different historical background, galloped cheerfully through the developing processes that went with the environment. It would have been difficult to make peons out of a people with the Mississippi valley hanging under their sunsets.

So the most constructive generalization to be drawn from the differentiations is that there, but for the grace of geography and history and economics—and God, if you like your scapegoats august—goes the 1940 annual banquet attendance of the Zenith Chamber of Commerce.

But the importance of the differentiations does not even lie in the specific width of our psychological separations from "the neighbors." It lies in the misunderstandings, the incompatibilities, the everlasting play of forces at cross purposes, which the separations have set up.

The 120,000,000 know, for instance—dimly and apathetically at the bottom; with knife-edged surgical realism at the top—that we are richer and more powerful than they, to a large extent because we were luckier in our original American real-estate selections; that we have somehow—with not very good *Latin* manners at any rate—confused our original sound judgment in left-over land masses with moral and economic merits. So the natural and not unhealthy envy of the luckless for the lucky has fed for generations below the Rio Grande on our peculiar pomposities, our condescending genialities and our self-assurance of superior virtue.

Out of such by-products of the differentiations, then, has come a chronic disposition on Latin America's part to distrust us—not always even fairly.

Most of the twenty republics have resented the Monroe Doctrine for nearly a half-century as an affront to their sovereignty and a hypocritical device for bringing about the eventual annexation of their territories. When our interests below the Rio Grande have conflicted with those of the European powers, Latin-American statesmen, as a class—unless their immediate self-interests were heartily involved—have rarely failed to support the Europeans.

Though Brazil and Guatemala, with other countries still more obviously under our influence, backed us up twenty-three years ago in the World War's first round, the crucial republics of Mexico and Argentina and, a little more diffidently, perhaps, Chile, were, if not officially pro-German, definitely anti-American.

At the 1938 Pan-American Congress at Lima the dominating Latin states joined together to whittle down Mr Hull's effort to form a "hemisphere front" against the totalitarian nations into an extravagantly loopholed declaration of good intentions. At the Panama and Havana conferences of 1939 and 1940 they only consented to more concrete measures of "solidarity," after their economic and religious ties with the totalitarians had been temporarily weakened by the second World War's outbreak.

Our other relationships have been hardly happier than the

strictly diplomatic. Our efforts at improving trade relations have been handicapped by the disinclination of Latin-American governments to put either their debts or their fiscal arrangements on a tradeworthy footing, and by internecine jealousies between the republics as to which would get the largest share of Uncle Sam's favors.

Our attempts at economic penetration have embroiled us almost invariably in Latin-American domestic politics. Punitively taxed by the graft-ridden and dictator-ruled states, or harassed like an invading army by leftist governments, our investors have found no secure footing anywhere.

Intellectual contacts on both sides have been on the whole—and somewhat self-consciously—little more than exchanges between specialists in exotics. In the sphere of political sympathies, when Latin-American leftist statesmen are not damning us as capitalist imperialists, rightist dictators are generally quarantining our democratic ideas and practices as a menace to public morals.

In a century and a quarter of talking about it, we have not, in a word, won Latin America's liking or understanding, friendship or co-operation. Latin-American relations have revolved during that period in an atmosphere in which the participants have seldom cherished the same aims, entertained the same concepts of themselves or each other, or meant the same things by the same language.

☆ ☆ ☆

The task of our foreign policy, then, in the moments when it has attempted realistic approaches seriously, has been to balance the aspirations of the prescription vendors—most of which are reasonably right, just aspirationally speaking—against the factual incompatibilities of things on the Latin-American front as they are.

This has not, of course, inhibited the State Department from occasional adventures in prescriptioneering on its own account. Mr Roosevelt's Good Neighbor policy, except as implemented with concrete programs, is inevitably an "emotional simplifier" of the basic problem of intimate adjustments; if only for the reason

[*8*]

that few peoples are less physically "neighbors" than ourselves and the Uruguayans.

Secretary of State Cordell Hull's reciprocal trade treaties were also harped on occasionally, before war tensions grew desperate, as a kind of old-home medicine-chest specific for the ills of the hemisphere. Undersecretary of State Sumner Welles is on the radio record with the no less perfectionist remedy than that, in our relations with the twenty republics, there should be no "shadow of suspicion or misunderstanding."

Mr Welles's perfectionism, however, assays some dilution from the fact that he is an old hand at dealing Latin-American compliments. And on the whole the Roosevelt II State Department has dealt with its hemisphere problems with unprecedented psychic acumen. It took its partial defeat at Lima with a minimum of moral pout and snobbery, and at Panama, in September 1939, it had its partial reward.

Its program for wartime economic co-operation between the republics was adopted practically without change, and its carefully developed project of banning belligerent naval operations from Western Hemisphere oceans and maintaining an interrepublican warship guard to police the disturbers away, was accepted so enthusiastically that the conference could actually be closed, for almost the first time in Latin-American history, only three days after schedule. Early Argentine and Uruguayan objections that it seemed more in keeping with old international-law rules to permit submarines access to American ports so long as they kept their flags flying and stayed only for their literal refueling needs, were maintained after a fashion, and indeed the final Conference action left the American governments free to exclude or admit submarines as their special neutrality emergencies dictated. But arguments on this point were free from the traditional Pan-American rancors. The Argentines made their point less like wilful obstructionists than like men in a friendly debate stating the case for the academic chiefly for the purpose of having the thesis better examined.

Yet it would be a mistake to represent the Panama result as a triumph over the incompatibilities. More realistically, it was a typically Latin-American reaction to a quick change in certain extremely concrete circumstances.

The United States, and Undersecretary of State Welles, came to Panama with the fiscal and economic power to ruin or succor a dozen or more republics whose trade ties and money links with Germany, via the barter export-import system and its Aski-mark accompaniments, had been completely disrupted by the war. Uncle Sam was thus due for a good deal of affectionate, and not wholly insincere, whisker-stroking if only because he had suddenly become the only banker and grocer on his street.

In addition, Washington's Panama conferees came to a Latin America disturbed about dim and frightening issues which large segments of United States opinion would probably be inclined to dismiss as "intangibles." The appealing legend, circulated so effectively throughout the twenty republics during the preceding few years, of totalitarianism as a world shield against social anarchy and bolshevist atheism, had broken down before the concrete fact of the new Hitler-Stalin comradeship. The comradeship, as Latin America saw it, might or might not grow into military alliance. But, at least while the Panama sessions lasted, Latin America felt a curious alarm from the vague threats from overseas to the religious and social order which the ruling interests and classes of the republics prize even above their independence of monopolist grocers.

It was a time to take shelter from indefinite perils somewhere. With Mr Welles's proposals of economic co-operation and naval quarantine, shelter was there.

Yet as the war has continued to alter world power balances, the results gained at Panama have seemed increasingly specious. What was originally a problem of minor economic co-operations and of keeping the war at arm's length from the hemisphere has suddenly become a problem of bargaining with new economic control systems in Europe; of consolidating the coasts of two continents for defense against attacks from abroad more terrible than Panama dreamed of.

Can peoples so alienated by misunderstandings and incompatibilities, distrustful of each other's capacities and motives, live under a cartel system rigidly regulating their exports and imports, and allowances of banking credit, even if there were no other way to save themselves from economic domination by the Nazis? Can countries, fearful of each other's military programs and political ambitions, fired by old and constantly reheated nationalistic jealousies, frame a common defense plan?

Some progress was made towards solving these problems at the conference of American Foreign Ministers which met at Havana during July, 1940. Yet there is still no assurance that a sudden German victory could not upset these solutions: the more easily because at Havana, as at Panama, the stream of incompatibilities flowed on. For instance, the delegates found Panama City, the host of the 1939 conference separated by sniffy prejudices regarding the "color line" from the American-born social and intellectual leaders of the Canal Zone. Zone society was suggesting its private views of the "good neighbor" policy by wittily nicknaming young Americans who married Panamanian debutantes "squaw men."

More than once, from the Latin side, the comment was to be overheard both before the Panama and the Havana conferences that at the worst a German victory might relieve Latin America of the threat of Yanqui imperialism; might actually make it easier for the twenty republics to retire, each to its own national selfhood, and live as it pleased.

☆   ☆   ☆

For the passion of the twenty republics for selfhood—as over and against the kindly and condescending disposition of the United States to remold "neighbor" selfhoods in its own culturally complacent image—is the crux of the Latin-American problem, rather than the so luminously plausible specialties of the prescriptioneers.

Our Latin-American relations are not a problem of economic or political or educational adjustments, or even of medical histories, so much as they are problems of getting us used to the fact that our national individualities are shockingly different. That the differences—in all that they imply of clashing tastes in all things

[*11*]

from business success methods to standards of sexual morals—are matters of course and probably beyond redemption; probably even beyond desirability of redemption.

The twenty-one selfhoods, indeed, might even become adjusted better if we and the "neighbors" stopped making such strenuously self-conscious efforts to make ourselves like each other better.

But to make even a beginning at such an enterprise in prescriptionless prescriptioneering, we need to understand what the selfhoods are like and what they sprang from.

First, they came out of geography; out of the body of the continents; if you prefer being emotional about it, out of the womb of the Western land mass.

CHAPTER II

Strictly Anatomical

THE BEST APPROACH to the anatomy of Latin-American nationalism is through the air.

By air, when the skies are clear, you overlook all day long vast circles of ground—ten thousand square miles per glance at the easy altitudes, twenty thousand at the medium heights, fifty thousand when you fly with the condors. And every hour of your flight, the circle changes.

When you have covered the fifteen thousand miles of the Pan-American Airways route from Brownsville, Texas, to Buenos Aires and Santiago and back, your eyes have rested on close to a million square miles of territory: more than the most strenuous explorers managed to survey in their hard-spent lifetimes; more than normally ardent train travelers and motorists manage to see in several decades. And you have done something more than "look at the scenery" through gaps in the foliage, through offshore haze of the shipping lanes, or the keyholes of railway-coach windows. You have looked at the framework of life for diverse societies, the ground plans for the living and working rooms of nations. You know now how continents are made.

It is, on purely esthetic grounds, an incredibly exhilarating experience.

A quarter of an hour below Brownsville, the last ragged Mexican truck farm fades away, and you are alone over the corn-colored tropical jungle, with fishing birds diving over the glittering sand-spits far below you into the green-and-gold Gulf waters. Slowly the hazy blue mountains grow on your western flank, pushing you languidly toward the seaboard. Out of Tampico you hover for a moment over the gray Pánuco River, then take off into mountains —small and opulently rounded mountains, first, spaced with the sunny curves of coffee and banana groves waved over by regiments of wind-stirred palms; then dark and evergreen-shrouded mountains, lonely and precipitous, where at vast intervals some mine or goatherds' village or a monastery ruin confronts the winds with the winter-bitten look of feudal fortresses.

Suddenly, jagged, blood-dark peaks and roaring cloud scuds are clawing at your sides in the 13,000-foot passes above the timber line; until, with a series of enormous spine-shattering jolts, you reach the peace of sunlight again over the wide, dusty Valley of Mexico.

In ways like this for fifteen thousand miles the loveliness of the earth's body uncovers itself beneath your plane in indefatigable pageant. In the hot spring wind the afternoon I left Mexico City for the south, dust whirls walked over the shining valley like a regiment of Jack's beanstalks gone dervish. Yet beyond the lava shoulder and blazing snow cone of Popocatepetl, we plunged suddenly into four hundred miles of cloud. The tropical valleys, when we saw them for rare instants between the torn mist fringes, were dark as curtained rooms. Then at Tapachula, on the Guatemala border, a lurid sun fought with thunderclouds over a violet and sulphurous Pacific. Huge streams of tropical rain drenched us, as we came into the frowsy little airport, suave to the body—after the upland droughts—as a gently medicated bath.

Again above the clouds, at fifteen thousand feet, the Guatemala passage was like a trek over snowfields in sculptured battlements, with the black volcano peaks thrust through like wind-scoured islands. Later, still on the air lane to El Salvador, the volcanoes were weather-rounded into prodigiously upright bosoms of forest, with blue and flamingo-colored lakes nestling between them in the heart of a green-and-mauve land. And over Honduras hung a sinister haze from the late dry season brush fires; and the Costa Rican hills were brown as August Berkshires. On the day when we slithered back and forth from ocean to ocean across Panama to the foot of the Colombian Andes, the palm mountains of the Isthmus were white under the lash of the wind.

Once, flying past Concepción volcano in the middle of Lake Nicaragua, I thought the waters quarreling around its foot in the clear sunlight were the bluest I had ever seen—until I looked away from the noon sun over the dark forested ridges southwestward and saw the Pacific.

☆   ☆   ☆

Yet slowly it dawns on even the most enravished traveler that the excitingly variegated beauty of the lands under his eye has a practical meaning: a meaning plain as the flush in fever; as descriptive of the limitations of life for the civilizations inhabiting them as a medical history.

Half an hour out of Brownsville the central facts in Latin America's economic-geographic anatomy begin to declare themselves. All night long, if you have approached Mexico by air across the United States, you have flown from Pittsburgh to Dallas over the Mississippi valley. All the early morning you have flown over the vast alluvial Texas plain.

Then, abruptly, half an hour out of Matamoros, flying south, the pleasant farm-dotted Rio Grande delta land stops. Swamp and jungle take its place; swamp and sandspit, swamp and more swamp take over the coast line, and for six thousand miles you will see no more wide farming plains watered by a river system.

The Pánuco cuts through softly rounded hills to the Gulf at Tampico, but its delta is a mere fingerprint. Vera Cruz is a city built on swamps and sandspits at the end of watercourses, more stagnant lagoons than creek mouths. So, from Tampico south to Turbo, the little morass-ringed Negro hamlet in Colombia where we took off for the Andes, are most of the Mexican and Central American ports. And so are many others.

Moreover, almost before you have begun to miss the delta lands, the reason for their absence makes its appearance—the mountains hanging on your western horizon. At Brownsville, less than two hours ago, the mountains were a thousand miles upstream at El

Paso. At Memphis, where the plane landed for a few moments last midnight, they were a thousand miles northeast at Pittsburgh —or more than half a transatlantic passage away at the Forks of the Missouri in the Montana Rockies. In between are the vast river systems, draining the mountain country, organizing the carriage of debris washed down from the peaks by the melting snows and the summer cloudbursts, endlessly working to build up— given a fair chance by engineering and human soil-use habits—new farm lands for old.

But to the south, from the Mexican coast line you can see the mountains. Between them and the sea there is no room to form river systems. Drenched by the enormous tropical rainfall, they are drained by an anarchy of torrents, and the coastal lowlands are their dumping sink.

There are local variations in the pattern, of course: lowlands where the sugar cane is not drowned out and banana plantations flourish; pleasant prairies rolling down to the sea from the older Brazilian mountains between Bahia and Pernambuco, with the cotton and sugar patches marching clear to the beaches. There are the beginnings of a reasonably swamp-free delta along the Magdalena River above Barranquilla, and along the Guayas in Ecuador a perfectly made one, as large, perhaps, as the Connecticut Valley below the Berkshires.

But in general much of Latin America must farm in its mountains, work and create wealth and life for itself in its mountains, because its coast lands are useless, its interior undeveloped. In almost every phase of Latin-American life that is worth considering, the anatomy of the mountains is the overwhelming conditioning factor.

For living in mountains is, in its way, an economic luxury. It is perfectly true that certain peoples do well at it. The Swiss, for example, live comfortably off their dairy herds, their toy-making, watches and their handicrafts. So, on the whole, do the Rocky Mountain States, off their prize potatoes and their protected sugar beets. So, as a rule, do peoples with the capital resources to work their own mines and a sufficiently balanced labor economy to assure their mine workers reasonable wages. They pay, in other words, for the privilege of living in the mountains by producing de-luxe or indispensable products within practicable shipping range of the world's principal markets. But the Balkan peoples, more remote from markets, and with less indispensable products and fewer skills, live poorly, while in the Himalayas the Afghans and the Tibetans scarcely, according to Western standards of comfort, live at all. Somewhere between the two extremes stand the Latin Americans.

Even before the brief flight from Tampico to Mexico City is over, the air traveler begins to see why. This mountain farming is expensive farming. Plowing the steep fields rolling so picturesquely over the lower summits, or slanting sunnily upward between pine-darkened precipices, requires more in man effort, if not in pesos, than plowing the Mississippi plain. Holding the soil in place on the mountain slopes or in the bottom lands of the stream-torn gorges, when tropical cloudbursts fall six inches to the hour with no flood engineers on call, is a personal feud against erosion such as rarely occurs even in nightmares of Washington's Interior Department. Forty miles to a railhead over the hard-surfaced highways of Idaho, with the year's potato crop tucked away in trucks in the pink of mechanical efficiency, is as simple as driving to town for the Wednesday-night movies. But forty miles to a railhead with a dozen cartloads of corn over the rain-bogged mud wagon trails of the Mexican mountains is an expedition requiring little less than a safari.

And when the Mexican farmer gets to the railhead, what happens? He must sell his corn in the market town to mountaineers poorer than himself, since if they had grown corn of their own this season they would not be buying it. Or he must ship it at the ruinous freight rates of mountain railroads down to some regional city or valley metropolis or port which is a center of mountaineers' penury. And if, instead of corn, his safari brings in some international commerce commodity like coffee or sugar or bananas, the difference is only fractional and not necessarily in the farmer's favor. He must still charge the burdensome freight rates against his profits—it makes no difference that his factors or his customers technically pay them—in order to ship to a world market already glutted.

No world markets bid against each other for the mountain plantation's products. The world markets are far away, and no specific Latin-American region produces anything in quantity that is specifically indispensable. No vast industrial populations on the plains or thriving seaport cities snap up the mountains' harvests because there are no plains, and the seaports—like the coasts for highlands' rainfall—are economic drainage dumps for the mountaineers' poverty. Mountain economy is expensive economy, and the Latin Americans, by their geographical circumstances from the Rio Grande to the Plate River systems, are essentially locked within it.

In being so locked, they are also confined within a vicious circle. Good roads would make their shipments to market cheaper and easier. Public flood-control works would ease their erosion problems. Mechanized implements and instruction in farming technology would make their farming more efficient and profitable —relieve it of unnecessary costs and of the perpetual need of race-stultifying man effort. But a mountain farm living from one bean and corn crop to the next cannot equip itself with the latest expensive gadget for cultivating and harvesting; or even with elsewhere discarded pre-1914 gadgets. The mountain republic's government cannot build concrete highways and flood-control works and maintain agricultural schools out of the taxes on mountaineer farmers who barely feed themselves; or out of the taxes on city and industrial populations which live by the mountain farm's all but pauperized purchasing power. The mountain farm cannot prosper until it has these things. And it cannot have them because it does not prosper.

All through Central America and below Panama this sickness of the mountain economy keeps pace with the mountains' beauty. Less than an hour from the Colombian eastern coast, you are flying over Andes. Higher and higher the vast regular ridges of the ranges run, like hazards on a golf course for gigantic deities before Chronos; knife-blades of frost and green jade thrust upward beyond the airs for the delectation of solar powers. On stormy afternoons your Scadta plane may fly nineteen thousand feet to clear them.

In between the vast valley floors lie, level as lakes of dark green land: Antioquía, about Medellín, bright with red and white herds in the fields; the Magdalena, at Bogotá, dark with orchards and winter vegetable patches; at Cali, the Cauca shimmering back into the heat haze the white-and-gold radiance of cotton and cane. There have been no such stretches of flat and arable land since you flew out of the Mexican plain over the shoulder of Popocatepetl. Nevertheless Colombia remains, plainly to the eye, mountain-locked in an anarchy of valleys.

No valley has outlet to the sea—and markets—except through mountain walls down precipitous and all but impassable gorges. No valley has natural intercommunication with another. Bogotá is just over an hour's flight from Medellín, barely the distance from Indianapolis to Columbus. Yet the railway, doubling back and forth over the lower ends of the intervening ranges, delivers you from one city to the other in from forty-eight to sixty hours. Cali is no farther from Bogotá than Cleveland from Chicago. But to plunge over even an approximate straight-line course from one to the other, you would need in your baggage equipment for arctic and Himalayan explorations. No government could build railroads and motor highways over those regiments of knifelike summits without the wealth of an empire to bear the cost and the shipping volume of an empire to justify it.

Now, to be sure, Colombia flies. Salesmen fly to their customers. Clients fly to their lawyers. Socialites of Bogotá and the valley centers fly to country house parties; corpses and family corteges fly to funerals; poor Indians fly to ask the government for jobs, or to relatives in trouble with the authorities away from home.

It is progressive; it promotes the national sense of unity—it is also, no doubt, inevitable—but there is another side to it. To the cost of living in mountains, Colombia, in a practical sense, has merely added the high price of airplane travel. Since you cannot fly Antioquía milk and beef to Bogotá and Cali, or Cauca cotton and cane to Medellín, her commerce still remains essentially intravalley commerce. Her main world export commodities, coffee and

[19]

minerals, still flow down to the seaports by costly and tortuous routes. Colombia's vast intrinsic wealth stays dammed up within the Andes hardly less than in the days, two decades ago, when Bogotá, three weeks upstream from Barranquilla by dangerous portages and a constantly deteriorating succession of river steamers, was the remotest capital of any functioning Western government. Certain inconveniences have been relieved, but the expensiveness of mountain economy has not been cured by any invention of the Wright brothers.

Neither has it been cured in Ecuador. The great 10,000-foot equatorial tableland lying about the foot of Cotopaxi and Chimborazo between Cajabamba and Otavalo will grow every fruit and every grain produced in western Europe. But what use are apples and pears and grapes and wheat and barley which must be hauled down Andean precipices and then sent five thousand miles overseas in order to reach markets which cannot absorb the fruits and grains they have already? Not even the workers on the sugar and cocoa plantations in the Ecuadorean coastal provinces can eat them. The mountains are too poor and too underpopulated to buy the plantations' products, except in driblets. The plantations are too poor to buy the products of the mountains.

And beyond Ecuador even the narrowly self-sufficient economy of the great valleys vanishes. Along the Peruvian coast, and for all but an hour of a full day's flight down the appalling worm-line's length of Chile, your plane moves over gray sand, yellow sand, brown sand, the copper-green sand of the nitrate countries. The coast, to be sure, is no longer a drainage dump for the mountains, because there is no longer any drainage. You have entered the great Humboldt current rainless belt, and for a distance as great as from Washington to Los Angeles you fly over desert. Even when you climb, on the way up to Arequipa and La Paz, over the gnarled coastal tongues of the mountains, you are flying over desert—granite desert instead of sand.

The mountains themselves are desert. All of two days they march beside you on your eastern flank in a line that becomes as monotonous as a parade of jeweled elephants holding each other's tails. But their flanks shimmer with tones of blue and obsidian and lapis lazuli, the colors of bare rock walls. The green jade knife-edges of the grassy Colombian summits have vanished. Only the glittering snowcaps show where moisture begins again. And from the Ecuadorean border to Ovalle, on the edge of the Chilean culti-vated lands at last, not a single green field that you see from the air will be without its border of wastelands.

Now and then at huge intervals the pattern is broken. Once to the hour, perhaps, narrow irrigation patches break out along the Peruvian shore. Now and then, a hundred miles apart in Central Peru—five hundred miles, perhaps, in northern Chile—at the bottom of some enormous canyon a narrow strip of green follows a river course up the bottoms, spangled with the tile roofs of ranch houses and little towns. Essentially the West Coast economy is a mountain economy further constricted—the economy of the oasis.

Or rather, a combination bringing out the worst features of both economies. For in these lonely canyon settlements no forty miles of perilous mud road leads to a market town or railhead. The railroads run to the mines—to Cuzco and Cerro de Pasco and the Bolivian tin mountains. But rails cannot be laid for the conven-ience of settlers up little ribbons of creek-grown grass no bigger than a New England township. Twisting coils of tire tracks across the sand may show where a highway is in embryo—mainly for the convenience of taxgatherers. Slowly, over the tire-lacerating granite and old lava, the road may even lead down to a little fringe of settlement about a few irrigated acres which passes for a seaport. But the seaport is a hundred miles away, two hundred, maybe three hundred. Why should the farmer in the canyon hamlet, with an extra cartload of corn or beans from a lucky year's harvest, even bother to know that the road is there?

Eventually, late on the second day, you fly out of it. The valleys of central Chile are as fertile as the California valleys. The roads, like the California highways, run easily down to the sea. Then, when you have flown eastward from Chile past the snow bulk of Aconcagua, you come out suddenly over the arid Argentine range country—a land as fine for cattle as the Wyoming high plains. Three hours more, and at Córdoba, you are looking down at limit-less green horizons of grain-teeming fields. Your six thousand miles are over, and you have come once more, in the deltas of the Paraná, the Paraguay and the Uruguay, to a great river system's alluvial plain.

Afterward come the rolling prairies of Uruguay and the sprawling immensity of Brazil. Yet the immensity has also, in contrast to the lands of the Cordillera, a kind of sprawling unity. There are jungles—hundreds of thousands of square miles of jungles leading down along the Iguazú toward the empty and melancholy plains of Paraguay; a million square miles of jungle choking the Amazon valley to the Andean foothills. But rivers pierce the jungles, and one can follow them to whatever trade offerings the jungle has. The roads and the railways can be built around it to the iron and manganese mines on the upper Paraguay, to tap the future wealth that may roll down from the Bolivian Andes, to haul the cattle away from the Paraguayan prairies when—if ever—the ticks are cleared from them and the cattle are there.

Brazil, too, for most of the two thousand miles from the Uruguayan border to Bahia, is a tumble of mountains, green and well watered and fertile as the prairies. But they are old mountains. As with our own Appalachians, erosion millions of years ago did its worst with them. The roads climb easily over their rounded summits and follow the soft contours of the valleys to the sea and valley railheads and trading centers. Their drainage is a matter of ancient adjustments. Their streams and short rivers plunge down between green and violet promontories to the ocean, building pleasant little deltas of coastal farm land, deepening harbors with their flow instead of filling swamps.

Through this vast tableland, the Brazilian—more hillsman than mountaineer—lives at a certain ease. He can trade with the plains and the cities. His harvests move easily overseas. He has the crops of the mountains, the coffee and the corn and grains of the temperate regions, the mountains' exhilarating climate and their beauty. The mountains do not lock him in. By the isolation of his tremendous distances, he is shut away, no doubt, from certain main currents of world life, and is, in his social habits, something of the same provincial the American pioneer was in the Mississippi valley a hundred years ago. But, even if only in a slight way, he belongs to the economy of a great land mass. He is not crushingly handicapped in a struggle for a footing in the economy of the world.

Yet nowhere in Latin America, not even in Brazil or in Argentina, is the mountain economy very far away. It conditions, after all, the psychology of the Mexicans, the Central Americans, the Colombians, the Venezuelans, the Peruvians—of sixty million people between the Rio Grande and the Chilean valleys.

Shut away with their trade resources on their vast, remote plateaus, they are poor and imperfectly informed, or even illiterate, because they can only afford poor schools. Remote they are, in the mass, untraveled. So they cling to old provincial habits of thought and customs and know little of the world.

Brooding generation after generation on what they lack—for most of them are conscious of it—they confront civilization at large with a provincial's jittery mistrust, both of the foreigner and of themselves.

The man from the next valley, they rationalize, may be smarter in horse trades, so it is well to keep him at arm's length, both in business relations and friendship. The foreigner from North America or Europe may suspect that we are lacking in culture. Hence the proper strategy is to overwhelm him with formal entertainment and extravagant displays of manners. The politicians of the next republic would undoubtedly like to exploit us. So it is sensible not to let diplomatic relations become too cordial —and for such subjects as political or economic co-ordination to remain undiscussable. The Yanquis are overwhelmingly stronger, and no doubt have materialistic designs on our resources. So outwitting them in business deals and local politics and making them faintly ridiculous, as often as the occasion offers, will establish our superior subtlety as well as help to keep them in their places.

Even the least logical of Latin America's political divisions, even the republics which barely function as economic units and cannot defend themselves, serve, while these ways of thought last, a need which runs deeper than practicalities. No Latin-American valley, in the teeth of these variegated passions for nationalism, will be ruled from other people's mountains. No

Latin-American politician will benefit, discipline or even exploit a people not his own. Ecuador in continuing to be Ecuador and Honduras in continuing to be Honduras preserve something more precious to the mountaineer than horse sense.

Thus, out of the viruses of the continental anatomy, the passion of the republics for nationalistic selfhood grows. And in obvious and compelling ways the republics of the plains and the river systems, too, are influenced by it.

The Brazilians live in lazy, hand-to-mouth sufficiency off the tropics' physical abundance. Many Argentines, from their cattle and grain lands and the world commerce of Buenos Aires, live a life almost as rich in sophisticated pleasures and the gadgetry of creature comforts—barring central heating—as the Chicagoans. Uruguay's little suburban civilization about Montevideo is as compact as, and only a little less comfortable than, Denmark's. Though the Paraguayans, on their tick-ridden prairie, are as poor as the Bolivians in their two-mile-high oasis, they are conscious at least that their river systems unite them with the world.

Each of the lowland nations reflects, with delighted vanity, that she is richer or whiter or more sophisticated than the mountain peoples; more important, more crucial to the world's political balances, more worthy of civilization's respectful obeisances. But the world is far away and may not understand this. The world-at-large, being addicted to simplicities, is inclined to lump all Latin Americans together. It does not always clearly distinguish the Argentine from the Guatemalan, the Brazilian from the Ecuadorean, even when he lives in Paris and keeps race horses and mistresses from the Folies Bergères.

The part of the Latin-American world which does not belong to the mountain economy is perpetually hagridden, in short, by an inner compulsion to prove that it belongs to something better; that racially and culturally, in sophistication and military power, each lowland political division constitutes an immeasurably superior society. In effect, to demonstrate that they are above the petty nationalisms of the mountains, the river and plains republics go in for cults of national selfhood even more showy and Balkanized.

Argentine foreign policy must be touchy and unco-operative in international undertakings to show that Argentina is a world power which needs to court no other power's good opinion. Argentine manners are surly—apologize to your Argentine fellow passenger for lurching against him in the aisle of your airplane, and you will soon learn how surly—to show that no citizen of the strong republic needs to practice the mountaineer provincial's methods of ingratiation.

Brazil, on the other hand, must associate with the world powers to feel one of them: must sit in their councils with an uneasy will to be charming, follow them in their wars and their political slogans. While her statesmen in the past have made handsome speeches on the peculiar affinities between Rio de Janeiro and Washington, Brazil by no means has always turned her back on the gaudy bait of totalitarian friendship. And where the Argentine frowns at even the normal courtesies, the Brazilian, if you let an hour go by without complimenting him on his sympathy with American viewpoints, is desolate.

Geography, the shape of the continents, has thus made the plains and river republics provincials along with the mountain nations. Poor or relatively rich, at the ends of the world's trade lanes or isolated, the twenty republics are proud with a sensitive, often a seemingly pompous and silly pride, because they are afraid of the judgments of strangers.

Slowly, perhaps, certain power-age forces—air travel's assaults on the barriers of sheer distance, the mass sophistication that comes over the radio, world standardization of industrial methods—may modify this aloofness, dull the edges of these suspicions and prejudices. But while the land masses remain as they are, the psychological fixations of provincialism are hardly to be removed by the mere wishful thinking of experts and diplomats. The jealous individualism of the republics is a Latin-American policy's first reality.

Yet along with so much individualism go curious traces of cultural and emotional dependence upon an older world. In spite of the republics' sensitive pride in the local life flavors which isolation has preserved, they have not been able to turn their backs upon Europe as a people could do whose business was filling a great river valley, with western mountains and a still more distant western ocean before its eyes.

Brazil fills no western valleys because its valleys are jungle; and the mountains that loom over the tree fronds on the mud-rushing upper rivers are Bolivian and Peruvian, rather than Brazilian, mountains.

Hence, even the most glamorous and self-sufficient of the Latin-American population centers have been bound more closely to Madrid and Rome, or to pre-*Blitzkrieg* Paris than to each other or to any compelling sense of common destiny.

By a never quite broken umbilical impulse, the republics are a little less separate from Europe's political passions and wars than Nebraska—or even Washington—is. They are less separate to the extent that a phrase like "to hell with abroad" lacks meaning for them.

After all, the Spanish and Portuguese colonial settlements came out of Europe's first onset of wars for the modern balance-of-power system. Colonies were precious because they would give Spain the gold with which to fight the wars for Philip the Second's sixteenth-century brand of Hitlerism. Later it was out of the nineteenth-century wars for the balance of power that the republics wrested their independence.

It is a curious fact about the twenty republics that they are tied to older civilizations by history almost as much as they are separated from each other—and from ourselves—by geography.

CHAPTER III

History As Hangover

F ROM WASHINGTON I can drive forty miles to Manassas or seventy miles to Gettysburg and see houses still pockmarked from the shooting in a war seventy-five years ago. Or down at the Capitol, the guides will show me vague stains under the paint on the sector of the original wall beneath the Rotunda staircase. "Where the British tried to burn us out in 1814," they say. "The scorch marks have never quite worn off."

But in Rio de Janeiro a few months ago when we were driving out to the Country Club, friends pointed out a pleasant villa dizzily perched on a sea cliff hundreds of feet above the highway. Its windows were shattered, and there were strange, gaping holes in its walls like an estate mansion washed up by a Long Island hurricane. "The Fascists' hangout," the friends explained briefly. "On the night of the putsch, while the shock troops of the gang were downtown in the palace trying to kill the President, the navy stood offshore and whaled the hell out of it!"

Or, in Mexico, on the paved highway toward Cuernavaca and Taxco, as you climb toward the top of the pass through the western Sierras, you come startlingly, in a tangled grass plot in front of the mountain forest, on a huddle of thirteen cheap metal crosses. Thirteen generals died here before the firing squad one morning in 1927, a rough wooden sign declares, as a warning to all soldiers and civilians tempted in their loyalty to the republic.

There is more in these contrasts than a simple difference between sight-seeing items for tourists. In the United States evidences of political violence are preserved as fairly academic holy relics. Houses battered by the Civil War, stones scorched by the flames of invasion essentially are museum pieces. In Latin America violence is something that happened in 1927, or last year, or yesterday, and can easily happen again tomorrow: a normal manifestation of current practical politics. It is no more archaically quaint than a Washington lobbyist buying a drink for a congressman. Violence in Latin America is a product of history, but it is also a living process in a history that marches on.

Gettysburg's painted battle relics and the crosses by a Mexican roadside point, in fact, to an impasse of understanding between Yankee and Latin-American cultures more subtle and far more drastic than the differences between their geographical environments. For history in the United States is primarily the study of conditions which the nation has left behind. In Latin America history is a pattern of living which, generation after generation, through all the technological and political changes from the sixteenth to the twentieth centuries, has been zealously repeated.

The development of the United States, indeed, has been almost a flight from historical inheritance. The settlement process itself was, for most of the colonials, a deliberate escape from the British social and religious hierarchy and from what was left of British feudalism. The pioneering age of the nineteenth century was an escape from the social and economic restraints of the old seaboard colonial life. All the "New Deals" proposed from Populism to Roosevelt II have been efforts to shake off social and economic stratifications imposed upon the continent by the machine age's first plutocrats.

This instinct toward easy divorcement from the past has given to United States history a series of constantly shifting emphases—a quality of almost lightninglike change. To today's huge practical problem of adapting the nation's production plant to the economy of the power era, the passions of the slavery struggle and the windy states'-rights debates of Webster and Calhoun seem hardly more pertinent than a Bayeux tapestry; Mr Coolidge's pious thrift maxims hardly less dead than Cotton Mather's observations on witches.

But in Latin America change comes in longer sweeps—when

it comes at all. Spain exported feudalism to the overseas colonies, and feudalism still colors the life and practical politics of the twenty republics. Spain founded her agrarian economy in the colonies by converting the discipline of the Indian tribes into a peonage. Today, except in the few republics where the Indians have vanished, the way to the improvement of Latin-American rural life still lies mainly in adapting economic reforms to tribal psychology and folkways. And since tribal discipline exists for vengeance and war as well as for work, and feudalism includes a contract between leader and follower to sack cities, and to kill, or be killed by, the group enemies, in Latin America you have violence.

Such fundamentals are no archaeological remains with the dust of centuries on them. On the contrary, history walks through the traffic jams of Buenos Aires and Rio de Janeiro and follows the wooden plow of the Andean peon in Peru as patently as the shadow of Daniel Boone once stalked through the California gold rush. As an Ecuadorean friend who studied his United States during prohibition put it, "With us, history is still alive—as alive and tangible as a hangover."

Nor is it necessary in order to be on speaking terms with Latin-American history to master the tangled political life stories of each of the twenty republics. Too often "learning" Latin-American history—from the campaigns of the wars of independence to the latest complexion change in Bolivian dictatorships—means losing sight of the major conditioning forces in a jungle of parochial details.

What counts most in history as an aid to a realistic interpretation of Latin America are three overwhelming factors: the settlement process; the propinquity and blood mixture of master and enserfed races; and the set of values developed through the colonial period and intensified, in the century since independence, by nationalism.

☆　　　　☆　　　　☆

In even the shortest journeys about any long-inhabited Latin countryside, the naked eye can trace the original settlement process with astonishing clearness. The pattern seldom greatly varies. When you see a town or a ranch house dating even from fairly deep in the nineteenth century, it harks back in its essential accouterments to the sixteenth.

The ranchero's mansion is a stockaded fortress. The thick outer wall about the courtyards and the family premises was built to withstand cannon shot. The massive hardwood timbers of the entrance gate would shed battering rams and bullets as well as arrows. Within, behind the central buildings' thick masonry, lies a crabbed labyrinth of larders and counting rooms, *salas* and bed-chambers, built to be defended from staircase to staircase and from door to door.

The older towns reflect the days when they were the hacienda's military complement. No towns were built in Latin America of a straggle of log huts in a forest clearing like Lincoln's New Salem. When a Spanish explorer raised his sword above the cross at some promising spot in an Andean valley or along a pampa river, and announced that the Royal City of the Holy Miracles of St Christopher was founded, it was no signal for speculations in suburban real estate. His little army broke ranks, but not to stake claims to residential lots in a future metropolis. Instead, at the end of the first season, a plausible replica of the little fortress-like towns of Andalusia and Aragon had arisen.

Wall flush to wall, its stone and adobe houses stood along narrow, straight streets, easily enfiladed by gunfire from the central Plaza de las Armas, where no invader could be at ease until the last patio had been captured and the last musketeer shot dead behind his window.

Spain, in a word, built in the colonies to perpetuate the feudalism it had known at home. For seven centuries before Columbus its feudal kings had fought each other. Neighbor had fought neighbor, and equal had fought equal for lands and the power of the State. Together, in an endless and agonizing series of raids and counterraids, they had fought the racial and religious enemies, the Moors.

Yet more was involved than the simple questions of habit and imitation. The same type of feudal captain who had made the wars of Pedro the Cruel led the Spanish pioneer into his adventure of settlement, and therefore he must expect the same conflicts. Millions of pagan Indians resented his conquest, so he must be prepared for the same racial dangers. If the Spanish ranch house was a fortress and the Latin-American town was built as a highly defensive urban community instead of as a hamlet for frontier individualists, there were good reasons for it.

The contrast with the settlement process in North America was enormous. The British colonist threw away the molds of British society almost from the moment he booked his passage. From Maine to Georgia, from the moment his axe sank into a tree, he was casting new ones. The planters' society that he built in our South was as different from the life of the Devonshire squirearchy as the life of the crabbed Yankee farmer in his Berkshire-hill acres was from the cap-touching yeoman's in Surrey. Wooden-housed Boston of Ben Franklin's childhood was as different from Queen Anne's London as today Ketchikan, Alaska, is from Greenwich Village.

Moreover, with the passage of time in Latin America, the mold of the Spanish inheritance actually hardened. Geography, which favored and assisted the British colonist's differentiations from England, trapped the Spanish pioneer in a narrow and imitative provincialism.

For North American settlement moved in waves. The first wave occupied the tidewater seaboard lands in the seventeenth century. Shortly after 1700 the second began pushing up the rivers, until by the Revolution it had washed over the first mountain ranges and was seeping into the nearer valleys. The post-Revolutionary population swept into the immediate trans-Allegheny lands, while the nineteenth century's first generation filled up the wooded prairies as far as the first tier of states beyond the Mississippi. The wave of the 1850s leaped half a continent to claim California and Oregon, and still there was force enough left in the undertow to subdue, in the post-Civil War decades, the states of the high prairies, the cattle ranges and the mountains.

Despite the vast distances and the scanty transportation of the colonial period there was always about the North American frontier an intercommunicating solidarity, almost a sociability. The men who broke the Carolina soils to rice and indigo culture shared common experience with the men who fought the Pequot wars in New England. Boston merchants and Virginia tobacco planters had common economic problems. Morgan's riflemen from beyond the Shenandoah, and Ethan Allen's Green Mountain boys, out of their frontier background, spoke a common political language. The North American pioneers advanced a common front against the wilderness, with the result that their very differentiations from each other united them increasingly in the bond of still greater differentiations from England. Out of this frontier individualism itself there grew, instinctively at first, and later consciously, a common nationalism that was to triumph over local and regional self-interest and to withstand even the contest of slave and free economies.

In Latin America, on the other hand, there was but a single major wave of settlement. No compact line of white civilization could be founded in a fever-stricken and agriculturally useless tidewater; for geography forbade it. The first Spanish and Portuguese colonists had to make at once for the highlands in order simply to be safe from murderous diseases and to feed themselves.

Nor in the highlands was it, as with the North American colonists, a question of driving primitive savages from their hunting grounds and clearing the forests for farmsteads. From Mexico to Bolivia the vast cultivated areas of the great Indian civilizations stood ready for the conqueror's expropriation, and huge populations—far too huge to be driven off or exterminated—were ripe for serfdom in the conquering race's economy.

Remote, however, as the Indian agricultural centers were in their mountain-locked valleys, the amazing settlement wave swept almost at once into regions remotely beyond them. The original pioneers had no sooner assured their food supply in the granaries of Peru and Mexico than they were racing down eastern slopes of the Andes and up through the Sierras of northern Mexico, raiding the jungles of Central America and the far southern pampas, in a hunt for souls and gold.

It was, in its way, the most arduous, the most flamboyantly

heroic exploit in the history of human migrations. In the first fifty years after Columbus certainly not more than two hundred thousand Spaniards and Portuguese came to the New World. In all probability the number who survived the perils of voyage and acclimatization was far less than one hundred thousand. Yet this small horde within the span of a short individual lifetime made an adequate over-all survey of the eight million square miles of the Latin-American land mass, explored and prospected its mountain chains from northern Mexico to Patagonia, charted its main river systems and founded, with only a few significant exceptions, the principal cities of Latin America today.

Rio de Janeiro and Montevideo were to come later, but by 1542 every other important Atlantic seaport of Spanish and Portuguese America was in operation from Vera Cruz to Buenos Aires. On the Pacific, Acapulco in Mexico stood ready to receive the galleons from the Philippines, while Pedro de Valdivia's arquebusiers, in the intervals between their wars with the Araucanian Indians, were building Valparaiso. Mexico City, Panama and Lima were already functioning as regional metropolises. Cali and Bogotá were rising in their moonily remote valleys, and Quito on its frosty equatorial tableland. Asunción stood on its sun-cooked prairie as far above tidewater on the Paraguay as Cairo, Illinois, is from New Orleans, while in Mexico the mining settlements spread out fanwise beyond Guadalajara and Zacatecas toward the Rio Grande. The great agricultural valleys of Peru and Mexico were hardly less dotted with towns and monasteries than in the 1930s.

It was as if the North American land mass had been explored from Cape Nome to Florida, the Rockies and the Appalachians prospected, the Mississippi and the Columbia river systems mapped, Klondike and California gold discovered, and Denver, Seattle, Chicago, Atlanta and every other American city today above a hundred thousand population founded within fifty years after Jamestown. Yet even this does not give a strictly accurate analogy. It is as if, in the North American chronology of settlement, this had been accomplished before Jamestown, within half a century after John and Sebastian Cabot's 1497 landfall for England at Newfoundland.

But it was also curiously as if Chicago and Seattle, Miami and the Klondike had been established in hermetically sealed compartments—a kind of communications vacuum. For the Spanish settlement process established no common front against the wilderness, but separate frontiers by dozens and scores.

Down to the nineteenth century Mexico and Peru heard of each other mainly through shadowy rumors, hardly less vague than the shadowy legends by which Inca and Aztec civilizations heard of each other in the years before Columbus. From Bogotá to Lima today is an easy all-daylight flight by airplane. But the rare Colombian provincial who had business with the Spanish viceroy at Lima two centuries ago, unless he cared to risk the perils of the llama paths over the high Andes, knew that it might take him many months to go and come by way of Panama; that a passage by way of Spain might actually be shorter in time, and cheaper. Buenos Aires—also under the jurisdiction of Lima until late in the eighteenth century—knew that the way to the capital ran either up the rivers two thousand miles and over the gigantic Bolivian Andes, or, once in five years, perhaps, if a ship happened to be sailing, by way of the Straits of Magellan. Asunción on its lonely hinterland was as locked away from the world as St Louis would be without railways and its corn belt.

Enormous and romantic, the great wave of Spanish colonization had washed over a continental land mass and its 20,000-foot ranges to deposit enduring settlements in mountain pools and prairie ponds and far-separated coastal inlets. With the Indians' land, the Indians' gold and the Indians themselves, the Spanish colonists, however, had inherited the Indians' immense isolation. Bound to the Indians by economic needs and associations, bound to Spain by their segregated helplessness, the Spanish frontiers were condemned in advance to a passionate localism out of which the life and politics of contemporary Latin America take their rise.

☆   ☆   ☆

From the end of the settlement saga, the history of Latin America is largely the chronicle of localism's hazards. In the isolated towns and feudal-estate neighborhoods built on the patterns of home, there was little incitement to change. Many essential patterns of life in Spain and Portugal tended to be repeated through sheer inertia.

Nor could colonies, separated by such far distances, and lacking contacts with each other, develop concentrated or even locally effective resistance to the mother countries' regimentations. So further patterns of imitation were imposed by orders from above. Spain and Portugal decreed what the colonies' political systems should be, how colonial society should be graded, defined religious orthodoxy, and heard no objections. By their system of licensing printing presses and booksellers, Madrid and Lisbon determined what the colonists should read, and by a rigorous control of exports and imports, what they should wear, eat and manufacture. There was considerable smuggling—more of British rum and French luxury articles than of books, incidentally—but nothing suggesting a revolutionary protest.

Thus, by the end of the sixteenth century, the colonists had settled down into a routine of dressing and amusing themselves like Spaniards; courting and secluding their women like Spaniards, obeying Spanish laws, observing Spanish conventions and taboos of thought and conduct, and accepting the gradations of Spanish society and the colonial bureaucracy as the primal facts of the social order.

There was, in fact, no other alternative. The Spanish and Portuguese administrative systems supplied the shipping on which the economic life of the colonies depended, as well as munitions and soldiers for their protection against the oppressed Indian masses. And what the administrative systems furnished, the administrative systems could withhold. Obviously, the mother countries' powers were not to be offended by frontier nonconformities. If, along with homeland architecture, Spain and Portugal wanted homeland social and political institutions rebuilt in the colonies, the colonists had plenty of practical reasons for doing as ordered.

But, especially in the racial situation, more was involved than Madrid's and Lisbon's regimentation policies. Unlike the North American colonists who, once they had cleared the neighboring forests of Indians, were free to experiment with home-grown institutions in a more or less pleasant sylvan laboratory, the Latin frontiers had to face perpetually the problem of dominance over vast Indian subject populations. At the end of the colonial era in the 1820s, less than two million whites, from Mexico to Bolivia, ruled, on their remote plateaus and in their mountain-locked valleys, over an agrarian and mining sweatshop of from five to eight million Indians. On the Atlantic coasts, from Cuba to Buenos Aires, another two million whites ran a slave empire of close to four million Negroes and Indians combined. Indeed, during the greater part of the colonial period the disproportion between master and enserfed races was far greater. The sweatshop and slave empires as of 1600 were controlled by barely two hundred thousand Spaniards and Portuguese, and it is unlikely that the white population passed the million mark until the first quarter of the eighteenth century.

The whites, at any rate, solved the problem of dominance as master races customarily solve it. Like Englishmen dressing for dinner in the jungle, they emphasized the racial and traditional mores—the stiffness of Spanish etiquette, the elaborateness of Spanish manners, the hierarchies of Spanish social and official life —in order to make the gulf between themselves and the subject populations more palpable. From the viceroys in Lima and Mexico City down to the village notary and the discharged private soldier on his tiny land grant, white society was a civilization on parade before dangerous inferiors. It had to be Spanish, with an authoritarian virtuosity and an extra provincial flourish, in order to preserve itself.

The rapid mixture of races in the colonies, far from weakening this phase of the imitative impulse, actually strengthened it. For the whites, the observance of Spanish forms was merely a bit of expedient social strategy, with perhaps a touch of homesickness. For the fractionally Indian descendants of Spanish fathers and Indian mothers, it was literally a means of social salvation. The white prospector might, after all, live a few years in an Indian hut in the mountains and still remain a Spaniard. But the mestizo who did not live in a Spanish house, eat Spanish food, cultivate Spanish vices, and manage the punctilio of Spanish manners with a trifle more exhibitionism than the viceroy, lived in perpetual danger of being reclaimed by the servile race from which his mother came. And the rare Indian "full-blood" whose wealth or tribal authority entitled him to buy one of the prized certificates of "whiteness" had, if possible, even more motives for accepting Spanish ways and values than the mestizo.

Finally, to all these forces making for a static and imitative society, should be added a still subtler compulsion: the deep inferiority sense of Indian, mestizo and colonial-born white alike, before the Spaniards from Spain.

On the segregated Latin frontiers, no common front of pioneer humor made fun of the pretentious mannerisms of royal governors, or laughed at officers, in the way Yankees laughed at General Braddock's red-coated regulars as third-rate Indian fighters. The officials, the court and political favorites whom Spain sent to the colonies were manifestly sent there to train the provincials in the refinements of Spanish living; and colonial society, with a sense of uneasy social inadequacy, accepted their values of snobbery.

The Spanish aristocracy scorned trade, for example, so the colonial aristocracy scorned commercial pursuits with the peculiar hauteur of parvenus. Spain revered titles, so lucky miners and hacienda proprietors from Mexico to La Plata spent fortunes buying titles of colonial nobility which barely permitted them to sit at table with a Spanish captain general's subsecretary. It was the age of Don Juan Tenorio, and Spain was quietly dissolute. So the young sprigs of the colonial first families in the universities of Lima and Mexico City, or in their European educational tours from Salamanca to Vienna, imitated Casanova with a maximum of ostentatious flourish.

But even more than in these fields of private vanity, the colonials hankered after distinction through public office. For all but the lowest and strictly local grades of posts in the overseas administrative system were reserved to native-born Spaniards, and ineligibility to office stood forth as the supreme tangible brand of the colonials' inferiority.

So the Latin-American towns swarmed with aristocratic lawyers

—ten and twenty attorneys to the case, despite the constant artificial stimulus to litigation. For a successful lawyer might look forward to something more than fees. As a petty town judge or municipal prosecutor, as notary or local recorder, he might actually, someday, set his foot on the lower rungs of the sacred bureaucracy. And as a potential arm of the court, a certain pseudo-official status could be enjoyed even by a lawyer who was briefless.

Heads of families mortgaged their properties and went into debt to the usurers to buy themselves the empty honors of membership in the colonial municipal councils. Fathers and mothers spent the revenues of mines and vast landed estates purchasing royal army commissions for their sons which, for colonials, could lead only to down-at-the-heels captaincies; purchasing ecclesiastical posts which, at best, could lead to a place only in an archbishop's household.

Thus, when the New Freemen of the Wars of Liberation emerged in the 1820s from the three-centuries-long conditioning process of the colonial period, it was in a state of almost sexual frustration for office, for power and for authentic symbols of individual and social consequence. The republics which their arms and their intrigues founded had an overwhelming primary purpose: to provide their starving vanities the satisfactions which Spain had withheld.

☆   ☆   ☆

With independence in Latin America few things materially changed. The Braganza king in Portugal was replaced in Brazil by the Braganza emperor in Rio de Janeiro. Simón Bolívar, the ablest of the liberating statesmen, ruled over the greater part of the old Lima viceroyalty, from Venezuela to Bolivia, as a benevolent semidespot. When the Bolivarian federation in the late 1820s fell apart into five republics, the presidential dictators who seized the reins of authority proved to be both more despotic and considerably less benevolent.

Mexico, in reactionary zeal, outdid South America. Her independence was achieved through a coup of conservative army officers dissatisfied with the liberal Spanish constitution of 1820, and the new nation's first ruler, Iturbide, styled himself the Emperor Agustin I. After he was overthrown and killed—while still blue-printing orders of nobility and selling dukedoms and lesser titles to the highest bidders—he was succeeded during the greater part of a century by mountebank despots masquerading as presidents.

The Buenos Aires city politicians entered into a forty years' war with the cattle barons of the pampas over the control of the Argentine dictatorship. In Chile, more simply, the privileges of the colonial bureaucracy were merely transferred to a ruling oligarchy of city banking families and landed aristocrats. In far-away Paraguay an eccentric hinterland intellectual by the name of Dr José Gaspar Rodríguez de Francia applied the technique of the Holy Inquisition to the extermination of political opponents.

Bureaucratic posts were tripled and quadrupled in numbers and thrown open to deserving politicians, subservient senates and congresses. Provincial legislatures sprang up in a hundred centers to assist the feeble municipal councils in the labors of government—and to make more jobs. The plains and the mountains swarmed with newly enlisted—and considerably overofficered—armies, while fleetless admirals and commodores tripped over each other in the seaport cantinas.

The New Freemen held the offices now, and the republics spawned offices with their best tropical fecundity, but the basic authoritarian principles of government remained the same. All the more because they had been starved for authority for ten generations, office was something the ruling Latin Americans proposed to enjoy.

What change there was, was mainly in the direction of atavism. Spain through her military power—and even more through the consciousness of the segregated frontiers that petty local insurrections would get them nowhere—had maintained a kind of static order in the colonies. Now that the bonds were released, there was a relapse into feudalism.

It was a nineteenth-century feudalism curiously colored with political job lust. The general in command at Arequipa knew that if he could march on Lima and overthrow the dictator-president, he and his followers could divide the precious offices; that if he promised his officers the key jobs in the republic, and promised the rank and file protection from prosecution in the pleasant duties they would have of ravaging the countryside, they would follow him in the adventure. If also he would promise jobs to a few town intellectuals and politicians who could serve as apologists and propagandists, and promotions to a few members of the presidential bodyguard whose treacheries might prove useful, he knew where potent and strategic allies could be had.

Essentially, the *caudillos* and revolutionary leaders made with their followers the same compacts that a medieval robber baron made with his fief-holders and fighting retainers. Each general owned his army as a personal possession; each army owed its primary fighting allegiance to its general, as the Spanish feudal bands owed allegiance to El Cid Campeador or to Pedro the Cruel. And from the Rio Grande to the pampas, Latin America became the feudal bands' battleground.

Mexico had nearly as many changes of administration in the 1840s as there were years in the decade. Peru had eight dictators in 1845 alone. Where order was restored, as under Rosas in the Argentine and under Porfirio Diaz in Mexico in the late nineteenth century, it was through rewarding the faithful with the spoils of the State and forestalling opposition feudalists with a typically czarist terrorism. Long unused to warfare in the quiet colonial centuries, the fortresslike haciendas and the barrackslike towns suddenly developed an immense utility in practical politics.

Along with the relapse into feudalism went an enormous increase in official corruption. For there was more to Latin-American politics than a mere lust for office. Those who won offices had to be supported in a style to which officeholders preferred to become accustomed. Presidents, to show that they were "as good as" viceroys, must live like royalty. Cabinet members must live like captain generals. Army officers, to demonstrate their authority, must live better than civilians. Members of the bureaucracy, to show that they outranked ordinary citizens—as the lowest clerks in the Spanish colonial establishment had done before them—must set a richer table and live in finer houses than the neighbors.

Officeholders, too, to "keep face," must show that they possessed the subtle official abstraction—influence. Even the most minor sub-executive, if he could not get all his male relatives to the second degree of cousinship on the public pay roll, felt himself disgraced in his normal political potency. So, in addition to the corruption and the disorders, every official pay roll bogged down under the weight of brothers and nephews and in-laws.

Economically, politically and socially, each republic lived in a perpetual vicious circle. While the feudal wars destroyed their taxable resources and interfered with the collection of the revenues, the officeholders grafted. The presidents, the cabinet members, the important generals and the political inner circles cultivated the grandee style of living by selling the favors of the state to privilege seekers, and by frankly expropriating the property of their political enemies. The lesser fry sold petty favors for cash and stole the revenues. And when the next feudal band swept into office on the wings of revolution, there was more of the same.

☆   ☆   ☆

There were exceptions, of course. During the lifetime of its empire, down to 1889, Brazil was spared from feudal anarchy by the habit of obedience to royal authority. Chile's ruling oligarchy, by adroitly intertwining the army's economic interests with its own, managed to keep substantial order in the republic until its prosperity as a caste collapsed in the postwar depression of the 1920s.

In all the republics individual officeholders made lonely and conscientious efforts to discharge their duties for the public good. In many of the republics sincere reformers even rose, at long intervals, to the presidency. But the wicked administrative spirit was stronger than the idealistic flesh. The statesmen who outlawed graft as the perquisite of office were continually at the mercy of rivals whose appeal lay in promising graft. Latin America, as things turned out, was lifted from the mire of feudal anarchy less by its pioneers in civic virtue than by its more ruthless robber barons.

One by one, out of the struggle of adventurers, men rose to power—Rosas in the Argentine, Santa Cruz and Castilla in Peru, Guzmán Blanco in Venezuela, Diaz in Mexico—who were able to bring their republics for a few years or a lifetime some experience with the practical peace of despotism. In their varying fields they developed the tricks of dictatorial government. They learned how to control the armies by pampering the right cliques of officers. They learned how to dispose of enemies and potential rebels against their authority by the quiet terrorism of espionage and the well-timed use of firing squads. They learned the trick of providing themselves with the fantastic and extraordinary powers they needed by having constitutions amended and freak laws passed under the guns of the soldiers.

Some of them even learned to adapt their regimes to the superficial processes of formal democracy. Elections could be held on schedule, an open rivalry between discreetly controlled parties could sometimes be permitted—provided the leaders understood each other's needs in practical politics and the armies stood guard. Even graft could be eliminated by a more virtuous dictator's ruthlessness, or at least kept to a scale which the republics could afford.

Thus, gradually, out of the experiments of the earlier dictators arose the patterns of contemporary Latin-American politics. Violence threatens government below the Rio Grande; and so government rules by the threat of violence above.

Latin-American government is still a pattern of despotism, much as the monarchies which followed the age of feudal disorders in Europe were despotic. It is designed for order, for compelling peace with authority—for manipulating men in politics, rather than releasing their energies in freedom for economic achievement.

CHAPTER IV

Economic Millstones

J UAN DE LA CRUZ is a wizened old gentleman of seventy-odd whose teeth are somewhere between a memory and a ground plan for a cosmic ruin, and who, when he has not happened to pick up a pair of time-tattered sandals in somebody's dump heap, is usually barefooted. After taking in the haphazard collection of cotton rags in which Juan de la Cruz clothes himself, and looking his rather vacant expression in the eye, you would probably be reconvinced of the merits of poorhouses. If you met him in downtown Cleveland or Omaha carrying a 150-pound packing case on his back through the heart of traffic, you would be tempted to call a policeman or telephone the Associated Charities. If he was doing this of his own accord, you would say to yourself, Señor de la Cruz is too eccentric to be at large. If somebody was forcing him to do it, surely there must be "a law against" taking advantage of an old man's economic impotence to make him a beast of burden.

But Mexico City sees Juan de la Cruz threading his way along the crowded sidewalks of the Avenida Madero or the Avenida Isabella la Católica every day at a pace halfway between a fast walk and a dogtrot, and never gives his 150-pound burden a thought. Señor de la Cruz has a casual economic virtue not unlike the economic virtue of some small bit of labor-saving gadgetry in an American restaurant kitchen: the charm of cheapness. He will carry your grandfather's armchair, or your barrel of china, or a sizable piece of heavy machinery half a dozen miles across Mexico City for half a peso—not quite a dime to you, Señor Norte Americano—where the horse drayman will charge anywhere from one to two pesos, and the motor truck may charge anywhere up to five.

What with two crosstown expeditions and a lucky assortment of shorter portages, Juan de la Cruz on an extraordinarily successful day can make as much as two and a half pesos—or all of fifty cents before the 1939 silver plunge. But such days are rare and are counterbalanced by days when Señor de la Cruz, being unpleasantly plagued with competitors, gets no work at all. It is probable that his daily earnings, not counting time out for Sundays, national holidays and religious fiestas, average somewhere between twenty and thirty cents.

On thirty cents a day Señor de la Cruz is hardly noticeable as a customer for modern industry. He buys, in fact, practically nothing that his ancestors did not buy before the machine age. A little corn and beans and a rare pound of the cheapest coffee for his groceries; now and then a candle for light and a little charcoal for fuel when his woman can pick up no sticks or convenient combustibles on near-by dump heaps; still more rarely a can of beer or pulque for his fiestas. He lives in a moldering 'dobe hovel, dirt-floored and one-windowed, as devoid of modern conveniences as the accommodations for the proletarian under the Aztecs and considerably more sunk in dilapidation. Once every year or two he visits one of the cheaper city markets to renew his rags with third-hand shirt or patched pair of third-hand trousers—or, more simply, arranges some week to take his pay from a generous client in cast-off clothing rather than in centavos. The household comfort gadgets which the United States and Great Britain, and until recently Germany, export to Mexico with such pleasing expectations of profit, the excellent clothing produced by the Mexican textile industry, are as astronomically beyond his personal economy as rib roasts and Rolls-Royces.

Yet Mexico City, except in certain rising radical and intellectual circles, is scarcely any more disturbed about Señor de la Cruz's being underequipped with purchasing power than about his being overloaded with cargo. As a piece of rather primitive machinery—a means of getting a packing case from one side of town to the other more cheaply than automobiles will carry it—Mexico City may consider him useful, even admirable. As a potential contributor to the general social prosperity, it frankly ignores him.

Señor de la Cruz, in fact, dates from an economy in which purchasing power was scarcely an objective—an essentially feudal economy which held parochial self-sufficiency, the subordination of the working masses and getting the work done cheaply to be the supreme goals of a civilized society.

Nor is Señor de la Cruz, though a survival, in any sense a quaint and outlandish oddity. In agriculture, in the lower ranks of industry, in the manual trades and in domestic service as well as in transportation, probably better than half the population of Latin America between the Rio Grande and Patagonia are not appreciably better off. If he typifies the past, he is a symbol of the dead hand of the past in the twenty republics' economics. He is a living proof of the controlling reality in the whole problem of our economic relations with Latin America—the fact that the lands to the south of us are half in and half out of the machine age.

☆   ☆   ☆

No economy's development has been more logical, or is more easily traced. Once more, the primary forces conditioning development can best be stated in a contrast.

In the British North American colonies, and subsequently in the United States, the inhabitants for three hundred years, or until the coming of technological unemployment, faced the problem of exploiting a continental agriculture and developing a continental industrial plant with a shortage of labor. Probably less than a million Indians occupied the entire area of continental United States, and of the hundred or two hundred thousand who came in contact with the pre-Revolutionary waves of British settlement, few, or none, were culturally adaptable to colonial labor processes. In Latin America, on the other hand, except in the pampas and the plantation lands of the Brazilian highlands, the problem was to develop a series of separate parochial economies founded on an enormous glut of man power.

It is true that the aborigines did not adapt themselves readily to

European labor processes, and that over wide areas it was all but impossible to make them work at all. Nevertheless, from Mexico to Bolivia the original fifty thousand to one hundred thousand Spaniards of the settlement saga inherited, in effect as the raw material for serfdom, the populations of the Aztec, the Maya, the Inca and the Chibcha empires—a total of somewhere between twenty million and thirty million Indians. On the Atlantic coasts where the Caribs died under the whip of the Spanish overseers and the wilder Brazilian Indians fled into the forests from the Portuguese, the losses were quickly overcome by the importation of Negroes from Africa. Although the numerical gap between the white and subject races slowly narrowed during the three centuries of colonial period, man strength remained the cheapest of the Latin-dominated New World's commodities.

During those three centuries the essential Latin-American economy developed. Because of the vast distances between the separate frontiers, it necessarily, like the feudal economy, placed an enormous emphasis on local self-sufficiency. Not only were Mexico and Peru separate economic units in a far more exclusive sense than Georgia and Connecticut were separate units, but the Cuzco valley and the lake-freshened plains about Guadalajara and the mining region about Charcas—now Sucre, Bolivia—were separate units. The vast missions of the Jesuits in Paraguay and interior Brazil, with their shops and their art crafts and their systems of crop rotation and storage, were hardly less independent of the world than the lamaseries of central Tibet. The remote haciendas fed and clothed their workers, made farming tools and built houses from materials on the ground with the self-sufficient completeness of a medieval manor. Only the European luxuries of the ruling family and the more modest comforts of the overseeing staff had to be brought in from elsewhere; and these during an emergency period of months or even years could be dispensed with.

Like feudalism, too, each of these separate economies placed an emphasis on keeping the serfs in subjection. Prosperous Indians, Indians who could look to anyone but the hacienda master or the mine owner for their next meal and their next year's allotment of cotton garments, would have refused the yoke of semi-enforced labor. Indians in a position to save real money from wages to buy farms—or guns—of their own would have been dangerous to the whole scheme of Spanish mastery. So there was more behind the cheapness of labor in colonial Latin America than the mere excess of supply over demand. Labor had to be kept in a state of acute economic helplessness—for the masses the self-sufficiency of the local economies was always meager—in order that the master race should be safe from servile insurrection. Indeed, all the prejudices of Southern industrial feudalism in the United States against Negro social advancement and larger purchasing power were graphically foreshadowed.

Yet it is doubtful if, in view of Spain's basic economic program for the colonies, there could have been any considerable volume of wealth to share with the working masses. For despite all the local self-sufficiency and the vast gulfs of distance and separate interests between the frontiers, the economic activities of the colonies were subservient to a single purpose. From Mexico to the neglected Argentine, the colonial economy, as Spain saw it and directed it, was a one-crop economy.

The crop was precious metals. All the self-sufficiency which hacienda and valley farming area and province built up so painstakingly was for one purpose only: that there should be free economic energy at the top of colonial society to seek for and exploit silver and gold. The toil of the Indians in the fields was not designed to put colonial populations on the routes of world-foodstuffs commerce, or even to feed Spain. Food was grown, cloths were woven, that a population of mine entrepreneurs and prospectors and workers might be supported.

Statistics of colonial exports tell the story with impressive clarity. In 1747, for example, long after the colonial economy had been fully organized and production was flourishing, the Spanish colonies sent to Spain 34,600,000 pesos in gold, silver and precious stones compared with less than 4,000,000 pesos' worth of all other products. The exports of the British North American colonies to

England and the West Indian dependencies in the 1740s included, besides fish, furs and naval stores, practically the whole range of colonial agricultural production.

In spite, then, of the unpopular Navigation Acts which required all colonial trade to be conducted through England, the remotest frontier farm of the northern colonies had a frontage, real or potential, on the stream of international commerce. In Brazil and the overseas New Spains, all agriculture except for a few tobacco and sugar plantations, as well as all industry save for a few exotic occupations like vicuña hunting and cochineal collecting, was locked away in the thin self-containment of petty local areas by a vast circle of silver and gold.

Under these circumstances, an economy grew up so curiously self-centered as to have an almost other-worldly touch. At the top there was money—hard money in old family coin chests, money buried in hacienda and city mansion treasure vaults, in bars and ingots beyond the dreams of any current banker's avarice: money smelted down into exquisite, though sometimes gaudy, church ornaments to impress the impoverished with the ineffable fiscal stability of God. Yet so far as their effect on general living standards or even on price levels was concerned, the huge individual fortunes drawn from the Sierras and the Andes might as well have been sunk under a mound in Kentucky or entombed with the Pharaohs.

The rich could not spend their wealth on wages. Indian prosperity was not to be encouraged, and anyway, for every labor service the mining Croesus needed performed, a hundred hands competed for a pittance. Neither could the rich man's hoard be spent on the products of colonial industry, for Spain forbade colonial industry. It could not be spent on colonial agriculture. The abundance of the food necessities which agriculture produced for each local area at a bare subsistence labor cost could be had for a song on virtually a barter basis. And there was a definite limit to the amount a few rich families could eat in any case. The big money had to be spent exclusively on luxuries imported from Spain, or on the Church, which used it primarily to gratify its own specialized tastes in luxuries. Hence, slowly the great fortunes whose spending could have spread the wealth down among the masses and stimulated in the colonies a prosperity as lush as California's in the generation after the gold rush, drained away to the motherland.

Since the money at the top failed to reach the proletariat, the masses themselves developed a fallacious preference for a low-cost economy. The Indian, after all, bought extra bits of bright cloth for his women, occasional delicacies for his family fiestas now and then, and even hired services from other Indians. If these articles were not produced and these services rendered by workmen as poor as or poorer than himself, he could not afford them. If the poor whites in the town shops and clerical posts, the mestizo small farmers and skilled workers could not keep down the costs of their own helpers and domestic servants, could not buy the local products at little better than barter prices, how could they lay by enough from their meager incomes to maintain their own end of the furious colonial social competition by stocking their houses with gadgets from Spain? Cheap labor and low prices seemed for the poor, indeed, a kind of substitute for sharing the wealth in their masters' strongboxes—a shoddy substitute, no doubt, but one that seemed worth clinging to. It was almost as if Juan de la Cruz were created by the economic ambitions of his own kind.

Yet in labor's very abundance there were other powerful conditioning factors. There were so many hands for the work to be done that the Spanish mine bosses and hacienda overseers saw little object in organizing the work efficiently. If Francisco García was slovenly with the hoe and with the machete in the sugar patch, forty other exact duplicates of Francisco García could be sent over the ground after him, and the sugar somehow brought to harvest. If men staggering toward death under their excessive ore loads stumbled over each other in the mine stopes, neither the overloading nor the mine accident statistics seemed important. However much the individual unit lagged in production, the gold would be got out, and gold would buy trinkets from Madrid. And when Pedro or Mario fell in his tracks, while the gold flowed, successors were available by tens of thousands.

In comparison with the United States frontier, where every

hand counted, economic leadership on the Spanish frontier grew up with a curiously slack sense of industrial management. To get together the largest gang possible, to overload it with tasks and burdens, to drive it with whips when necessary, yet to treat the individual worker's physical and mental efficiency with total indifference—this was the only method which colonial Latin America knew. Nor, under such a working system, was slackness confined to the economic leaders. When the laborer shared his work and his pittance living standards with millions precisely like himself, what incentive did he have to improve on the methods handed down from ancestors any more than the masters had? Why should the gang in the mines or the fields organize itself to work more efficiently when neither bosses nor any factor in the entire social system offered rewards for efficient performance?

Such a system, moreover, tended to block technological improvements no less than it discouraged intelligent management. In an economy overcrowded with hands, there was no sense in importing tools to perform any tasks which hands could perform without tools. Why install winches in mines, for example, when regiments of Indian backs stood ready to carry ore up forty-five-degree passages without winches? The crude gadgets with which toil was lightened and production increased in European and North American industry and agriculture during the seventeenth and eighteenth centuries seemed, to the Latin-American colonial economy, mere engines of wastage and social corruption. Cheap as they were, they cost more than hand labor working for beans and tortillas. The faster they were introduced, the more the masses would be encouraged to live in beggary and idleness.

Thus, during the entire colonial era, the New Spains and the New Portugal in Brazil were so obsessed with the internal economic problem of keeping their vast glut of man power busy and disciplined that it was scarcely even possible for them to consider themselves as citizens of a larger economic world. No free capital hankered for investment, for the gold and silver at the top went to Spain; while on their hand-to-mouth standards at the bottom the working masses neither created capital by their savings nor knew that it could be created. Except where new mines were discovered, no entrepreneur adventurers longed for new frontiers to conquer, for new frontiers merely meant more workers to feed and organize for the picayune profits—or losses—of local self-sufficiency.

Vaguely the hacienda proprietors and the artisans in the small industries of the towns were discontented with the restrictive policy of the mother countries which confined their trade to Spanish and Portuguese ports and vessels and outlawed manufactories altogether. But smuggling arrangements with easily corrupted customs officials eased these privations. Too much world commerce might give the working masses a desire for things which were not for peons. It was as well, perhaps, if peons should not know that such conveniences as world commerce existed. The wealth of a colony consisted in something else besides export and import statistics: in man power to be used recklessly, to be wasted and squandered—as surprised and naïve heirs squander sudden riches.

So, for three conditioning centuries, the little provincial areas meagerly fed and clothed and housed themselves and their curiously localized economies droned on. If the master class had gold and silver, or flourished in physical abundance on their haciendas, the aims of the economic organization of society were satisfied. If Francisco García had beans and cornmeal and a palm thatch over his hovel, it was well. If he lacked these things, he sat in the shade of the church doorway and begged for them; or he died, and, economically, there was no perceptible difference. Francisco Garcías swarmed in millions. Neither he nor any other problem on the economic landscape seemed worth fighting over or working very hard to solve. High and low, the Latin colonial world accepted these conditions with a resigned and fatalistic assumption that no other conditions were possible in the world.

Not even the independence movement seems seriously to have sought a cure of these basic economic evils. Spanish taxation policies and colonial trade restrictions were included, to be sure, among the Latin people's fighting grievances, but the emphasis was different from the protests of the Philadelphia Continental Congress. The Latin-American colonists fought to enter world commerce and to control their own taxation systems for the benefit of the great hacienda and estancia proprietors. The North Americans fought to open new frontiers and new world-trade opportunities to their masses as well as to the ruling capitalists. Far more savagely than against mass economic abuses, the passions of the Latin revolutionaries burned against the social and political exclusiveness of Spanish autocracy—and its control of the offices.

Without fluid capital, then, lacking technological skills and equipment and experience in industrial management, the enfranchised Latin Americans entered the laissez-faire competitive struggle of the nineteenth-century world as economic innocents. Their training and their habits equipped them for one economic service only: to use the glut of cheap man power to glut the world with cheap raw materials.

☆   ☆   ☆

As an inheritance from the colonial economies, there persisted, too, in the new republics, the instinctive conviction that cheap labor was the economic state's greatest asset; that at all costs cheap labor should be preserved.

It was an objective which for several generations ruled out automatically most of the lines of activity which were basic in the economic development of the United States. Manufactories were out. The heirs of a peon agricultural and ore-bearing civilization could no more have found their way about in factories and competed with the skilled workmen of Europe and the old-fashioned Yankee tinkerers than they could have invented rocket ships.

Staple agriculture was hardly more promising. The narrow valleys of the Sierras and the Andes might produce their local quota of corn and beans and cereals, but not even cheap labor could make up for the cost of transporting the vast bulk of grain crops down the mountains to the ports and overseas to Europe, to say nothing of the fact that there was more often shortage than excess. Europe, too, down past the middle of the century was fairly self-sufficient in agriculture, and what she lacked in lean years could be supplied from the developing resources of the Mississippi valley. So even the natural grain belt of the Argentine pampas lay useless and unutilized until late in the 1870s.

The republics, then, had to find their market in fields of production where European agriculture was helpless or where the competitive power of their cheap land and labor was supreme. Europe produced hides, for instance. But on the Argentine and the Uruguayan plains the cattle ran wild. The hordes of gauchos who vaguely tended them lived on the free meat of the slaughtered carcasses rather than on wages. So Argentine hides could compete in the world markets in spite of the cost of haulage. Sheep, too, grazed on the practically valueless pampas. Their wool would undersell the products of the English moors and the Spanish uplands. Furthermore, from Mexico as far as the southern temperate zone, the republics had a free field, down to the last quarter of the nineteenth century, in practically the whole range of tropical agricultural produce. For coffee and sugar and cocoa—crops which cheap and unskilled labor could raise with a minimum of effort—could not be produced in Europe.

Yet relative prosperity in the tropical-products field actually intensified rather than corrected the trend toward modern, cheap labor economy. On the coffee and cocoa plantations the laborers had only to be paid their pittance wages for the few weeks of the year when they worked in the tending and harvesting seasons. The rest of the time, on the little kitchen-garden plots which the shrewd generosity of the employers allotted them, they could shift for themselves.

Thus as the export of tropical products came to be the dominant industry in most of the nations from Central America to the southern frost line, the evils of a moneyless proletariat grew with the foreign-trade statistics. It was as if the basic living standards for farmers in the United States were fixed by a group with a purchasing power even less than that of Arkansas share croppers.

Today on the Brazilian coffee fazendas, within a few miles of cities equipped with all the modern facilities for spending and civilized living, there are still hundreds of thousands of families whose cash incomes seldom exceed $15 a year.

There remained the mines. But the mines proved no more a

source of economic salvation to the republics than tropical exports. Many of the best veins had been worked thin by the time independence arrived, and almost without exception the operating properties were overripe for technical renovation. New lodes stood ready for exploitation, and new discoveries were yet to be made, but the republics, bogged down by the debts and destructions of the wars, lacked the capital to develop resources requiring enormous investments.

And in the wars of political feudalism which followed independence, the mines were the first targets. Generals on their way to presidential palaces looted the mines of their treasure to line their pockets and their military pay chests as automatically as their ragged armies slaughtered hacienda cattle for their daily nourishment. Generals on their way out of office into banditry or exile destroyed mine works in impartial profusion with the conscientious purpose of hampering, at whatever the cost, the looting intentions of their enemies and successors. In the vast bill of destruction of $418,000,000 which the Colombian economist, Sanín Cano, charges against Latin-American revolutionaries between 1824 and 1924, mines bore a share far beyond even their proportion to the national wealth of the republics.

Few economic structures could have withstood such a process of repetitive ravishment. Within a generation of independence, in fact, the native mining aristocracy practically collapsed under it. With hardly more than negligible exceptions, the Latin-American mines were either mortgaged by, or in hock to, the governments, or owned nominally by gold-poor or silver-poor local aristocrats without funds to operate them.

The result was, of course, foreign economic penetration. British and French, and later German and United States capital could flow into the republics in sufficient volume to repair the damages, make the necessary renovations, bring mining processes up to date and exploit the hitherto undeveloped properties. But the price it charged was, inevitably, possession. So by the beginning of the twentieth century hardly a mining property in Latin America of first or second consequence belonged wholly to Latin-American owners or poured its dividends into the streams of Latin-American economy.

Foreign ownership, however, did no more than fractionally change the Latin-American wage and living-standards situation. For wages were still fixed by the weakness of the group at the bottom—the moneyless agrarian proletariat. In an economy where the plantation laborers often worked for less than $10 cash income a year, the miner, in spite of his harsher and more constant toil and the higher prices of food and fuel in his barren mountain villages, might consider himself fortunate if he earned $100. And as Latin-American gold competed with California and Klondike gold in world markets, as Mexican silver competed with Nevada and Colorado silver, and Chilean copper with Rhodesia and Arizona copper, low wages increasingly became the differential on which the foreign overlords of the mines staked their hope of profits.

Cash wages, it is true—agricultural as well as mining—moved slowly upward during the long expanding period of the international-credit economy between the 1860s and 1929, but the Latin-American scales lagged behind those of the United States and western Europe with a steady persistence. The Latin-American worker's income bought him little more, relatively, of the living comforts of civilization in the boom years of the 1920s than in his pastoral seclusion of the 1840s. In Mexico it rather definitely, according to the latest studies on the subject, brought him less than in the last days of the colonial period.

There were, naturally, exceptional times and exceptional areas. The 1914 war's boom brought something like bonanza wages for a time to workers in the Chilean nitrate fields, to Mexican and Chilean copper miners. Oil fields "came in," along with the freshet of demand for gasoline from the automotive industries, in Mexico, Venezuela, Colombia, Peru and the Argentine. For a few score thousand roustabouts of the industry it meant slightly better wages than in the mines, and for a good many thousand skilled workers and semitechnicians, living standards on a par with those of petty foremen in European factories. The larger capitals and the more important seaports, invaded by foreign branch offices and industries, took on a tinge of modern metropolitan economics and gave birth to a petty bourgeoisie of white-collar workers living substantially as well as similar classes do in Rome or did in pre-Civil War Madrid.

In Uruguay and the Argentine, change was more basic and affected all classes. As the industrial masses tripled and quadrupled their numbers in the European factory centers, Europe's capacity to feed itself passed, and bread-hungry nations called for the wheat of the pampas. The hide-hunting gauchos, living off the meat of half-wild cows, were transformed into farm laborers, and with the invention of refrigeration in meat packing, the wild herds were replaced by blooded Herefords. Far-southern republics developed, in fact, for the first time in Latin-American history, a crucial labor shortage—and solved it by importing five millions of peasants from the low-wage countries of southern Europe.

Nevertheless, from the southern states of Brazil to Patagonia, vast gains took place in the fifty years from the 1870s to the 1920s, both in money wages and living standards. Argentine farm laborers made as much as $1.50 a day in the boom years, lived in houses where the gaucho had lived in hovels, ate a balanced and fairly bountiful diet where the gaucho had existed like a preying carnivorous beast.

In spite of these locally beneficial factors, however, the basic incubus remained. Latin America was swamped in the poverty of its working masses. Where wages were pittances, national incomes were also pittances. Where national incomes were pittances, no purchasing power was available to support large-scale national industries; no capital could be saved up to develop national resources. No funds were available, either through taxation or philanthropy, for general educational programs which would bring the masses abreast of modern technological progress.

For capital, for technical supervision, for equipment and the gadgets of modern comfort, the republics had to turn increasingly to the United States and Europe—to go increasingly into debt to the United States and Europe—as the pace of their superficial modernization was speeded. And as the debt deepened, the narrow control of their own meager economies, which the republics had originally possessed, passed increasingly out of their hands.

One by one, in the wake of the mines, the tropical-products planta-tions, the banking systems, the more prosperous upland haciendas, the new railroads that opened up new frontiers, and new factories, built to relieve their dependence on alien industrial skills, slipped slowly into the control of the foreigners. They slipped away faster, if anything, during the years of the first World War boom than before; fatter dividends attracting more possession-impassioned investors. This is one reason, perhaps, why certain statesmen look on the somewhat desperate efforts of the United States to manage their second World War economics for them with less than child-like trust and hopefulness.

One thing, however, as the interest and dividends drained away to London, New York and Paris, the republics still incontestably owned: the dregs of their natural economies—the low-wage pro-letariat.

☆   ☆   ☆

When you travel extensively in Latin America, you begin to realize factually what this handicap means.

No statistician, to be sure, has the slightest idea what the average annual income in Latin America is. It varies considerably from Mexico to Magallanes; it varies materially from class to class. But one thing to the naked eye is manifest—its insufficiency.

The head of a press association bureau in Rio de Janeiro won-ders, for instance, how his bright young men on from $8 to $20 a week manage to marry, raise children and support—as the Brazil-ian convention requires of their virility and white-collar social station—mistresses. He does not wonder why they look jaded and undernourished.

At a cocktail party in Ecuador you ask your host why a gentle-man of his obvious worldly sophistication chooses to live in a far-away mountain-hamlet like Quito.

"Because," he tells you frankly, "my income in normal times (with which since 1929 I have had no experience) sometimes comes to as much as $125 a month. Here, on $90 a month, I live on a two-acre suburban estate and keep three servants. But in whose restaurant would I have to wash dishes in order to live on $125 a month on Long Island?"

Your American hostess, whose butler and two maids are serving you champagne in a Central American capital, along with a feast approximating a state banquet, asks with not quite mock tearfulness how she and her husband may be expected to live on a first lieutenant's pay when they are transferred back to New York. "Why, my cook here," she mourns, "costs me exactly as much for a month as a cleaning woman back there will cost me for eight hours."

She exaggerates slightly, but the broad patterns of comparison are unmistakable. You do not know statistically what all cooks and bus boys earn from Valdivia, Chile, to Tampico. But you do know that coffee, bananas, cocoa, sugar and cotton, from Mexico to southern Brazil, are tended, picked and prepared for export by labor which works for between twenty and fifty cents a day on less than a fourth of the days of the year.

You know that except for a few classes of expert mechanics, and in a few highly unionized areas of Mexico, most Latin-American mining is done for less than $1 a day. You know that unskilled and semiskilled labor in the cities works for from fifty cents to $1.50 a day, mostly on the dark side of the dollar sign, and that in the white-collar classes any young man who makes more than $1,000 a year is considered—mistress commitments and all—a definite catch for the neighborhood.

Not even in "modernized" Argentina is the situation exactly an economic victory. A Buenos Aires unskilled worker earns from $30 to $35 a month in an environment where the Argentine government's own statistics show that the subsistence minimum is close to $45 a month. The Argentine farm laborer, on from $15 to $22 a month, with his vegetable plot and his two or three pigs to raise, lives actually a trifle better.

But how can a $30-a-month ditchdigger in Buenos Aires—the last word in aristocracy for Latin-American unskilled workers—save money to buy a home, or a car, or a share of stock in his employer's enterprise? How can he, without considerable recklessness, buy a toothbrush or see an American movie? And how can a $3-a-month Quito or Managua house servant buy even a box of bobby pins or a Jersey City lipstick?

Nor do the evils of the situation shrink with time. On the contrary, since the turn of the century, the vicious circle has widened. For, once having entered the international low-wage competition, Latin America's twenty-to-fifty-cents-a-day tropical-plantation labor inevitably finds itself at the mercy of two-to-ten-cents-a-day labor.

Rubber has practically passed as Brazilian and Peruvian "big pay" export, because rubber can be grown more cheaply on plantations in the tropical Orient by East Indian or Malay coolies. Thirty-three years ago South America produced better than three fourths of the world's cocoa crop. Today Africa produces nearly two thirds of it. African Negroes, on a living standard a fraction above a savage's, grow it for less money. Chilean and Mexican copper must fight, in the European markets, a losing battle with Congo and Rhodesian copper.

In the tropical export fields where Latin America still holds its own or is advancing, a kind of spontaneous overproduction prevails. Brazil either burns surplus coffee by millions of pounds, or dumps it on the world markets to depress the economy of all the republics from Guatemala to Bolivia. Caught between the high-priced quality cottons of the United States and the low-production-cost cottons of Africa and the Oriental tropics, a dozen republics try to meet their problem of export by putting inferior and inadequately graded cottons on the market. Every economist and practical businessman the traveling American meets between Havana and Rio de Janeiro has an argument to offer for increasing Washington's sugar quotas. Even with twenty per capita demitasses to the day and two tablespoonfuls to the demitasse, Brazil is choked in sugar.

Yet constantly upward the pace of production of sugar and coffee and cotton runs. The labor is there on the plantations, and with each year's natural increase in the fecund tropical climate, more labor has to live. No chance for better farm land beckons it to new frontiers, for this labor would lack tools and the capital to exploit jungle and mountain farm land even if it were to be had for the asking. No openings for better-paid harvest-hand's work calls it to the little self-sufficient economies of the highland valleys. Industry and the rough work of the growing cities call away a few thousands each year, but the millions must live where they were born. They can live by one method only—producing more of the commodities of which the world has already more than enough. The low-wage economy thus drifts toward the point where it survives by deepening its penury.

It is easy, of course, to explain away the situation's difficulties. Mr Stuart Chase can write charmingly of the idyllic self-sufficiency of Mexican village life—first having picked his village with reasonable discretion. Romanticists insist that the peon without money enjoys a kind of other-worldly felicity in being independent of the machine age. Economic "one idea" men, from single taxers to Fascists, ignoring both the nature of politicians and the hazards of social experiment, insist that all evil can be exorcised by putting the right political medicine men in office and initiating the right program. The Latin-American upper classes and little "colonies" of Yankee works managers and salesmen and industrial property owners who represent American capital in the twenty republics offer a perpetual brief to the effect that Latin America is the best of all possible economic worlds as it is.

On his vegetable and banana patch the Latin-American worker eats, they chirp cheerily. He has no fuel expenses, his house can be built for the price of a pair of shoes in Omaha, his clothing costs less than an alarm clock. Since he is forever busy scratching for a bare living, he does not suffer from unemployment. If he belongs to the city proletariat, with his dollar a day or his seventy-five cents a day, he buys his food from a country proletariat which lives and produces on a vastly cheaper basis than himself. The peons of Latin America's rural slums, these upper-class philosophers proclaim, actually set a more bountiful table than Arkansas share croppers; the city laborer's $5 a week will buy more of the basic necessities in Rio de Janeiro or San Salvador than $25 a week will buy for the taxi driver's family on Manhattan Island. So what would the proletarians below the Rio Grande do with more money, if they had it? It is as if the whole problem of Latin-American economics hinged on the question of whether Juan de la Cruz is able to handle money with the discriminating wisdom of a branch-bank manager.

Actually, the problem runs distressingly deeper than that. What we have in Latin America is not so much peons without money as nations without money. For better or worse, societies have grown up which lack the mass aggregate wealth either to develop their own natural resources or to pay foreign capital for developing them; which lack the taxable resources to pay for the roads, the schools, the public works, the public-health services—all the physical gear a society requires in order to function as a participating member in a modern civilization.

But more is implied in this chronic shortage of cash income than Latin America's mere domestic poverty. In one way or another practically every phase of our relations with the twenty republics is affected by it. Governments without tax resources of their own are automatically tempted to lay ruinous taxes on foreign investors. Nations which see their natural resources drifting into foreign hands, the national incomes being paid out in dividends to foreign shareholders, inevitably seek to regain control of their economic destinies by the desperate means of expropriation. Programs for trade expansion cannot gain impressive headway in nations whose total available funds for purchasing abroad seldom run above $1,500,000,000. American competition with the "barter economy" of the Fascist powers necessarily will be handicapped by the fact that, for countries without cash purchasing power, barter agreements have an almost fatal fascination. Bright and tender-minded movements for better cultural understanding tend to be shipwrecked in republics which can barely afford schools to carry on the most elementary features of their own domestic cultures. The business of bringing a continent abreast of the power age is not to be performed swiftly while a society of 120 million people still needs Juan de la Cruz to carry its burdens.

One vital basis of our misunderstanding of Latin America lies, then, in the fact that we both ignore her economic lag and expect the impossible of her. We expect the twenty republics to function with respectful and contented docility on a slum income as the mineral and the tropical-products sweatshops of international capital, and at the same time we expect them to pay their way and conduct themselves as self-respecting equals.

CHAPTER V

Culture As Façade

In QUITO under gray and golden domes stand three of the most spectacular churches in the Western Hemisphere. They are heavy and massive and bear their own weight against a background of mountains so tall that only at noon under the equatorial sun is the town quite free from shadows. Yet they are at the same time light and lovely, delicate in curve and outline. When you look down on them from the slopes of Pichincha, their domes nod above the city like artificial golden flowers.

Within, the tone color of La Compañía de los Apostólicos is sheer gold. San Francisco is gold with the blue of the dawn sky filtering innocently through it. La Merced is gold, overlaid with a sinister dark crimson, like drying blood. Gold flashes from the ornaments of the stations of the cross and the favored saints' niches like the play of sunlight in a room half-shaded by wind-swept branches. On the central altars gold gleams in a kind of orchestration of opulence.

The vestments, the carvings of the seventeenth-century pulpits, the choir stalls and shrine gateways are only a little less rich than the gold. Now and then the guiding padre stops in your tour and calls your attention to a Murillo or El Greco—time-frayed and badly preserved, but an authentic old master.

Yet he also calls your attention to pious chromos by local amateurs of the nineteenth century, pictures as stiff and ungracefully lurid as the colored lithographs of Balkan War scenes one used to see in Greek shoe-shining parlors in the United States as late

[63]

as the 1920s. Side by side with virgins carved by the exquisite Spanish artisanship of the sixteenth century stand virgins which might have been hewed by local carpenters with their tongues in cheek.

"With God," the padre at La Merced informed me sententiously, "genius and good will rank the same."

Socially, there are even more significant discrepancies. Long before dawn in Quito, the thin mountain air is shaken by the ferocious bonging of church bells. "The servants' day begins at five," my Ecuadorean friends explained it, "so there must be Mass at four." Under your windows, then, when the tumult stops, you hear suddenly the "slip slip" sound of hundreds of sandaled feet walking to church through the piercing chill of the night mist. The $3-a-month proletariat is paying its duty to the golden shrine.

But this working proletariat is relatively rich compared with the one which you meet when you make your own church visit —the maimed and the blind, the crippled and the syphilitic crawling about the aisles and porticoes of magnificence to beg for five-centavo pieces of a coin worth seven cents on the dollar.

It was in Quito, too, that my fleas came back. The Managua and Tegucigalpa consignment had weakened their hold in neat San José, in Costa Rica, and fallen off altogether in scientifically sterilized Panama. The Colombian cities left me scatheless, and so had Guayaquil. Even my first two days in Quito produced no return in the affliction, but on the third they were suddenly at me in swarms.

"Ah," an Ecuadorean friend sympathized when I came to him for consolation and advice on local remedies. "So you have at last been to the churches?"

The churches are places where the poor, the crippled and the illiterate may go to admire the esthetic superiority of their betters. In their flea-infested magnificence there is, indeed, a kind of allegory of Latin America's inherited culture. For—except in specialized areas like Mexico, where old bonds are breaking, or Buenos Aires, which is as modernly urban as Chicago—culture, whether intellectual or esthetic, has never grown very far from its early roots and motivations. It is still the special province of the

[64]

aristocracy—a realm which the populace is only expected to enter as a dazzled spectator. Culture is a theatrical device with which you overawe the subject masses; a varnish with which you hide your essential poverty, the bleakness of the communal life, from friendly visitors of not too critical insight; an instrument admirably designed for exhibiting the virtuosity of favored individuals and classes but hardly, as yet, a medium through which a democratic society is expected to express or improve itself, or even to criticize the conditions under which it lives.

So, though in Quito you are seldom out of sight of the three most charming churches in Western Christendom, you never come within range of a cultural campaign for the eradication of fleas.

☆   ☆   ☆

This is not set down in dispraise of Quito, which—fleas notwithstanding—is one of the pleasantest towns of its size in Latin America. Quito is simply the product of its past. The startling contrasts between a pretentious cultural establishment at the top and an equally flamboyant poverty at the bottom are the logical product of all the forces that have entered into Latin-American history.

The Church, for example, came to Latin America with an already full-grown tradition of pretentiousness. All successful religions are pretentious—the Massachusetts Puritans no less so in theology and authoritative mannerisms than the Ecuadorean Catholics in ceremonial pomp and gaudy display of material riches—for fairly simple reasons. The glories of an unseen world can be sold as certainties to an instinctively skeptical race only through immensely dramatic showmanship.

Once established in Latin America, in any event, all the Church's motives for pretension were redoubled. Here were not merely Spanish peasants to be impressed with repetitions of ceremonies accepted as holy interpretations of the meaning of the universe for centuries. Here were millions of Indians to be held in subjection by fears of a hell and hopes of a heaven they had barely heard of; to be kept in order by their admiration of conquerors who had barely mastered them. To hold its authority in Spain, the Church merely had to be present where the peasants could seek it out. To hold its more perilous sway over a continent of barbarians hardly won from paganism, and at the same time to support the political powers of Spain with the terrors of its mystical rewards and punishments, the Church had literally, in every settlement from Mexico to Patagonia, to dominate the physical landscape.

The Church's culture was a culture of display, of pretense, of virtuosity—a culture of the "top ranks" deliberately contrived for the edification and mystification of the masses, because on no other terms, against such racial and numerical obstacles, could a culture imposed by the foreigner from abroad have survived.

And for the three colonial centuries (long enough to condition society), the Church was practically the only cultural establishment which the Latin-American masses knew at all.

When broader horizons dawned for the generation before independence, in the last quarter of the eighteenth century, the attitude of the new intellectuals toward the world of ideas was curiously like that of the padres toward their own special province. The mine and hacienda owners, reading their Diderot and Voltaire and the daring new books from Europe, the university students and the new crop of young lawyers and political theorists arguing the opinions of the French *philosophes* in the clubs and coffee houses, hardly conceived of intellectual culture as a force that sprang from the masses or bound them more closely to the masses. It was not a form of wealth that the masses could conceivably have a share in, but something as far above the bookless state of the subjugated Indians as the gold on the sacred altars was above their poverty. Culture was an exotic treasure that came from Europe like a piece of exquisite jewelry; a new badge of aristocratic distinction for proud colonial families wounded by the slight of their social subordination to officials from Spain. The new learning was something to dazzle equals with, to prove the young colonials cleverer than their official superiors. But Latin America was slow—and is slow today—to think of it as a medicine with which to inoculate the masses against poverty and ignorance.

Moreover, under the republics all the forces that made for pretentiousness strengthened. The republics were sovereign powers, yet they lived on for decade after decade in gross political disorder and economic squalor. The cultured man—the intellectual, the scholar, the artist—who managed to keep a certain integrity in such an environment had, to a degree, to disassociate himself from the life about him in order to prove his quality. In the world of thought or art or letters, he represented his republic—of which as a cultural society he might be secretly, and more than a little, ashamed. He must conform to European thought molds and to European modes of expression with an extra flourish, then, for two reasons: both to suggest that his native culture was stronger than it was, and to show that he was superior to it. Even when he took his material from his native background, the artist had to paint, and the novelist and the historian had to write like a sophisticated Parisian or a Madrid classicist, in order to prove how many cuts he was above the rank and file of revolutionists and political gangsters who gave coloration to the republics' politics.

It was a difficult climate for national cultures to develop in, but by no means unprecedented. Down at least until the Civil War and in many fields long afterward, writers and artists of the United States were equally occupied with the demonstration that they could escape the frontier's corrupting influences and perform as elegantly as the British.

Longfellow and Hawthorne yielded nothing to Tennyson and Thackeray on points of Victorian correctness. Cooper's Iroquois spoke Sir Walter Scott's jargon for feudal aristocrats without blemish, and Irving repeated the cadences—and the whimsies—of the London essayists of the early nineteenth century as faithfully as the historians of early Latin America reproduced the ponderosities of the Madrid scholars. American painters of the post-Revolutionary school cultivated the lyricism of eighteenth-century English portraitists and the romantic classicism of the French David with the assiduity of copyists who could risk no innovations. Poe was an original exotic, but an original exotic cast in European molds. Even today his esthetic theories and experiments are better understood by continental Europeans—and incidentally Latin Americans—than by his own fellow countrymen.

[67]

And when self-expression arrived, it came in rushes of uneasy exhibitionism—the "barbaric yawp" of Whitman, the self-conscious drolleries of Mark Twain, the cryptic style of Emerson, the crabbed individualism of Thoreau. Americans had been too long embarrassed in a world of Sydney Smiths roaring, "Who reads an American book?" to be quite free from the impulse to posture in a world where suddenly they were read. On this point, too, it may be worth mentioning, Latin America has repeated the process. Nowhere else in the world is the exhibitionism of the early Yankee self-expressionists better matched than in the flamboyant positiveness of Rivera murals.

With its artistic awakening of the 1920s and 1930s, Mexico has reached approximately the same stage in its progress toward self-expression that the United States reached with *Leaves of Grass* in the 1850s. Yet this statement in itself gives a false impression for Latin America as a whole. In Mexico self-expression has been reached only after profound social and economic revolutions. Elsewhere than in Mexico—and in Mexico itself except in painting and sculpture—the cultural climate of Latin America has changed chiefly with the changing fashions of Europe.

Art, literature and scholarship remain much as they were in colonial days, the province of an elite, and of an elite far more interested in demonstrating its ability to copy the patterns of Paris than in telling what the twenty republics have on their minds. Like polo in the Argentine, like the physical adornment of the Quito churches, culture in Latin America is itself a façade —a means of disguising the poverty of life rather than of expressing its vitality and richness.

"There is," the Peruvian critic García Calderón once wrote in a pregnant paragraph, "a strange divorce between its [Latin America's] turbulent politics and its refined art." The divorce is not to be contested, and historically it was no doubt inevitable, but it is typical of Latin-American criticism to boast that a vast gulf exists between culture and reality rather than to be distressed by it. Because of that gulf, Latin America's Whitmans remain undeveloped and her Paul Bunyans undiscovered. Because of it her culture remains a culture of ingratiation rather than of self-expression—and a further stumbling block to understanding between the Americas.

☆   ☆   ☆

The net effect of the situation is to infect culture, where it raises its head above the masses, with an empty and showy—and occasionally vulgar—pomposity. Like the excessively uniformed presidential palace guard troops in the better-tailored republics, learning and the arts, literature and intellectual accomplishment are constantly on parade, and they enjoy it.

Most obviously, perhaps, the tendency betrays itself in architecture. The Spanish colonial mansions and public buildings were stately and reticent, if often dull, but the average government palace built during the republics' later years is a voluptuary's dream of Gothic or Greco-Roman or Byzantine ostentation.

The Argentine Congressional Hall in Buenos Aires is as grandiloquent with terraces and porticoes and rows of flamboyant columns as a temple for Nero. The new Capitol at Havana, with its pillars of colored marble, its vast expanses of gilt and red plush, its enormous diamond in the center of the mosaic floor of the main *sala* at the feet of the gigantic gilded statue of "the Goddess of the Republic," represents a curious combination of a wedding cake and a Comstock Lode millionaire's ideal of opulence in marble halls. In Bogotá, the congressional buildings now being rushed to completion suggest a hybrid between the Acropolis and an Andalusian monastery. With two or three exceptions, every republic at one time or another in its periods of prosperity has spent its funds on the Second Empire magnificence of some Teatro Nacional in the capital city. Yet outside the two or three obvious metropolises, the dramatic fare offered the populace was confined to jaded stock companies from Spain, and the blighted edifices are now mainly used for Hollywood movies.

In the main, too, the official pace of ostentation has been eagerly copied by private builders. Curliques and cupolas flourish on top the office buildings of Rio de Janeiro and Buenos Aires as lavishly as gargoyles on medieval cathedrals. Lately, in cities like Bogotá and Mexico City, which are practically rebuilding their residential sections, the old conservative style of the plain-walled houses, with their iron-grilled windows built flush with the sidewalks, has been abandoned for the lusher gorgeousness of the Hollywood villa. In Quito, where a rash of miniature Robert Taylor palaces is breaking out in the town's swankiest suburb, this art form reaches a kind of all-Latin-American apogee. Not satisfied with a Southern California-Moorish mansion in gray stone with pink trimmings, fronting on the as yet undeveloped neighborhood plaza, the retired politician who built it has equipped the establishment with a minaret, full size.

The capitals and the larger towns bristle also with statuary no less than with architectural wonders. They are scarcely more melodramatic than many of the older statues in Washington, but in the small, compact plazas and shorter avenues of the Latin cities their concentration seems more ostentatious. Generals who were uncompromising dictators on earth and died in exile or before firing squads must ride to the wars again on prancing stallions or brandish their swords or their best oratorical gestures against the enemies of the fatherland. National—or local—poets must strike their best elocutionary poses; scholars stand before the world in the depressing dignity of their somber robes and classroom severity; politicians loom over tropical parks with statesmanship lowering from their brows.

Allegorical groups, mainly of ladies in various stages of classical nudity, must represent the national virtues and aspirations. Bolívar mounts a war horse in practically every central plaza of a consequential town from Caracas to La Paz; and in an astonishingly bold and artistically effective conception at a fork of two highways in Quito, he rides with his cavalry under the wings of condors. In Managua, Rubén Darío, probably the most competent modern poet Latin America has produced, but also one of the most competently Bohemian voluptuaries of nineteenth-century literature, stands in a scholar's gown with his hand outstretched in blessing over a marble boatload of overfat cherubs. So many hero generals of the Paraguayan War of the 1860s have been placed on gigantic male horses in the park bordering the sea wall at Rio de Janeiro that a waggish French resident christened it "the esplanade of stallions."

As one moves on through this continuing grove of statues, the display of local and regional worthies takes on a kind of synthetic quality. The monuments represent every degree of artistic merit —from the Civil War memorial type and the town stonecutter's tombstone virtuosity to works of extraordinary felicity, like the virile bronze memorial group and bas-reliefs, in Mendoza, Argentina, of San Martín's expedition for the liberation of Chile. The personages commemorated represent all degrees of human merit from local *caudillos* and panhandling politicians to men, like Bolívar, of unqualified greatness and vision. Yet, seen as a kind of sculptural convention, the statues register chiefly the vanities of patriotism. Nations are equals, they seem to proclaim in unison; therefore, all national heroes are equal and therefore all national heroes must have equally ornate statues.

So, along with San Martín in Mendoza, you have an heroic group for General Barrios in Guatemala City. General Barrios, you learn upon consultation with your textbooks, was an exceptionally competent dictator of Guatemala who died in battle in 1885 trying to extend his dictatorship over the four other Central American republics. So, along with the various equestrian Bolívars in the republics from Venezuela to Bolivia, you get, in Rio de Janeiro, the Duque de Caxias mounted on an even more imposing and more virile stallion. The Duque de Caxias was chiefly memorable, in the quiet days of the Brazilian empire, for having, at the end of five years of warfare and a series of appalling defeats for his superior forces, overwhelmed Dictator Francisco Solano López of little Paraguay by a ten-to-one preponderance of numbers.

The foreigner is seldom, under any circumstances, however, permitted to consider these discrepancies—either of sculptural merit or historical importance—critically. It is entirely appropriate for one's Cuban friends to remark with reference to the monument to Máximo Gómez, the charmingly uniformed old guerrilla leader on the Malecón in Havana, that the allegorical figure representing Cuban liberty sits under the horse's tail. It is proper for one's guide in Guayaquil to wisecrack over a bust of Pizarro in

[71]

a public park that "we keep this here to show that we Ecuadoreans, too, honor hypocrisy."

But from the foreigner no wisecrack is expected. This is national art—though in a surprisingly large majority of cases imported from France and Italy—and these are national heroes. Respect and awe, mingled perhaps with a little of the ignorant alien's naïve and apologetic curiosity, are the only attitudes accepted. One may ask what are the works for which Ecuador's national poet is distinguished, but not how good is an Ecuadorean poet.

☆ ☆ ☆

Often in Latin America it is as if the statues had communicated something of their spirit to literature and the intellectual life. Sculpture in general—and practically all Latin-American sculpture —is a technique for putting a man in a heroic pose and holding him there. It is the art which above all others disdains casualness. And so does the Latin-American intelligentsia. It is not, of course, that the intelligentsia has bad manners. The writers, the educators, the leaders of thought one meets in the centers of cultural activity greet one, as a rule, with a gracious modesty. They bubble with little jokes in deprecation of their personal attainments and professional interests. The authors one reads strive for suavity and delicate subtleties quite as often as for tropical lushness or shock-your-little-sister realism. Latin America is virtually the last of the continents where the "gentle essayist" still has a following.

Yet under all the conventional self-deprecation broods a kind of passionate earnestness. You are invited to a gathering of the intelligentsia, for instance. Everybody is *"doctór"*—*"doctór"* is the standard university degree in Latin America, "bachelor" being merely the reward of a course in the *colegio* or high school—and everyone uses it with the utmost formality. The poets, once the social civilities are over, recite their verses, with elocutionary gestures. The novelists and essayists read from their latest manuscripts. The professors discuss their fields of erudition with all the flourishes of the lecture platform.

The atmosphere, in short, is something between that of the

piece-speaking afternoon in the old-fashioned public school and the faculty meeting. Everyone is an important person. Everyone knows it, and everyone enjoys it. Minds are on parade, and while a certain amount of wit is unquestionably on display along with their other accouterments, any levity which interferes with the general dignity of the procession is regarded as a gross breach of manners.

For all this mildly exhibitionist austerity, there are, no doubt, abundant North American precedents. The intellectual Brahmins of Boston and Concord in the mid-nineteenth century also had a cultural façade to defend against alien detractors; and the pride of pedantry in which they armed themselves was rarely more than faintly punctured—certainly never deflated—by the persistent chirpiness of Dr Oliver Wendell Holmes. Even today in certain Boston groups where the sensitive tradition lingers, the occasion when Mark Twain presumed to address the assembled Titans with a broadside of personal wisecracks is remembered as a cosmic social catastrophe: an episodic insult in which the blasphemies of the Sin against the Holy Ghost and the nihilistic abandon of the 1938 hurricane are abominably mingled.

Thus the analysis of different cultural climates boils down, in a sense, to the fact that the Latin-American intellectuals share, at worst, a kind of parvenu pride in punditry with the lately flowering New Englanders—and certain parvenu fears of being seen off mental parade momentarily, and being taken for something less important than they are.

So in Bogotá's and Buenos Aires' more erudite circles a kind of pundits' formality reigns—modified, it is true, by ingratiating Latin manners—much as it did in the Boston Atheneum lectures of the 1850s. You can no more play with what is in your mind in Lima or Santiago than in Concord you could have "joshed" with Emerson about self-reliance. Learning is earnest in the twenty republics and is no more to be displayed frivolously than a ball gown is to be worn on a tennis court.

One evening, for instance, I was taken to call on an outstanding woman writer of South America. She was a formally cordial lady in her middle fifties, but there was none of the easygoing genial-

ity in her welcome that one finds between fellow craftsmen of the
writing business in the United States. The man who took me had
known her from early childhood, and the friendship between
their families dated back two generations. But obviously the part
expected of him in the proceedings was to remain in the background and admire her as the local Héloïse. Plainly, from the
moment the polite questions about mutual acquaintances were
over, this was to be a conversation between highbrows and on
a high intellectual plane.

Was I going to Peru? she asked me. If so, I would not like the
Peruvians. They were, she assured me, the incurable imperialists
of South America. Once they had ruled the continent from Lima,
and they had never accepted their descent to the position of a
mere republic. They still felt themselves superior to their neighbors in blood and culture; still schemed impotently to seize the
lands of the border republics and build from these a new Peruvian empire. Did we not realize these things in North America?
she inquired a bit chidingly. And for half an hour she lectured
me, in solemn classroom manner and with a display of vast historical erudition, on the thesis that all Peruvians were frustrated
Conquistadores.

She turned her attention to President Roosevelt. Was he a
Socialist? I made it clear that he fitted no orthodox definitions.
So, then, he must be a Communist or a Fascist? And if he was
neither, then he must be a laissez-faire individualist?

I struggled to explain that Mr Roosevelt has at various times
been tagged by all four names and that his policies appear to be
heirs of any number of ideologies.

"Do you North Americans really believe that a man can be
four political persons in one?" she smiled skeptically, and proceeded to enlighten my muddled mind. For half an hour she
expounded what Communism was, what Socialism was, and what
were the exact philosophical differences between Adam Smith and
Mussolini.

"Now," she demanded triumphantly when the lecture was
finished, "to which category does Mr Roosevelt belong?"

I stuck to my guns that Mr Roosevelt defied cataloguing; and

suddenly the atmosphere changed. My hostess's prodigious learning had failed to impress me, and, rather plainly, she was baffled.
To her insistently classifying mind a statesman must belong to
some specific school of political philosophy. Her manner said definitely that it was perverse, or worse, lowbrow, of a mere journalist
in the presence of a pundit to maintain otherwise.

From then on, I could feel the force of two struggling suspicions. Could I, for some malign reason, be trying to conceal Mr
Roosevelt's true ideological connections? Or could I, in some
sudden paroxysm of barbarous Yanqui humor, be trying to pull
a sage's leg?

Her dismissal was, if anything, a shade more formal than her
greeting. Quite evidently, North American journalists were to be
listed in her future categories as men without proper reverence
for things of the mind.

There are times, on the other hand, when it is difficult to get
a Latin-American pundit to discuss the matter in hand at all. I
called one day on one of South America's leading publishers. I
had one simple curiosity—to learn how the publishing business in
Latin America functions—how it scouts for and finds authors,
how it finances them, how it earns its profits. I stayed more than
two hours, but I never learned.

The publisher, an expansive and wholly hospitable gentleman,
began by asking me how George Washington during the Revolution financed his early munitions purchases. I didn't know the
answer; but he did, which pleased him greatly. He spent perhaps
fifteen minutes learnedly elucidating it—a discussion which led
him around eventually to the generalization that all hit-or-miss
enterprises like new publishing houses and wars of independence
have to do with their financing on a hand-to-mouth basis.

It was part of his personal philosophy, he expounded pleasantly,
and for the next hour he reviewed his personal philosophy, and
after that, his personal career and the history of his personal
friendships with celebrated European and Latin-American literary
figures. He was an amiable man without undue reticences, and
I have no doubt that if I could have deferred my other appoint-

ments until the next day, I could have learned all about the publishing business. But first it had to be impressed upon me that a meeting between a publisher and a professional writer was a strictly cultural rendezvous. If it took two hours to do this, mere information could wait.

Finally, there was the young Argentine who came to see me one day and confessed that he had written several novels. He had read *Gone with the Wind* and Emerson; and he was curious about United States literature—particularly Dreiser and Sinclair Lewis.

I described their works, their styles and their contributions to social insight in the best Spanish I could muster, while my visitor waited with polite impatience.

"But what schools do they belong to?" he asked as soon as a chance came.

I explained that they were both realists, but there the resemblance ended. Mr Dreiser's realism was melancholy and philosophical, even a little sentimental. Mr Lewis' realism was photographic and satirical. And so on.

"But I do not mean it exactly in that sense," Don Arturo interrupted gently. "I am interested in knowing what their associations are with the European literary groups. . . . Señor Dreiser, for example, he is very old, is he not? Would you say, then, that he writes in the tradition of Anatole France, or of Hauptmann or Sudermann? And Mr Lewis? Would you call him a Proustian? Or is his work more the style of the 'Men of Good Will' series?"

I feared, I told him, that Dreiser was chiefly Dreiser and Lewis, Lewis. Although both no doubt had their European mentors and their home-grown imitators, it was difficult for us in the United States to think of our authors as moving in set schools at all. We had only the grand divisions—the realists, the romanticists, the pulp writers and perhaps the humorists.

"It is a pity," said Don Arturo gravely. "It is difficult for us to read and appreciate your authors when we cannot place them in the categories to which we are accustomed.

"I, myself," he added, "am a Proustian."

☆   ☆   ☆

Such personal incidents are not put on the record to indicate a superiority of one type of culture over another but to point the differences between them. Between ourselves and the Latin Americans, the distinction is not fundamentally one of quality, but a profound difference of mainsprings.

To the literate Latin American, the culture of the North, cherishing its pragmatic values, standing in the streets and striving to express life and to analyze and explain its problems in terms of raw emotions and physical experience, seems to have abandoned itself to a brawling, materialistic bedlam. Latin America's culture, placing itself on a pedestal, striking statuesque poses, striving for the ideal life of the mind and the perfection of form rather than social usefulness, seems to us academic and emptily pretentious.

We educate for use. They suspect that we miss the whole aim of culture in not educating for ornament. Our scholars and savants tend to disparage their learning, strive not to be taken for literary personages; and college professors, in public, laugh at their virtuosities with the wisecrackers and the humorists. Can this be a symptom, the Latin mind wonders, that the North Americans do not even believe in the little culture they have?

We sin against their canons that wisdom should be gracious and hold itself above the common life to be admired like a jewel on an altar. They sin against our canons that wisdom should be "practical" and not take itself too seriously. In general, too, the Latin Americans are more aware of our sins than we are of theirs. A vast body of literature has grown up in the republics around the theory of the Uruguayan critic and philosopher, José Enrique Rodó, that Latin America's culture is the culture of Ariel, ours the cult of Caliban.

These mis-estimates of one another's cultural merits need not, I believe, present permanent barriers to friendship. But they cut much of the ground out from under the thesis that an easy solution of the problems of closer understanding with Latin America is to be found in cultural rapprochement. We shall not get cultural rapprochement merely by wishing it and making polite gestures. To win the respect of Latin-American intellectuals, more is needed than occasional patronizing reports from returned travelers that the intellectual tone of conversation in Bogotá and Buenos Aires is higher than in New Orleans. More is required than gracious banquet compliments to the merits of Latin-American writers, who, every literate Latin American knows, are seldom read above the Rio Grande.

"Cultural understanding" with the twenty republics is remote from reality until educated North Americans approach Latin-American art and thought with the same sense of historic backgrounds with which we approach British and French art and literature. We cannot be sure that Nazi and Fascist influence over the neighbor peoples will be less effective than ours until we come to feel the bloodstream motive powers behind their cultural and emotional lives.

CHAPTER VI

Certain Social Values

It would be unfair, no doubt, to mention the name of the Colombian city where I met Don Tomás. It was a sizable provincial metropolis, and nothing to be ashamed of. Furthermore, Don Tomás' forefathers had played an important part in its life for four hundred years. Yet I never met a man who was quite so afraid of being taken for a provincial. It would hurt him as much, I suspect, for me to reveal that a man of his accomplishments lives there as for me to tell his true name.

Don Tomás works in a vague way—apparently as a sort of official greeter—for an American corporation with wide interests in the region, and was assigned to the not too arduous task of guiding the strange journalist about town. We began with an evening walk.

In every little plaza, South American fashion, stood a statue of a founding father. "My ancestor," Don Tomás at each of these encounters would exclaim with an apologetic leer and a clipped British accent. "But it's all eyewash. Being related to all the local celebrities is such a bore, what?"

And Don Tomás would proceed to enlighten me on the exact degree of cousinship by which each of the founding fathers was related to the sixteenth-century Spanish nobility.

But in between statues his conversation was on livelier themes. There were the socialite lives to be described, for instance, of the sister in Paris, the brother in London, the cousins in Madrid, in New York and in Switzerland. "We're a strictly international family," Don Tomás boasted happily. "Polyglot as Biarritz, you know."

There were the years when he attended an English public school and was a footballer. "They say, you know," he explained, "that when a Colombian goes to an English school, he becomes more British than the British. Life without cricket still seems to me frightfully off form."

There was the year he had worked in New York. "Do you journalists see much of the Follies girls?" he inquired, a shade sniffishly. "Too dreadfully expensive, no doubt. But my cousins had ways of arranging little intimacies."

Spain, too, it appeared, gets in a young sophisticate's blood as well as England. "I suppose," Don Tomás confided airily, "I'm a bit of a throwback to my Castilian ancestors. But the first month after I came back here something extraordinary happened.

"I went to the bull fight. I went with two of the most beautiful girls in town, and the matador wasn't doing very well. Suddenly everything turned red before me. The next thing I remember I was down in the bull ring, with the scarf of one of the girls over my arm, trying to play matador myself. The bull roughed me up quite a bit—tossed me directly against the barrier, in fact. The girls, I gathered, felt quite disgraced over it. But you should have heard the cheers—and seen the flowers. . . . When all is said and done," he added, a trifle self-consciously, "Colombia prefers its men to be definitely *picador.*"

I remarked that that seemed to be the way with a good many countries—but that ideas of what constituted virility differed. Don Tomás was instantly in agreement.

"Now take you Americans," he said. "I think there are certain things wrong with you. You are much too sentimental about animals, for instance. It is very difficult for a Spaniard to realize that you have conquered a continent and built that tremendous material civilization of yours when you are distressed at the mere sight of blood in the bull ring. And you undoubtedly pamper your women. We Europeans—or perhaps I should say we Colombians —realize that women are only happy when they are, as you say it in New York, under control.

"But there is another side to you, do you realize it? I am going to tell you something that Americans did for me once. It is one of my most precious memories."

He told me. It appeared that Don Tomás is a Falangista—a member of the local branch of a little doctrinaire Colombian Fascist party. So one night a few months before my arrival he had taken it on himself to break up a meeting of a labor union single-handed.

"They may have been Communists, they may have been merely Socialists," Don Tomás explained cavalierly. "What difference does it make? What the Colombian masses need is discipline."

On this occasion, however, the masses had not recognized their need, and someone had shot Don Tomás in the arm. It was a mere flesh wound that cracked no bones, hardly more than a bullet graze. But Don Tomás was proud of it and showed me the still raw scar.

"And do you know what happened?" he went on excitedly. "They took me to the hospital, and within less than an hour half the American colony was in my room with flowers and Scotch whisky. The doctor told me, since all I had lost was a little blood, that whisky would be the best thing to build my strength up. So we made a lovely night of it.

"But I shall never forget it. I had never quite understood Americans before. This showed me something about them that I had failed to realize. In spite of all your pose of vulgarity and your talk about democracy, you are quicker than any other people in the world to recognize the virile, aristocratic gesture when you see it.

"And if you would like to meet some of the American colony now," Don Tomás added, his English getting a little less clipped as he got further away from football, "I shall be glad to take you to the saloon which they frequent."

So we went to the local cantina which bore the closest relation of any in town to the spots frequented by Dinty Moore, and I was greeted, as usually happens to the traveling Yankee below Panama, with a fairly close approximation of the courtesies of an American old-home week.

"Who's your new Falangista recruit?" the local telephone magnate bellowed. Other wisecrackers took me aside and in stage whispers told me of the perils of Falangista initiation rites—"every bit as bad," they assured me, "as the Kappa Beta Phi's." . . . "Where," they joshed Don Tomás when they learned that I was a traveling newspaperman, "did you get the money to hire a press agent?"

"I sell all the news from here," roared a slightly inebriated young giant who had once sold a paragraph to *Time* magazine. "Didn't you know all Colombian saloons were posted?"

At length, after the long Latin-American cocktail hour, we broke up; and to my considerable surprise Don Tomás parted from me with a solemn humility. "I wish to apologize," he said gloomily, "for the rudeness of my friends. They are good people, but they have rough ways. They do not understand the sensitiveness of men like yourself who appreciate Latin America."

I assured him that I understood the kidding technique—and even the barroom humor—of my fellow countrymen. No offense had been intended or received. But Don Tomás remained disconsolate. I had been insulted in the house, or at any rate the cantina, of his friends, and his humiliation was boundless.

It was a definite shock, then, when late at night Don Tomás entered the hotel cocktail lounge, where I was watching the dancing, and greeted me with the curt nod of a man who is dismissing you from his life permanently. Under the circumstances, naturally, I never heard the explanation of his mysterious coldness from his own lips. But it is fairly easy to surmise. Don Tomás had decided two things about me: his American circle had made fun of me, and I was a man too lost to considerations of personal dignity to resent it.

☆   ☆   ☆

I pick Don Tomás out of a crowd of Latin-American acquaintances, not because he is typical of Latin-American manners toward visiting firemen, but because he is a symptom of forces in Latin-American psychology which run deeper than manners—and indeed control manners. If Don Tomás had been a strictly traditional young provincial aristocrat, he would have shown me the local statues with a grave courtesy, never even mentioning that they were ancestors. He would have bought me drinks in his club or a strictly Spanish cantina, found pleasant, if rather indefinite, things to say about other American acquaintances, deprecated bull fighting as an ancient and probably incurable diversion, and gently dismissed the rows of the local Fascists with the labor movement as an inconsequential feud of local hotheads unlikely to affect the even flow of the home town's life stream. He might have been right and he might have been wrong in his estimate of social forces, but his attitude would have been one of philosophical retirement governed by his sense that, since things had not changed much in his valley in four hundred years, they were not likely to change greatly now. And if, after we parted, our paths crossed again, he would have greeted me with an exquisite cordiality.

But Don Tomás has broken—or at least is trying to break—with local customs and traditions. So at practically every point of a casual human contact, he is painfully unsure of himself. To show that he is not a provincial, he must be more British than the British, more bull-fighting than the Spaniards, more sophisticated than New York night-clubbers. To show that he is abreast of the ideas of the times, he must cultivate gorgeous adventures as a lone-wolf local Fascist. He must be so American that he even takes the face-saving side of an old-fashioned barroom joshing match seriously. Wherever, in a world of constant complications of ideas and mannerisms, a new idea or a new mannerism swims into his ken, he must respond to it with a flourish. In short, Don Tomás is uneasy and unhappy with himself unless he is being a successful show-off. If he is not being a successful show-off, someone might rate him as a failure at the man-of-the-world role he has cut out for himself.

Yet underneath there is more similarity between Don Tomás and the conventional Latin American than you might suppose. Don Tomás feels himself at ease in a world of changing ideas and customs only when, with occasional excessive whoops and false gestures, he is dimly struggling to adapt himself to them. His more orthodox contemporary dismisses the mere possibility of serious changes of ideas or customs with polite belittlement—since he is seldom quite impolite enough for open disdain. But both are hagridden by a single problem—what the world in general will think of them. Both come from a nation which is poor both in cash resources and low mass cultural standards, from a region remote and provincial. Both spring from a race which for three centuries was snubbed and looked down upon by the only people from the outside world its members ever saw—the officially superior Spaniards from Spain. That others, and especially foreigners, should recognize their importance is, in the social life of each, the consideration that is supremely important. One retreats behind a wall of polite custom to safeguard his dignity from criticism; the other, to be sure that he will create an impression, rushes off into callow exhibitionism. The techniques are distinct, but there is hardly much difference in objectives.

They are objectives, incidentally, which throw the windows open on practically the whole range of Latin-American social values. They are simple and highly personal values, on the whole. In a fairly broad sense, they can be expressed in two sentences. A man, if he has talents, or fancies that he has talents, must be admired for them. And a man must be safe from the snubs and the ridicule of the rest of society. What he has, what he has achieved, is relatively unimportant if his dignity is not respected and his amour-propre is not flattered. When due attention is paid to his dignity and his vanity, it makes little difference if he has achieved nothing and has nothing. Man as a social being is on parade in Latin America no less than his culture. When his existence as a person is saluted, he has justified himself.

For all these reasons the citizen of one of the twenty republics who travels abroad often seems, on the surface at least, exceptionally adaptable to foreign milieus. The Latin American picks up the slang, and scraps of the characteristic humor, of the United States almost before his English becomes comprehensible. In Paris, as most night-club major-domos will testify, his graces and gallantries frequently outshine those of the native experts. After a few weeks in London he can outclip the Oxford accent and out-freeze British reserve.

As with Don Tomás, however, these cosmopolitan modes do not always sit easily on him when he returns to the home front. He has put them on to please. But always in the back of his wisdom is the knowledge that the intimate social circle in his native metropolis will be better pleased if he rigidly observes the local customs. So he either sheds off the alien accomplishments with considerable inner struggle, or, being unable to shed them, faces life with a sense of insecurity and symptoms, at times, of painful emotional unbalance.

Within his republic's gates, in any event, he greets the presentable alien, as a rule, with a charming self-consciousness. Concentrating on the impression he makes, your Latin-American acquaintance invariably prefers to say pleasant things to you, to tell you pleasant news. If he has dark suspicions of Washington's diplomatic policies in the back of his mind, he tells you how much he admires American material civilization and what a beautiful ideal is conveyed by the Good Neighbor policy. If he has been stung by some slight to his nation in a wisecracking session with the local American colony, he tells you what a stroke of fortune it would be for hemisphere solidarity if Latin America could be penetrated by Norte Americanos as simpatico as yourself. If it is twenty miles over an abominable road to where you are going, he will tell you that it is twelve miles over an excellent dirt road bordered with delightful scenery.

He laughs at your polite witticisms with the air of a connoisseur enravished by such drollery. When you obviously grope for words in Spanish, he informs you that you have an exquisite accent. On the other hand, if your accent is so bad that he has to ask you to repeat every second phrase, he compliments you on the marvelous flow of words you have. You are pleased with him, and the more he recognizes your pleasure, the more his social virtuosity shines. You cannot possibly—no matter what your foreign standard of values—look down on him as a poor provincial while he is saying such agreeable things to you. He is saving face, as it were—outegoing your ego—with deft courtesies and pretty compliments.

[85]

But not all of the denouements are pretty. Out of the goodness of his heart, for instance, your Latin acquaintance has announced that he will call for you at eleven o'clock tomorrow morning with a car and take you for a tour of the city. Eleven o'clock arrives, but no one comes; nor at twelve o'clock; nor at one o'clock. No one comes at all. Some inconvenience has arisen—work to be done, a lady to be visited, or simply the failure of an alarm clock to go off. After all, the thrill of extending an invitation has been experienced, and the foreigner's gratitude has already been enjoyed, so why bother about the aftermath? It does not occur to your pseudo-host to telephone you about the difficulty. It would be embarrassing to explain the failure to keep an appointment. The ego would not be quite sufficiently triumphant. So you wait—being careful, however, in proportion to your understanding of the customs of the country, not to wait too long.

After such an experience, you are unlikely to see your acquaintance again. He is even capable of declining invitations to gatherings where you are likely to be present, in order to avoid you. But if by unlucky accident you do meet him, he is murmurous with gracious plausibilities. He was called out of the city by a family illness. The friend whom he instructed to inform you was also, in the middle of the night, stricken with an illness. Or the stupid messenger he sent could not find you, or the numerous efforts he made to telephone you of an unexpected business crisis in his life were foiled by some menial on the hotel staff who did not understand your Nordic name.

If you play the game with an innocent air of sympathetic understanding, you are back on the same footing again. You may even receive other invitations. But if you let the slightest intimation of the caustic creep into your tone or your look, you are rated as a barbarian who has failed to respond to a gentleman's courtesy. Only by feeling that you accept him as a man of honor and are completely fooled by him does your pseudo-host regain the sense of superiority which preserves his happiness.

But not all of your Latin-American contacts are of this strictly social character. The customs and immigration officials one meets at the frontiers, the police who sign your tourist permit cards and check on your journeys, the clerks in the railway and travel agencies are hardly in a position to gratify the ego by trading compliments and invitations. So if there is anything which carries a stronger impression of *ne plus ultra* dignity than the port of a petty Latin-American bureaucrat sitting in judgment on the petty problems of traveling compatriots and touring aliens, I should like to meet it.

There was the unforgettable young man—tall as a beanpole and solemn as a nest of Presbyterian owls—who met me on my arrival one Saturday night at the rain-sodden port of Buenaventura on the Colombian Pacific coast, to take off for Ecuador the following Monday morning. He attended to the "official difficulties" of travelers on the Panagra airlines, he explained in English, and had I my *pase salvo?*

A *pase salvo* is a document explaining that, having no contagious disease, police involvements, tax obligations or bad debts outstanding, the traveler is free to leave Colombia. It takes usually a full day in the Bogotá police offices to get one, and when the evidence is at all muddied, anywhere from two days to two weeks. But in Bogotá, due to certain amenities reserved for visiting journalists, the chief of the national police establishment had given me a letter stating that in my case the *pase salvo* could be waived.

"But that is impossible," the young man told me mournfully. "No one has ever left Buenaventura without a *pase salvo*. I will have to cancel your reservation for the Monday plane, then, and advance it to the Thursday plane. It is possible that you will not be able to leave until a week from Monday. You may even have to go back to Bogotá to get it."

He was not, it was plain to see, a disagreeable young man by nature. It was not gloomy joy at my predicament which registered in his attitude but rather the gloom of an acute disappointment in himself. His job was to meet all outgoing Panagra passengers and check their *pases salvos* for technical correctness. In trying to get out of Buenaventura without a *pase salvo*, I was affronting his whole idea of his official importance. It was as if I had come all the way to Buenaventura deliberately to hurt his feelings.

I flourished my letter from the national police commandant.

[*87*]

"But that is not a *pase salvo*," he reproached me.

"But," I argued, "it says specifically that I do not need a *pase salvo*."

"The captain of the port," he countered, "is prohibited by law from letting anyone leave the republic without a *pase salvo*."

"Then when can I see the captain of the port?" I pleaded.

"I regret to say," he informed me stiffly, "that it will be impossible to see the captain of the port at any time before your plane departs. It is Saturday night, and his office is closed. It will be closed all day Sunday. The captain of the port will be present Monday morning for the departure of the plane, but it will then be too late to adjust your difficulty. Besides, without a *pase salvo* it would be inconceivable to the captain of the port that you should have any business to discuss with him."

"Then, I should like to telephone him," I ventured.

"It is impossible," he blocked me, "to telephone the captain of the port on business except during office hours." He sighed resignedly. "There is no other solution—I must change your reservation to Thursday. By Monday evening it should be possible for you to find out whether you can get your *pase salvo* here or whether you will have to return to Bogotá for it."

I did what is necessary in such cases—told him that if he canceled my reservation without permission I should cite him to the chief of the national police as a dangerous character—and sought out his local bosses. Within an hour, as a result, I was seated pleasantly over highballs with the port captain, the police chief's letter had been accepted as a super-*pase salvo,* and all was arranged.

But the young man at the take-off on Monday morning bade me farewell with the same haughty formality he would have used toward a guest who had made slighting remarks about the family silver. "You are very fortunate," he muttered coldly. "But, remember, some other time the failure to have a *pase salvo* might cost you two weeks."

Momentarily, at least, I had destroyed for him a precious possession—the ability to hold the traveling public and imperious foreigners in thrall through the sacred majesty of red tape. On the petty point of routine with which he is charged, he has to dominate his company's clients in order to feel himself a person. When a case arises where he cannot dominate, the whole edifice of his personal self-respect crumbles. He feels like a man whose virility has been slurred under circumstances of acute public humiliation.

☆   ☆   ☆

Once you recognize this yearning for dominance as a primary stimulus, you are in touch with an explanation for practically the whole range of Latin-American social action. The petty official must dominate by forcing his petty public to run through the red-tape mill to the last ringer—or he is less than a man. Your social acquaintance must dominate you by charm, by superior knowledge of the local ritual of customs, by conferring obligations upon you—or feel himself ill at ease. Don Tomás, who has largely abandoned local conventions and is too poor to confer obligations, is unhappy unless he is advertising the pungency of his character through a more or less antic exhibitionism. There is no psychological ease in Latin America without mastery over someone—without demonstrating one's superiority at least to one's immediate world.

Translated to the political sphere, these appetites color the whole spirit of Latin-American government. The Latin-American political leader whose enemies do not fear him, whose friends and associates do not defer to him, flatter him and on all points of importance in public policy slavishly agree with him, thinks of himself, and is laughed at by his public, as a leader without authority. When he rises to the presidency, then, the leader must compel an absolute obedience from his own faction and stifle the criticism of his opponents, or seem less than virile. To exercise power less than ruthlessly is a sign of weakness. To this extent, if a Latin-American leader does not come into office with a lust for despotic power, he is compelled, by his practical political necessities, to develop it.

Few Latin-American presidents, for example, have been able to sustain the activities of a vigorous opposition in Congress. If the opposition is vigorous, so Latin-American psychology reasons, there must be something feeble in the president.

Hence, a long list of tried and traditional methods have grown up for disciplining Congresses. In its gentler forms, discipline may be no more than a matter of buying off the opposition. If there is graft in the republic—and there often is—the most vocally critical senators and deputies of the minority can be silenced by being cut in on it. Or a few key disturbers can be tactfully removed by appointing them to prominent legation and embassy posts in the diplomatic service, a solution which combines the practical effects of silencing a critic with the advantages of polite exile.

But a president who has to buy off his opposition still has to struggle against public suspicion that he paid off because he was afraid. The more serious the opposition is, the more necessary it is for his reputation as a statesman of mastery to silence it by strokes of physical power. This may be accomplished by several methods—at all of which the normal Latin-American political leader is instinctively an expert.

The opposition can be expelled from Congress, for instance. Charges may be made that the minority members were corruptly elected, and, since the Latin-American president who does not hold his courts in the hollow of his political hand would be an unthinkable idealist, there is no question of getting convictions—and removals from office—out of the judiciary.

Or the opposition leaders may be brought before military tribunals for trial on charges—sometimes, but not invariably, trumped up—of devious treasonable intrigues and conspiracies. If guilty—and while a president controls his army, they are always guilty—they can be disposed of by whatever methods, from exile to the firing squad, the sternness of the emergency seems to require. Or Congress may be induced, under a little adroit gun pressure from the army, to declare a state of alarm or emergency, for the duration of which congressional criticism, or even congressional sessions, are indefinitely adjourned.

But the preferred, and perhaps most common, method begins at the grassroots. The Latin-American statesman who most successfully registers mastery does so by preventing the election of any opposition politicians at all. If it becomes known in the provinces, for example, that to run for office against the president's party is a sure-fire way of courting trouble with the police and the military authorities, of losing the friendship of the courts and the local bureaucracy and of putting the government's influence against one's interest in business and the professions, there are not likely to be many candidates. Even if there are candidates, there are not likely to be many voters. Why stand up and be counted with the opposition when it means risking the loss of a job or a jail term on a phony charge?

Latin Americans have various engaging wisecracks to cover the situation. "Voting against the majority is like catching the fever," they say in Mexico. "You may not die, but it will certainly leave you weakened." In Guatemala they put it somewhat more grimly: "If your widow likes flowers, make a speech against Ubico."

In Cuba a defeated antigovernment candidate for Congress told me a delightful story of how an opposition can be crushed by malpractice in arithmetic.

"My mother might lie to me and my wife might lie to me," he said, "and all my brothers and sisters might lie to me. But I know that when I went into my precinct polling booth that morning I voted for myself; and they didn't even count that."

In short, the typical Latin-American administration does not keep its prestige and maintain itself in authority by exchanging heftier buffets with the opposition. The opposition does not win by giving the president's party harder blows than it takes. It wins by working underground in intrigues and conspiracies until it can overthrow the president by some outbreak of violence and disloyalty among his ostensible supporters. There is another Latin-American proverb, indeed, to cover this point. "A truly effective opposition," I was told in Venezuela in a strange parody on a famous Bunker Hill aphorism, "never advertises itself until it can shoot at the white of their eyes."

And when the opposition shoots, or seduces, its way into power, the same grim suppression job is to be done all over again. If it is weak, if it has come in on a liberal pronunciamiento, it must repress criticism all the more sternly in its practical politics in order to show that no citizen dares to take its authority lightly.

There are exceptions to this picture as a simplified, over-all pattern of Latin-American politics, of course. The opposition has a fairly free field to express what is on its mind about the government in Colombia and Costa Rica. The worst dangers its candidates confront at elections are from the government party's vote counters. In the Argentine and Uruguay criticism and debate are free in normal times, and elections are free except when disorders occur—and they are fairly easily invoked—requiring the supervision of the army. Venezuela is breaking away from a long era of repression and permitting both Congress and the newspapers to debate public issues openly. Chile, in spite of the numerous "states of emergency" restrictions provoked by her numerous revolutions since the economic collapse of the 1920s, relapsed into liberalism late in 1938 long enough to permit an opposition to triumph in a presidential election.

But six republics whose governmental methods are partial exceptions to the general pattern do not void the rule for twenty republics. In general, Latin-American government is an institution of inerrant majesty, not the product of democratic political cooperation or competition. And Latin-American rulers, moved by the basic Latin-American social values, feel secure only behind the guns of smart palace guards and the quiet of criticisms suppressed.

☆   ☆   ☆

There is nothing exotic, however, about these political necessities. The ordinary citizen, in his daily round of encounters and clashes with friends, competitors and enemies in his personal social cosmos, must keep his mastery of the situation as effectively as the dictator preserves his state with rifles and repressions.

This is a point which explains many things about Latin America—its fantastically perfect manners, the enormous conservatism of its customs, its cult of lugubrious personal dignity, its attitude toward women, its intense family cohesions. Without these safeguards to his vanity, the Latin American feels himself naked to the scorn of his depreciators.

You cannot make fun of a man whose manners are flawless, for instance, or think harshly of a man who has just flattered you. So your Latin-American acquaintance makes an elaborate ritual of the smaller courtesies. All the proper inquiries must be made concerning your health and your family's health, all due compliments must be paid your personal merits and your professional attainments. Who enters a doorway first is a matter of profound etiquette.

All but the smallest newspaper offices maintain reception rooms where due honors can be paid to important subscribers and distinguished visitors, and in them, when you call, you are seated on the sofa on the proper side of the editor in exactly the same manner as visiting royalty at the White House. When you visit a local entrepreneur on business, anywhere from fifteen minutes to several days, depending on the size of your enterprise, must be devoted to strictly polite civilities. Your customer, or the gentleman whose customer you are about to become, must establish himself as a man of charm and put you under obligations to him for his courtesies, before the perilous business of dickering begins.

Neither can you conceivably hold a social advantage over a man who knows his local customs better than you. So to a greater or less degree all over Latin America, custom is sacred. Men in their business relations with foreigners may relax the bonds considerably in their cocktail-hour and golf-course intimacies, and the smarter social groups cultivate European and North American games and diversions with ostentatious enthusiasm. Yet basic custom remains a subtle and silent barrier both to contaminations from abroad and to the foreigner's critical appraisal.

No Latin-American social group—except rare circles of bohemian intellectuals in the larger cities—cultivates any diversions which seriously affect the integrity of its basic forms. No foreigner is accepted by any social group who does not conform to its conventions to the letter. A young American, for example, who even intimated that he would like to take the daughter of a respectable Latin-American family to dinner or the theater unchaperoned would be dropped from the household's list of receivable acquaintances as quickly as an announced seducer, regardless of his matrimonial eligibility on other counts and the grade-A moral record he might have back home.

Behind the walls of its subtle formalities, the Latin-American community sits with a feeling of complacent safety, always in a position to exclude the foreigner as a barbarian who does not measure up to the standards of gentlefolk. After all, the foreigner cannot laugh even at the provincialism of an aristocracy by whose standards he is not quite acceptable and to whose intimate gatherings he is not asked.

In result, progress toward intimate understanding between foreign and Latin-American elements is almost incredibly difficult even when they are in constant contact with each other. Familiarity with the local customs remains for generation after generation the token of the Latin's superiority to the outsider, the handle of his advantage over a potentially critical outside world. So customs change slowly, and when they do change, the new custom is as inflexible as the old. And always there are subtle conventions within the open and obvious conventions to remind the alien, while his hosts' ingratiating compliments flow on, that as an outlander he is admissible on sufferance only; to hold him, even as his simpatico qualities are being praised, at arm's length from the threshold of easygoing and informal friendship.

Equally important, the Latin American's sense of dignity is to be considered. It is not, in the usual sense, a pompous dignity. About his personal success and attainments, the Latin American is far less likely to brag than the Anglo-Saxon in his natural state. Since self-deprecation is called for in his code of good manners, he has as many little jokes to offer at the expense of his peculiarities, his peccadilloes and even his merits as the average American would think of at several college reunions.

Yet underneath he takes his standing, whatever it is from the highest to the lowest, with the utmost seriousness. The answer to his little deprecations is, in fact, to announce that his failings are imaginary and that you have even more humorous deprecations to offer. If you let them pass without this bit of by-play, you are

likely to discover, from a sudden change of manner, that you have
hurt his feelings. If you should happen to commit the unfor-
givable sin of taking his lead and trying to laugh with him at
failings he has not yet mentioned, the chances are that you will
have a permanent enemy on your hands. Anything like the give-
and-take of an ordinary American nineteenth-hole "kidding
match" is scarcely thinkable between Latin Americans, even in
intimate friendships. As between Latins and foreigners, if such
familiarities are attempted, it takes on all the grimness of a fighting international incident.

No degree of intimacy quite breaks down these barriers. "I
thought I married my husband because we shared a common sense
of humor," the young Swedish ex-wife of a rich Argentine estancia
proprietor confided to me in Buenos Aires. "In Paris, where we
met, he seemed to see so much of the amusing side of the things
we did and the people we met that I actually thought I was falling in love with a quiet humorist. But from the moment we
started for home with a boatload of Argentines everything
changed. He was lugubrious as far as Rio; and on the last lap,
from Rio down to Buenos Aires, he was positively—or was it
plain viciously?—morose.

"And for the next two years all I got was instructions on when,
where and with whom not to laugh, and scoldings for being
frivolous in the wrong places. He was continually rubbing it in
that if we weren't solemn and formal on all occasions, something
dreadful would happen to his reputation.

"I still suspect," she added, "if I could get him back to Paris as
it was, where he didn't feel himself on parade all the time, that I
could fall in love with him all over again. But we simply had to
end it. I couldn't take being the wife of a man who lived for his
dignity first and me afterward."

Dignity, unquestionably, runs more to the morose side in the
Argentine than elsewhere in Latin America, yet its tight lacings
are to be felt in social amenities everywhere. It would be hard, for
instance, even to imagine a dinner party so intimate that a wife
could indulge in affectionate jibes at her husband's minor frailties
before the guests, after the established Franco-British-North

American fashion, without creating something of a social scandal.

Nor is this touchiness the special province of the social upper brackets. Laugh at your new servant's awkwardness in a Latin-American household, and the chances are fifty to one that you will have a temperamental explosion on your hands. Scold your servants harshly—or fail even to offset a mild correction with due compliments on their merits—and you may wake up next morning without servants. When things are missed about the household, something may be salvaged by mentioning casually that certain precious articles have been lost and that you expect them to be found. But accuse a servant of theft directly, and, no matter how red-handed the evidence, your chances of seeing either the servant or your lost bauble again have been virtually tossed out the window. No one in Latin America sinks to a point in the social and economic scale where he is willing to work for an employer who both knows that he steals and lacks the breeding to refrain from mentioning it.

☆   ☆   ☆

Since a man who has dignity is a man who cannot be made fun of, a Latin American must especially hold his pose of mastery in the field where ridicule comes easiest. Above everything else, he must manage his women.

There are, in a sense, three parts to the obligation. A man must bind his wife and mistresses to him by chains of such poignant sexual satisfaction that infidelity is unthinkable to them. He must at the same time prove his mastery over his household by keeping all female dependents, daughters, sisters, maiden aunts and dowagers, in a state of flawless discretion and virtue. And he must also, when the slightest opportunity presents or seems to present itself—as occasional American girls have learned to their interest or their sorrow—register conquering virility by proving himself irresistible as a seducer.

He can think of sex, in other words—and as a rule he thinks of it with fairly tropical constancy—only in terms of mastery or its absolute opposite—humiliation. There is, for him, no happy medium between being cock of his barnyard or being ridiculous.

Practically every phase of Latin-American social life is colored by this attitude. One meets Latin-American women under the orthodox circumstances, of course. At receptions and cocktail and dinner parties they swarm as numerously as they do in the United States, and always they are full of agreeable small talk and pleasant compliments. But there the matter ends. It is no more possible for the unattached traveling male below the Rio Grande to take the wife of his Latin-American friend out to luncheon, to call formally on his unmarried sister or virgin daughter, or to drop in for an evening with the family circle, than it would have been to take the daughter of a Charleston "first family" off for an unchaperoned week end before the Civil War. Her men would assume that even if the gringo were so unaccountably lacking in virility as to fail to attempt the worst under such provocative circumstances, the lady's reputation would be irretrievably ruined.

Nor is it appreciably easier for the traveling stranger to include the wife of a friend in the courtesies extended to the husband. At least a dozen times in various Latin-American centers I have invited gentlemen who had been helpful to me, and whose wives I had met casually on one or more formal occasions, to dine with me under strictly circumspect auspices, as a couple. Always the gentlemen accepted, and always they made rather unconvincing excuses for the wives.

In a sense, perhaps, Don Ramón García may have explained the subtleties behind this reluctance. He and a friendly American couple were dining with me at a pleasant—and certainly not scandalous—night club in Mexico City, Señora García having sent the usual regrets.

"But don't you ever bring Señora García here?" the young American matron asked him, when for perhaps the fifth time Don Ramón mentioned politely that he was finding the evening agreeable.

Don Ramón slipped into English, and with the naïveté that comes with struggling with a foreign language put his problem directly:

"It is perfectly right for American ladies to come to this place," he said, "because everyone in Mexico realizes that American ladies go everywhere. But if I bring Mrs García here, perhaps I meet the chief of my bureau in the government or my official superiors dancing with the girls who come here to dance for the establishment, and perhaps they think she is not my wife."

Moreover, if the male outlander must struggle to know Latin America without women friends to help him, the task is not greatly eased even for women visitors who fail to observe the ruling conventions religiously. In spite of the fact that her "virtue" may be technically credited and respected, the woman from the United States remains (except to a pioneering minority of her Latin sisters) the emancipated rebel, the distinctly perilous iconoclast. It may not be a "bad" woman who drives her own car, lunches and dines and goes to the theater with men as she pleases and dares to descend on a cocktail party without either duenna or escort. But definitely she is a potential contaminating influence. Such hoydens must be kept at arm's length if the ancient customs by which virtue and male mastery are preserved are to be safe from corruption.

More things, however, are affected by the cult of male mastery than international understanding and the tone of social formality. I asked the head of an American news bureau in one of the larger South American capitals one day why his reporters had such a drawn look about the eyes and gave such a melancholy impression of physical and sartorial seediness. Was his outfit going in for the old-fashioned imperialist custom of sweatshopping the natives?

"Actually," he said, "my staff makes from $18 to $25 a week, which is considerably better than the average on the local newspapers. But you have to remember that each one of my reporters is a journalist and a professional man, and therefore a gentleman. And as a gentleman, he has to marry young—to show that he is economically above minor cautions—and beget several children as soon as possible to carry on a gentleman's line. But also, to show that he is a true blue-blood, as soon as possible after marriage, he must begin keeping a mistress. Sometimes two mistresses.

"On from $20 to $25 a week, this leads to undernourishment— and no doubt to various other forms of exhaustion."

Yet, despite the accent on sex, Latin America gives singularly the impression of a land without women. In the glittering night clubs of the larger metropolises where American jazz and native tropical rhythms call to youth to enjoy itself, table after table is filled with young men without girls. The middle-aged and the elderly solid citizens have their women on parade—wives and daughters in the strictly respectable establishments, mistresses elsewhere—but not the generation fittest to enjoy it. On the streets and around the little plazas at night, pale and unhappy-looking boys follow with hungry eyes the girls in a thousand towns—girls blooming with a kind of mannequin-on-display beauty at being so manifestly desired, yet hardly girls looking for comradely under-standing, or girls, beyond its biological adventures, to share a life with. The social emphasis on male mastery seems, indeed, to have produced a cult of sex without quite producing men and women who are fully alive to each other.

On the other hand, once a marriage is made, the Latin American finds an almost idyllic protection for his sense of importance in the exclusiveness of the family itself. You can never laugh at a Latin American because of his family background, or scorn him because his children are unruly (they almost never are!) or make fun of him because of his Oedipus complexes or his wife's silliness or because he is henpecked, or for any of the thousand reasons that Americans make light fun of their best friends and think nothing of it. For until you are an intimate friend of long standing and bound to one or more of its male members by innumerable ties of mutual obligation, you are unlikely to see a Latin-American family circle at all. To traveling strangers and friendly acquaintances, no matter how personable or well recommended, and often to inti-mate business and professional associates as well, the family circle is as impenetrable as a bank directorate to a WPA ditchdigger. Whatever may be the rank of its members in the local social cosmos, the family remains a center of exclusiveness from which every conceivable human relationship which threatens the Latin's self-esteem can be banished.

But there is more to the family than mere impenetrability. It is the hogtight, fighting corporation for advancing the self-esteem of the members as well as a wall of reserve to shield it. In part, this

[99]

cohesiveness is physical. Though modern urban living conditions are breaking the tendency down, the Latin-American family unquestionably is most comfortable when it lives beneath a single roof as a vast hive of parents, grandparents, sons and daughters; of in-laws, maiden aunts, bachelor uncles and widowed elders—all under the control of a ruling patriarch or matriarch.

In the richer establishments the married sons and daughters may live in separate houses provided by the paternal bounty, but usually close by, and, whether close by or not, definitely under the parental authority. In poorer districts, when overcrowding makes communal living impossible, the married children in their separate establishments are still hardly less at the beck and call of the head of the family than those who are lucky enough to be able to live at home. The thought of unmarried sons and daughters leaving home to live their own lives, or merely to be nearer their work, is as heretically unthinkable to the normal Latin-American family group as airing domestic scandal in public.

Out of this intense physical cohesiveness grows, instinctively, a cohesive pattern of action. The family lives together; therefore, it functions as an economic unit. If one of its members is wealthy or locally important, his wealth or his prominence is expected to be used for the advancement of all. If one of the members has political influence, that influence is supposed to be at the disposal of the least consequential of avuncular in-laws. If one member lands a job at a time when others in the charmed circle are jobless, the lucky one is expected to organize himself—or herself—as an employment agency of one to take care of the needs of the luckless. "Hire a cook," runs a pleasant South American proverb, "and you start an inn to feed her relatives."

Nepotism, in result, ranks throughout Latin America as a no less respectable virtue than putting on mourning. The Latin-American capitalist makes room for relatives of all degrees of consanguinity in his business as naturally as he feeds his children. The lawyer or physician makes room at least for his son in his office and is expected by the rest of the clan to handle their cases gratis. A man in a high government post is expected, at the very least, to take care of such blood relations and in-laws as are having trouble in supporting themselves in private industry. The rank and file of clerks and minor jobholders are rated as to their political potency by ability to get other family members on the pay roll and procure them small official favors.

In any job-seeking operation, furthermore, it is considered eminently proper that the family spokesman should take the initiative. I was in the Rio de Janeiro branch headquarters of a large American corporation one morning talking with the manager, when an elderly and obviously aristocratic Brazilian gentleman's card was presented.

After ten minutes' conversation with him in the private sanctuary, my host came back and reported.

"In the States," he said, "if a young man sent his uncle around to do his job soliciting for him, you'd think he must be phony. But that's what this old boy has been doing; and here, though it isn't universal, it's the only really formally correct way of starting things. This man is the head of the family—they're an enormous clan of about forty-seven, most of them living in one old mansion. I know him socially in a casual way. So, to the family's eyes, in sending him here to break the ice, they're really paying me a compliment.

"Anyway, he comes here this morning and tells me all. His nephew Guillermo has a sterling character and a charming personality and has had training in our line and would like to go to work for us. Tomorrow, God and I being willing, he will bring the young man around and introduce him to me, and if he makes a good impression, I can ask him back the next day so that we can finally talk business alone.

"The funny thing is, Guillermo may be all right in spite of it. After all, there are two ways of looking at it—our way and theirs. According to their way, if the old man hadn't called first, Guillermo would have thought the family wasn't backing him up in his job hunt. On the other hand, if Guillermo had gone out and got the job on his own without bringing his uncle into it, the old man would have felt that his authority wasn't being properly respected. And if I showed by the wink of an eyelash that I was off Guillermo because the old man had taken the initiative, the whole family would consider themselves insulted, and I'd be just another gringo savage who didn't understand nice people."

☆   ☆   ☆

There are, of course, in this complicated pattern of traditions, conventions and prejudices certain elements which tend to create an affinity between Latin Americans and Fascists. Latins love the pomp and display of petty dignities, the outward trappings of discipline and the strut of hierarchical overlords, whether in family life or in government. Where the Germans of the pre-Hitler starving time were attracted to the Nazi circus by the bread it offered along with more stagey enticements, the Latin Americans love a brightly stage-managed, garishly uniformed circus for its own sake.

But it would be too simple to say that Latins are predestined to the Fascist orbit merely because they take a somewhat childlike joy in such pageantries. Within them is a hard core of individualism—often of ruthlessly self-seeking individualism which Fascism, with its subordination of the individual to the state, contemptuously scorns.

It is hardly individualism as a North American understands it. In Latin America, where a man is "built up" by the forms he uses, the impressions he creates, the dignities and reticences he preserves, the little private vanities he lives by may be more important than realities; are, perhaps, the crucial realities.

To intimate, however, that one man's realism is another man's poison, states a serious problem in adjustment: An adjustment likely to be no easier for Nazi penetrators, cultural or military, than it has proved for the "missionaries" of Gringo democracy from the North.

CHAPTER VII

How Latin Americans Get Ahead

The standard success methods in Latin America are inevitably adjusted to the social values. The elements which make up the prestige of a prominent citizen there are subtly different from the elements which give a man strength and leadership in his community in the United States.

A young man "on the make" in Latin America becomes a personage by following a special type of self-levitation process. In general, it might be put this way: it is more important for him to garner the symbols of prestige and success than to bother about records of achievement. The titles he can win, the influence he can wield, the important people he can be seen with are his stock in trade rather than his production chart on the boss's books down at the office.

There is not, either in a racial or derogatory sense, anything exclusively Latin-American about it. From ancient Greece to postwar Germany, a great many otherwise competent and highly diverse peoples have preferred the symbols to the realities of success, largely in proportion to the deficiency of material opportunities in their economic environments.

Nevertheless, one is often surprised at the naïve frankness with which Latin Americans declare their objectives.

There was the bright young man, for instance, a kind of combination headwaiter and reception clerk for visitors from the United States, in the hotel where I stopped in San Salvador. He spoke excellent English. He was expert and trustworthy on all local problems from politics to taxi drivers' temperaments. We became friends in a casual fashion, but hardly such friends that I was prepared for his application for a job.

On the evening before I left, he filed it. I was a staff member of the New York *Post,* was I not? I therefore knew the editor very well, no? If he wrote that night a letter to the editor asking him for an appointment as the *Post's* El Salvador correspondent, would I not, out of friendship and consideration for the kindness he had been so happy to show me, send it north with my cordial indorsements?

I demurred—on purely practical grounds. "Why, the New York *Post* wouldn't need a news dispatch from El Salvador that the press associations wouldn't carry, once in five years," I discouraged him.

"I fully understand," he protested a trifle haughtily. "I should not expect to use such a position to make money."

"But have you had newspaper experience?" I asked him.

"Not of the slightest," he said airily.

"Then why should you want a job for which you have had no preparation and at which you couldn't possibly make any money?"

"It would give me a great deal of prestige here," he said simply. "It would greatly impress my *patrón* at the hotel and would give me a standing with the most important politicians in the republic."

He was perfectly serious about it. I tried to soften the blow by explaining that American newspapers, as a matter of cruel policy, did not go in for honorary correspondents. But his disappointment remained. "I do not see why," he pleaded, "when it would cost them nothing." His farewells were cool, and quite plainly he felt that both I and American journalism had let him down without cause.

Prestige, however, is not always a matter of such relatively inexpensive honors. Years ago I had known Don Calixto (to misname him) when he was a political exile in the United States. So when I found him working as an important brain-truster under a Mexican cabinet minister, our reunion was something of a gala occasion.

When we met for dinner, however, I was slightly embarrassed to be told that I was expected to be his guest for my entire stay in Mexico City. Where would I like to dine?

I left it to him.

"If you are willing to accept me as a mentor," Don Calixto proposed, with exquisite formality, "I shall give you your choice of two places—the town's most fashionable night club and the town's most pretentious whorehouse. . . .

"I should rather go to these than to the quieter restaurants," he went on frankly. "Many of my superiors will be there. It will be helpful to me to be seen with a foreign journalist who has been interviewed in the papers."

We compromised on the night club, and a little later made still another compromise. I told Don Calixto that, happy as I was in his hospitality, it seemed more fitting that a journalist on an expense account should just for one night entertain an old friend for dinner. He accepted with alacrity, and promptly invited half a dozen superior and inferior officials to our table for drinks and light refreshments.

A few days later, after further civilities had been extended, Don Calixto came to me with another suggestion. He knew that I was interested in making a motor trip to the government sugar cooperative at Zacatapec, 150 miles from Mexico City. In fact, for a day or two there had been some desultory talk about getting me a government car. But Don Calixto's new grand plan swept these petty economies aside.

"You are a man on a large expense account," he said reverently. "It would be perfectly possible—no?—for you to hire a car and take me and my cabinet minister to Zacatapec. And then, in the evening on the return trip, you could give a small intimate dinner for the minister in the hotel at Cuernavaca, no?

"I need not tell you how helpful this will be to you in your efforts to gain the confidence of the higher government circles. As for me, nothing you could possibly do would raise your old friend's prestige so high with the cabinet. . . . Shall I initiate the arrangements?"

Fortunately, American friends saved me. They had suggested

stopping off with me at Zacatapec on their way to a week end in Taxco. It was barely possible to persuade Don Calixto that by withdrawing from their party at the last minute I should leave them desolate and inconvenienced.

Afterward, he did no more than gently chide me about it. But it was easy to see that he considered a man who would not use an expense account to make a display of lavishness before a cabinet minister a child in the affairs of the world. The fact that a cold auditor in New York might have objected to an item of $150 for entertaining high dignitaries was wholly beyond him. If not to heighten prestige, what were expense accounts for?

☆   ☆   ☆

In general, the pattern of the Latin-American success story differs from the Horatio Alger patterns hardly less than these incidents differ from the biography of Abraham Lincoln. It is not that the upper-crust society in Latin America forms a closed corporation or that rising from the ranks is peculiarly difficult. On the contrary, Latin-American history is full of stories of peons who have become dictators, private soldiers who have become millionaires, members of the ostensibly subject races who have become generals and aristocrats. The disorders of the republics, the possibilities of graft and intrigue, the fascinations which ostentatious personalities have for the uncritical Latin public smooth the upward path for gifted adventurers in politics and business as neatly as it is smoothed anywhere in the world.

About the technique of rising from the bottom, however, there is a subtle difference from the model performances recommended by moralists elsewhere. Latin-American opinion seldom admires its public hero of the moment for the difficulties he has conquered or the struggles he has made. It admires him for the slickness with which he has left all traces of his origins behind. So while Lincolnesque ascents from obscurity are wholly practicable, a Lincoln cut to the Latin-American pattern would have established himself, from the moment the barest possibility of eminence glimmered before him, as a general of the Illinois militia and a Springfield socialite.

HOW LATIN AMERICANS GET AHEAD

The first maneuver of a young man on the make, then, is to get himself enrolled in the white-collar classes. For the son of a worker's family, an office job represents almost as precious a boon as an election to the French Academy to a Parisian novelist. As a bookkeeper's apprentice he sits over his figures, or operates a comptometer, with the melancholy dignity of a judge pronouncing doom in court. Nothing can hurry him, nothing can ruffle him—except an affront to his calculated poise. He is *caballero* now, a man of standing and importance, and all petty excitements are below him.

The whole tempo of his life changes. He no longer goes to the coffee bars and the cantinas frequented by the working classes. If he marries, he is expected to pick a girl whose brothers are also office workers. If his salary is so small that it does not permit him to marry into the class to which he aspires, it is considered laudable of him to remain a lifelong bachelor. If he has any surplus for recreation at all, his style in mistresses is expected to change as well as his taste in brothels. No matter how sweltering the local climate, it is as unthinkable that he should do his work, or be seen in public, without a coat and tie as that he should appear in the plaza in a G string.

He has a position to sustain, and sustaining it is more important than anything that has to do with the mere performance of the job. He is so infatuated with the position, indeed, that there is a better than even chance that, indifferent to promotions and only vaguely concerned with raises, he will stay on the bottom rung of the white-collar ladder for the rest of his life in a state of blissful, vegetable complacency. If he loses the job, he may posture about town indefinitely as a genteel lounger. If no further jobs in his "class" are forthcoming, eventually he may sink gracefully into the status of a moral derelict. The one thing that is next to impossible, despite economic problems, is his return to the laboring classes.

If, however, the young man is ambitious, his procedure has little to do with office routine. He may let his production record languish for days at a time, while he schemes for an assignment to a task which will bring him to the attention of the main boss. He will slight his immediate superiors to do the head man a spectacular favor. If he has cousins or in-laws or old schoolmates who have slightly better white-collar jobs elsewhere, he may spend his whole social life cultivating intense intimacies in circles whose blood and emotional bonds require them to speak well of him. By a kind of natural instinct he realizes that the best openings for advancement are likely to lie with competitors, and he assiduously makes friends of the clerks and subexecutives of rival firms.

When the time comes for him to move toward a new job or a promotion, it is the people he knows, the favors he has done, the intrigues he has managed and the charm he exudes which are his chief recommendations. Indeed, if the record is mentioned at all in an application interview, he is apt to show faint signs of annoyance. It goes without saying that a gentleman with such interesting connections and references has a sound working record. He has prestige—what more can an employer want? And once elevated above the rank and file of subordinate white-collar jobholders, his business standing will be fixed almost entirely by the generals and politicians he knows and drinks with, the clubs he belongs to, the horses he bets on and the favors he knows how to trade.

When he goes on still further and becomes an independent capitalist, his rating will be set in the community less by his financial balances and his executive efficiency than by the lavishness with which he lives, the eminent personages he is seen with, the circles of control into which he is able to bluff his way, or buy it. Being able to buy or bluff your way into the controlling circles is Latin-American business strategy in its supreme form.

☆　　　☆　　　☆

A similar formula applies in politics. Politics differs from the United States model, among other things, in the fact that it is a means of social climbing itself. The young man from a worker's family who lands himself a government post or wangles himself an elective job becomes *caballero* from the moment the new dignities are conferred no less automatically than his bookkeeper cousin. To change his style of dress and manners, to cultivate gaudier tastes in friends and amusements is precisely what his own following expects of him.

Suppose, then, that our young man gets far enough along to be elected to congress. No one expects him to make himself a record as an expert legislator or party wheel horse or logroller for his district. He may display his prowess in ardent oratory on occasion, but his main job is to outshine other luminaries and to intrigue with the right people for his advancement. His standing with his constituency depends less on what he knows about their interests than on how many cabinet ministers he knows on a favor-trading basis and what his chances are of landing a cabinet post for himself.

His outlook for promotion depends largely on his capacity for intrigue. Since, with the exception of three or four republics, he has practically no chance to win an election on a platform of honest opposition to the president's party, he must hold onto his seat by cultivating the friendship of the people who run the government. If he is looking for a higher post—a seat in the senate or a governorship—it will come to him through superiors who have a virtual power of appointment.

The young man's problem is, therefore, to bind his superiors to him by ties of personal obligation regardless of the cost. If he provides the president with better entertainment than the rival politicians in the next-door state capital when the chief executive goes visiting, it makes no difference what he mortgages to secure his triumph, from whom he borrows or how much. To a shrewd manager an investment in presidential favor pays dividends enough to take care of sound professional obligations when the next list of executive appointments is made.

Other significant favors, however, can be—at least in the fiscal sense—less expensive. A rising political gentleman who turns over his mistress to a cabinet minister, or procures a definitely dazzling one for the new military commandant in his province, may also count himself several steps ahead in the promotion line. Nor will his constituents think any worse of him as these delicate matters are circulated in local gossip.

Furthermore, along with ingratiating himself with his superiors, the young man must tirelessly watch over developments in practical politics for more dramatic openings favorable to his advancement. Keeping one's eye alert for signs of dissension and trouble in the higher ranks, or symptoms of public disorder, is far more important than lying awake nights thinking up new ways of distinguishing himself in the public service.

Is a cabinet minister about to be dropped or a senator from his province in danger of being politely exiled on a diplomatic mission? Is a state governor—particularly the governor of his own state—having trouble keeping his public disciplined or getting into deep water with his finances? If so, the politician who has the first inside tip on the scandal and redoubles his ingratiation efforts in due season will be interestingly to the front in the scrimmage line when the successorship is decided.

Governors' troubles are particularly interesting to all Latin-American politicians below the grade of cabinet minister for sound practical reasons. In a large and representative group of republics the constitutions permit the president, when the solvency or the public order of a state is menaced, to remove an elective governor and appoint an acting governor, or *interventor,* to function for the duration of the emergency with dictatorial powers. Not only are the jobs agreeable and often reasonably permanent—there are at least half a dozen republics in Latin America in which the states have not seen an elective governor for more than a decade—but an *interventor* who uses his special powers shrewdly can within a comparatively few months convert the state whose destinies have been entrusted to him into a disciplined personal principality. Thereafter, he is a figure to be reckoned with in national politics. If the state is large and powerful, especially if it is rich enough, he may be in line, in the next national crisis, for the presidency itself.

Consequently, among Latin-American practical politicians, there is a continuous bull market on interventorships—and, by extraordinary coincidence, an insistent trend toward the undermining of the authority of governors. The young man whose secret agents—and few political officeholders in Latin America above the

grade of street sweeper are without a fairly sizable flock of hangers-on and active retainers—can foment a few mobs or a military
outbreak in an unpopular governor's bailiwick, or entrap a few
high state officers in a financial scandal, can be first to the president's ear with the inside news of the "emergency" and first with
the insinuation that he would like the interventorship. Definitely
the politician who knows who is going to get into trouble,
and how best to get rivals into trouble, is the man who is going
places.

Next, however, to ingratiating himself with the ruling circle, the
rising politico's problem is to keep in the good graces of the circle
which may be in power next year or next decade. Here it is not a
question of keeping on a friendly footing with an open opposition
party in congress, for in most Latin-American congresses the opposition party is either absent or powerless. It is a question of
finding out which group of politicians, more or less within the
ruling circle, is planning a coup against the sitting administration,
or which group of generals is planning a revolt against the president; and above all of accurately measuring its chances of winning.
To the rising young man, much more important than his duty to
the public service is the necessity of keeping abreast of current
intrigue.

His difficulties are multiplied by the number of intrigues he
knows about. He can dismiss the lesser ones as visionary, of course.
The borderline cases, until they have grown or withered as the
fates decide, may be placated with an extra display of personal
politeness to the leaders. But the intrigues which seriously threaten
the overturn of the government tax even the Latin American's
easy talents. He must keep far enough aloof from the intriguers
so that, if their attempt fails, he will not be listed by a vengeful
government among the "conspirators." On the other hand, he must
register so much general sympathy for the plotters, bind themselves to his interests by so many personal and political favors
that, if their attempt does come off, they will consider him one of
them.

Many a Latin-American politician of otherwise notable gifts
has been stopped in mid-career, or even faced a firing squad, for

imperfect balancing under such circumstances. But innumerable gentlemen who, with an engaging duplicity, have devoted themselves to the delicate arts of winning friends by conferring favors and of charming rivals have managed to survive.

Thus, whenever the curtain goes up on a new political emergency —whether the old-fashioned revolution or some new drive toward local totalitarianism—the practical politician is apt to be discovered at a juggling act involving two shining accomplishments: persuading his friends in the government faction that he is only associating with the intriguers in order to spy on them; and insinuating to the revolutionary faction that they can rely on his support in the crisis and that his support will be crucial.

Once on my travels an observant Argentine journalist put the formula for political success in an ironic nutshell. "With you," he said, "the effective politician must be a man of enormous energy. He may operate some vast machine for controlling the votes of millions, or he may spend his time endlessly flattering the people in oratory, or he may build up his prestige by serious statesmanship. But with us the idyllically successful politician needs to do only two things: travel so light on commitments that he can join any political faction at any time, provided it is destined to be the winning faction; and at the same time build up such personal influence and following that the winners will receive him with shouts of triumph even if he omits to join them until their victory has been attained."

☆   ☆   ☆

Political success formulas deserve this relatively exhaustive discussion, I believe, for the simple reason that politics in one way or another clutters up most of the highways to success in the twenty republics. In the United States it is possible for a man to become, say, a successful corporation lawyer or carve out a distinguished career for himself in scholarship, the arts or sciences without ever making the acquaintance of a practical politician. In Latin America, if politics does not open all doors to success, at least it has the power to keep them closed.

The lawyer who does not enjoy a favorable standing with the ruling political faction in his republic is, as the saying goes in Latin America, "unlucky for his clients." It is not that Latin-American courts are corrupt or corruptible in the ordinary sense. The courts simply belong to the political system. It is as natural for them to rule generally for the controlling administration and for the friends of the administration as for the congressmen to vote for the president's recommendations or for soldiers to obey orders. While the successful lawyer in general practice need not be "in politics" in order to guarantee his standing, he must recognize where the centers of political control are, and, in the friendships he cultivates and the favors he does, show them due deference.

The journalist faces a still stiffer handicap. In more than half the republics an opposition press is at the mercy of censorships and arbitrary suspension orders. Except in countries of long-established liberal traditions like Colombia and Costa Rica, and here and there, as in Mexico City and Buenos Aires, where the press is powerful enough to be dangerous, the reporter whose paper is on the off side of the ruling faction gets no news.

On the other hand, the juiciest practical rewards of the profession are paid for political conformity. In Havana, for instance, newspaper salaries are virtually fixed on the assumption that the working journalist will derive from one to three fourths of his income from a government sinecure which requires him to do little besides sign occasional official papers. The reporter without a place on the public pay roll can practically consider himself suspected as a subversive influence.

Publishers feel the impact of this pressure politics no less than reporters. Even where he runs no risk of suspension or permanent closing, the Latin-American publisher is under constant menace. Politicians may send warnings down the line in the business community—for example, that the favor of the government depends upon where they bestow their advertising. A quiet tip to the police may stop newsstand sales, or a wink from the treasury department may shut off banking credit.

Under these circumstances the successful newspaperman is known by the politicians he professionally strings along with. In final result, inevitably, he strings along uncritically with whatever politicians happen to be in power. The most successful "chain publisher" in Brazil, for instance, boasts cynically among his intimates that he has supported every brand of administration the republic has had for a generation, and is capable of every brand of journalistic inconsistency except a taste for underdogs.

Success in business offers similar, if more subtle, problems. For the elaborate codes of labor, sanitation, fire safety and corporate practice with which most of the Latin-American governments safeguard their economic purity—not to mention their interesting schedules of special and punitive taxes—can be used to give the politician the whip hand over the businessman no less efficaciously than the press can be disciplined by censorship.

The system—while full of detailed refinements and subject to certain qualifications varying from country to country—is basically simple. The banker, the merchant, the manufacturer who is generous with discounts and easy with credit to his political customers finds the enforcement of these complicated statutes mysteriously relaxed. The competitor who tries to get along without courting political friends in high places is likely to find himself at the constant—and often ruinously expensive—disadvantage of having to obey all red-tape restrictions and pay all imposts in full.

"The uncollected account of a politician," a Nicaraguan friend once enlightened me, "may be regarded as a form of capital investment."

☆   ☆   ☆

A far more important short cut to success in Latin America, however, than either business or the civil professions lies, in all but a few of the republics, through the army.

But the army is also a branch of politics. Indeed, except in Costa Rica, where the militia is smaller than the school-teaching force, and in Colombia, where no army has revolted against the government for almost a century, the typical Latin-American army functions as the control department of politics.

So, while there are excellent professional soldiers in Latin America, soldiering is rarely, in the sense in which West Pointers and officers of the Western European powers conceive it, a strictly professional career. The young officer may virtuously make himself an expert in modern military tactics and gadgetry, and there is considerable evidence that the contemporary breed of Latin-American subalterns work harder at their strictly professional tasks than do the civilian politicians. His main business, however, as a practical careerist, is to attach himself as intimately as possible to the cliques of the generals who keep presidents in power, or, when the hour of their opportunity strikes, know how to oust presidents and control the succession. The art of being a successful officer, then, is precisely the same as the art of being a successful congressman. One plays one's cards with the winning side—always keeping an eye open to the chance that some general with superior gifts for intrigue will overthrow the ruling generals.

Under these circumstances the military careerist rarely thinks of promotions in terms of seniority and professional merit. He thinks of it in terms of crises in army politics and of crises in his republic's affairs in which the army becomes the dominating factor in national politics. The lieutenant who leaps overnight into a colonelship, the captain who dreams of jumping the intervening grades to a generalship, needs to know when the revolution is coming and who is going to engineer it successfully far more than he needs to know his trajectories or his trench tools. "Come the revolution" anywhere in Latin America, the officers who stayed with the losers can count on two fates: being cashiered or bogged down indefinitely in the obscurity of low grades and unimportant commands. The swank and thrills of high command, the lures of pay and meteoric advancement are for the young men whose shrewdness as army politicians enabled them to pick winners.

The practicalities of the promotion problem, then, give all subalterns in Latin America and most of the less distinguished general officers a permanent curiosity about revolutions—if not a specific partiality for revolutions. And while the same considerations usually inspire a high practical devotion to the regime in the officers at the top, the forces they command are not necessarily strong enough to stand against the massed weight of ambitious insubordination from below. Revolutions have happened in Latin America—and still happen occasionally—for no very specific reason except that the yearning for promotions, too long frustrated in a static period, washes over the dam of the high command's excessively interested loyalty.

But not always. For the officer who has come to the top through the routine revolutionary formula also knows, if he is wise, how to foil excessive ambition in those who come after.

Of this type of shrewdness I cite the case of General Pedro Aurelio de Góes Monteiro, chief of staff of the Brazilian army, as an all-time Latin-American classic.

General Góes Monteiro is without question one of the ablest professional soldiers in Latin America. Ten years ago he was a somewhat obscure lieutenant colonel, pleasantly looked down upon by the flashier members of the high command as a military highbrow.

In 1930, however, when Getulio Vargas stepped into a difficult election situation and proclaimed himself president, Góes Monteiro went with Vargas. His troop deployments aided crucially in the success of the coup; and in 1932, when the state of São Paulo attempted a revolution, his campaign against a powerful army of state troops and revolting federal regiments was a masterpiece of maneuvering and relatively bloodless tactical victories. As military mentor of the Vargas regime, he was named chief of staff and has since, according to the realistic Latin-American custom of taking military mentors seriously, been permitted to name the ministers of war and have a say in all the major policies of the Vargas government.

For nine years General Góes Monteiro has ruled the Brazilian army, with the result that, except for intimates in the Monteiro circle, dramatic promotions have been long overdue. So in May 1938, when the presidential night guard at Guanabara Palace turned revolutionist for the night and attempted to shoot the President, a curious thing happened. There were no troop deployments at all. President Vargas, with the help of two faithful personal bodyguards and his daughter, shot it out with the guard company for several hours until the police came to the rescue. General Góes Monteiro kept the troops in barracks.

No disloyalty was involved. If anything, General Góes Monteiro's prestige with the Vargas regime and the public was increased by the omission. The chief of staff merely knew that to turn several thousand practical military careerists loose on the streets of Rio de Janeiro on a night of revolution, with their minds full of success maxims, might be—fatal, among other things, to the future success of General Góes Monteiro.

CHAPTER VIII

Conditioned Thinking

THE LATIN-AMERICAN MIND works substantially as its enormous complex of values and inherited experiences, of physical and historical conditioning forces, requires it to. There is nothing unusual in this. Original individual minds occur in every society. But the thinking processes of large groups—of nations, great racial and cultural divisions—are shaped in the forcing bed of environment.

Mere blood-stream inheritance may be no more than a minor influence. In the United States citizens without a drop of British blood in their veins think, in their political decisions and their ethical judgments, more like Englishmen than like their racial brothers in the original homeland. Distant in time though it is, British ideological inheritance has colored the education they have received, the values they have been taught to respect, from the moment their immigrating ancestors first saw an American shore line.

On the other hand, Americans of technically "pure" British descent are constantly shocking Englishmen by their departures from what every subject of King George regards as mentally orthodox. Three centuries on a frontier, a century and a half without royalty and official "upper classes"—to mention simply the outstanding differentiating factors—have modified almost beyond recognition the stereotyped concepts and values which the original "one-hundred-per-cent Anglo-Saxon" Americans brought across the ocean. Unquestionably we are more "like" Englishmen than we are like Belgians or Brazilians. We and the British, however, are distant mental kinfolk, not identical twins. Environment and the huge differences in the experiences we have undergone since the seventeenth century would not have permitted us to remain identical twins, even if we had wanted to and tried hard.

Latin-American thinking also differs from that in its ancestral home, from Spanish and continental European thinking, much as ours differs from the British. More important to us, Latin-American mental processes vary from those in the United States as, item by item, the Latin-American's environment, historical inheritance and body of experience are different from ours.

Even this highly inclusive statement hardly expresses the difficulties, within the Western Hemisphere, of achieving anything like mental comradeship. Inside the Latin-American world itself there are differences in values and thinking processes hardly less sharp and dramatic than those between distinct races. When one compares the Mexican gift for malicious satire, for instance, with the grave pomposity of the Argentine ruling classes which hardly tolerate humor at all, one all but despairs of classifying the Latin-American mind as a unit. Between the easygoing and gaiety-loving Brazilians whose wars are relatively bloodless, and who hate long terms of imprisonment even for political prisoners, and the dour Salvadoreans, with their boasts of massacring revolutionists in thousands and their passional crimes which daily fill the republic's newspapers with "murder stories" replete with knife thrusts and mutilations, the gap seems as wide as between Parisians and Balkan peasants.

Yet there is such a thing as the Latin-American mind if only in its differentiations from the mind of North America. Back of our mental processes in the North stand certain basic attitudes: self-confidence; the complacency of acknowledged power; the pride of a society able to afford and achieve vast enterprises; the sense of being at home in the contemporary world, no matter how patently at times we may fumble our interests in it.

Back of mental processes to the south stand poverty, provincialism, the haunting sense of military and economic inadequacy in a world of vastly stronger forces; above all, the fear that if these weaknesses are exposed, the outsider, with his wealth and power, will take advantage of them to humiliate and despoil.

Minds work from these basic attitudes, in the two great divisions of our hemisphere, as directly as skilled debaters argue from stated premises. But the premises here are almost incomparably different. Hence it so often develops, both in our disagreements and in our exchanges of civilities with the Latin Americans, that, in the deeper psychological sense, we are not "talking the same language"; that, at times of tension in our diplomatic or personal relations, we suddenly find ourselves staring at neighbors amazed at the gulfs between us.

☆   ☆   ☆

Provincialism and the unsureness of self that lurk in its background explain, first of all, the Latin-American mind's overwhelmingly self-centered quality. It achieves impersonal and analytical viewpoints, casually critical attitudes and, above all, self-criticism only with the utmost difficulty. Even when it seems to achieve them, there is often less of true impersonality than of striving for an Olympian pose. Prick the posture with a mildly Socratic question or a sharp contradiction of opinion, and you are likely to have an *affaire internationale* on your hands.

These are factors which often explain the incredible in our Latin-American difficulties. One day in Rio, for instance, a taxi driver whom I had asked to take me to the American Embassy delivered me to an office with a sign, "United States Products Company," over the doorway.

He opened the cab for me to alight. "Embaixada dos Estados Unidos," he said briskly.

"But this is the United States Products Company," I objected.

"Embaixada dos Estados Unidos," he insisted, plainly bristling.

I forced him to read the sign. It changed his argument but not his attitude. "That's where you said you wanted to go," he raged at me. "I am a good taxi driver. I know every place in Rio de Janeiro. If I do not take you where you want to go, it is because you do not speak good Portuguese."

It was a case of brawl or abandon him, and I abandoned. In time, if not in money, it was cheaper to take another taxicab than to force an irate Brazilian taxi driver to lose an argument.

The incredible, however, is sometimes less personal and more significant. Let's consider as a case study the mobs which tried to stone the United States Embassy in Mexico City in June 1939, after Francisco Sarabia, Mexico's outstanding flier, had been killed in a take-off from Washington, D. C.

From the realistic Yankee viewpoint the demonstration was wholly fantastic. Sarabia had just made a nonstop flight from Mexico City to New York; and while the exploit was not strictly unprecedented, he had been received—by the President and the highest military authorities, among others—as a genuinely appealing good-will messenger between republics. As investigation later proved, Sarabia's fall was caused by the presence of wisps of rag sucked into the gas-feed mechanism by some freak action of the air-intake devices, which no saboteur could conceivably have calculated. Certainly, unless he had an enemy with a mad genius for estimating air-intake forces, not a soul north of the Rio Grande resented Sarabia's success, wished him ill or would have harmed him.

Yet the mobs—before proof of any cause for the accident could have been provided—shouted in the Mexico City streets that his engine had been sabotaged and the gringos had murdered him. To North American reasoning, such an outburst could only be explained as evidence of an enormous Fascist plot to poison Mexican-American relations, or as proof of some extraordinary malevolence of the Mexican mind. No doubt Fascist agitators made the most of a rich opportunity, as certain Mexican officials suggested, but it was hardly a question of malevolence. In its suspicions, the Mexican mind obviously reasoned in a straight line from the passionately self-centered premise.

To the rioters (as doubtless to thousands of other Mexicans who with difficulty and reluctance suppressed the same suspicions which animated the riots) the clue to the Sarabia tragedy lay in the fact that the dead aviator had made his great flight at a time of extreme tension in Mexican-American relations over the oil-expropriations issue. Point by point, the deductive process would be about as follows:

The oil interests, since the controversy was bitter, would hate all Mexicans as enemies, and, since Mexicans were enemies, all oil magnates, employees and sympathizers would feel humiliated by any Mexican's triumph. Feeling humiliated, they would hanker after revenge, or at least would naturally consult together on ways and means of shattering the triumphant one's prestige. The oil interests, in other words, had a motive for killing Sarabia, a motive strictly in accord with Latin America's fundamental psychological values. For when your enemy gains "face" in Latin America, you lose it. His success is as intolerable to you as a pain in the stomach.

Having rationalized the motive, then, out of inner psychological experiences, the lush Mexican imagination was equal to the rest of the task. It invented the legend that oil-company hirelings poured water into Sarabia's gasoline, or jimmied his engine, and did kill him. And having invented the legend, it believed it with furious emotional sincerity.

As a rule, however, the self-centered quality expresses itself in considerably more subtle stratagems. And here an instructive case history can be found in Argentine tactics as of the 1938 Pan-American Conference at Lima.

The Argentine Republic has lots of reasons for trying from time to time to put Uncle Sam's nose out of joint. Some of them are what any businessman would recognize as sound reasons. Prior to the agonizing fiasco of long-overdue negotiations in 1939, Argentina was given a several years' polite run-around in her efforts to make a reciprocal trade treaty with the United States. Less politely, she has been insistently slapped down in her efforts to sell her beef in American markets. Consequently the Buenos Aires statesmen spend a good deal of their time devising maneuvers which tend to embarrass Washington's diplomatic projects and trade relations generally. Enough embarrassments, they feel not illogically, might induce Uncle Sam to be reasonable.

Furthermore, Argentina is skeptical of any Washington policy which looks like an effort to line up the Western Hemisphere nations in anything suggesting an anti-European, or even an anti-

Nazi, block. Export trade is more important to the Argentine than to most of the Western republics, and nearly three quarters of hers is with Europe. Argentina, as several Buenos Aires governments have seen it, will have to take care of threats to her independence and territorial integrity when, as, and if war or the emergencies of totalitarian peace should prove her in error. Meanwhile she cannot afford to offend her meat and wheat buyers, Nazi or otherwise.

Other motives for coolness toward Uncle Sam, though, are more strictly subjective. Toward the rest of the Latin-American republics, the Argentine is a good deal in the position of the first son of the family to put on long pants. The big wheat and beef country has got over the habit of "government by revolution" better than most of the smaller brothers. It is richer, more sophisticated, more advanced in technical plant and more potent in a military way than the others.

All this gives a young republic an enormous amount of dignity to live up to. And the best way to live up to it, as Argentines see it, is to show that, no matter what happens, Argentine policy cannot be influenced or controlled by the stronger neighbor in the far North. So, just to be sure that no one will take them for "push overs" for Washington, Argentine leaders are inclined to look for points to differ about even when their interests or objectives happen, in a given situation, to be more or less parallel with those of the United States.

With all these impulses in the background, the Argentine approached the 1938 Lima Conference. The ground was carefully prepared. Several weeks before the Conference, a book by former Foreign Minister Carlos Saavedra Lamas—Nobel Peace Prize winner several years ago for his efforts to end the Paraguayan-Bolivian War—was widely circulated. Against the main Conference objective of the Washington statesmen (a declaration of hemisphere solidarity against aggressions by the totalitarian powers) Dr Saavedra Lamas opened all his guns. Any union on a hemisphere-solidarity program with the United States, his thesis declared flatly, meant submission to the domination of Washington.

Next, Dr José Maria Cantilo, the succeeding Foreign Minister, came to Lima for the opening session on a warship. He colored the psychology of the proceedings to the best of his ability by making a speech. Ostensibly the speech was full of compliments. It praised Secretary of State Hull's oratory, and it praised his ideals. Everyone agreed, Dr Cantilo said, that the hemisphere's defense problems were common problems. Mr Hull had shown his usual wisdom and frankness by bringing the question into the open. But, Dr Cantilo went on, Argentina did not consider any declarations which might be interpreted as reflecting on any European nation to be necessary or desirable.

And here the Argentine chief spokesman inserted his key sentence: "Just as the United States maintains its Open Door policy with China," he said, "and were led to interest themselves in the Hawaiian Islands; and, after the war with Spain, to obtain the cession of the Philippines—in other words, to maintain a policy not exclusively American—so do the interests which the River Plate countries have in their European markets weigh on their national and international policies."

In some seventy words, Dr Cantilo had cited three of the outstanding past imperialistic adventures of the United States, all of them unpopular in Latin America. And he cited them before a Latin-American audience as reasons why the twenty republics should not collaborate in a present-day Washington policy.

Following this delicate puncture operation, the Argentine delegation filed a "hemisphere solidarity" declaration of their own. Its chief characteristic was its innocuousness. It stated in a general way that the American nations disapproved of aggression by foreign powers, but suggested no concrete measures for action against aggression if it came. All expressions were carefully deleted from it which the totalitarian powers might interpret at being aimed at themselves. In effect, the Argentines were against aggression somewhat as Calvin Coolidge's preacher was "against sin."

The intent was open and obvious. Although Argentina at the moment was having far more difficulties with Nazi propagandists than was the United States, Uncle Sam was not to be permitted, if any Argentine stratagem could prevent it, to enjoy the prestige of winning a Conference ideological victory.

As things turned out, the Argentine program partially miscarried. The nineteen other Latin Americans stood closer to Mr Hull than to Buenos Aires on the aggression issue; and toward the end of the Conference, the Argentines, in order to avoid being branded as obstructionists, were forced to accept a compromise. The final "Declaration of Lima" did not have all the teeth in it that Mr Hull wanted, but it was a long way from the original Argentine design for a declaration without any teeth at all.

From the Washington point of view, it was a minor disagreement over phraseologies in which the United States had lost a good deal even though it had saved something. But to the self-centered Argentine mind, it was a Yankee triumph, and to a republic proud of never yielding to Washington on issues, painfully compromising. Such a stain could be wiped out only by an equal and opposite anti-United States counterstroke. So the politicians in Buenos Aires, totaling up their list of other grievances, did a little consciously dramatic timing. Within a week the counterstroke came. The Argentine fiscal authorities ordered sudden drastic changes in the customs and exchange regulations on shipments from the United States which, in the next six months, caused a 49-per-cent reduction in Argentina's Yankee imports. Argentine families paid several hundred dollars more for their Detroit motorcars as a result, and the dispute over trade balances had, after all, very little to do with the Lima argument over aggressor nations. But Argentina had thrown off the stigma of the Lima concession and proved once more that she was free from the imperialistic influence of the northern colossus.

☆   ☆   ☆

As one of its weapons in the constant battle for this type of mastery, the Latin mind has developed another trait often amazing to the less dialectically expert Anglo-Saxons—its uncanny genius for shifting issues.

You win an argument from your Latin-American friend on points, for instance, or seemingly dispose of him on the facts in evidence. Suddenly you find that this was not the question you were debating at all—or was simply one of the discussion's minor phases.

A more than usually choice instance of this occurred in the 1938 diplomatic correspondence between Great Britain and Mexico over the oil expropriations. The British in their notes sought to raise the entire issue of alien property rights under Mexican law and constitution, plus the question of whether the British oil interests had behaved themselves in Mexico. The Mexican reply airily ignored virtually this whole element in the protest. Furthermore, though strong complaints could have been made of the conduct of the oil corporations in their labor policies and their attitude toward the Mexican courts, and a powerful case for expropriation could have been built up on Mexico's economic necessities, these opportunities were dismissed no less cavalierly.

Certainly, a long series of "events and circumstances" had led up to the seizure of the properties, Foreign Minister Eduardo Hay's communication to London admitted; but "the validity of the expropriation does not depend exclusively on circumstances." And Señor Hay continued:

My government deems it necessary to place on record that there is a universally accepted principle of international law which attributes to all sovereign and independent countries the right to expropriate in the public interest with payment and adequate compensation; moreover, this principle has been considered and held to mean that the grounds of the public interest may be determined by every state at its own discretion, with such latitude as conditions, social, and of every other kind, may require. . . .

The note continued more caustically:

If the documents had been examined, His Majesty's government would undoubtedly have understood that the Mexican nationality of the expropriated companies debars them [the British government] from affording international support to their demands . . . and would have grasped the full legal character of the case.

Thus, the note concludes, the expropriation must be "adjudged legal and valid in itself."

The whole structure of the argument, in a word, was built up on the stratospheric issue of sovereignty to prevent a discussion of the pros and cons of the expropriation policy on its merits. For that matter the law had been built up likewise. The "documents" to which Minister Hay referred the London Foreign Office were the Mexican statutes declaring that foreign shareholders in Mexican corporations, by the mere act of purchasing Mexican securities, forfeited their rights to secure diplomatic support for their grievances from their home governments. Mexico had put herself in the happy position where, officially and as a matter of strict rationalization, she was able to regard any protest against expropriation as a hand laid more or less feloniously on her holiest liberties.

In diplomatic controversies with the Latin Americans, shifts of the issue, in fact, are rather more than less often in the direction of ideal concepts like philosophical sovereignty. For the Latin-American mind tends to feel itself peculiarly superior in a realm of blithe perfectionism to the too materialistic neighbors from the north. Swimming in a pellucid pool of absolutes and abstractions, it can look out on fellow creatures bogged down in the swamps of mere practicality as Calibans to its superrefined Ariel.

A list toward perfectionism, however, has not always encouraged perfect harmony within the hemisphere. Elsewhere, some of the crimes committed in the name of the Monroe Doctrine will be given due consideration. But it should also be put into the record that some of the protective knight errantries which certain Latin Americans have called for under its aegis might have led to embarrassing consequences.

The first Brazilian minister to the United States, José Silvestre Rebello, began his mission in 1825, for example, with a frank appeal to Secretary of State John Quincy Adams for a military alliance against Portugal. Portugal might seek to reconquer Brazil at any moment, ran the Brazilian's argument. The United States was opposed to the extension of European political systems anywhere in the hemisphere. Therefore a military alliance against a potential reconqueror was a strictly logical development.

Rebello was politely discouraged, but his rationalizing talents were shortly put in the shade by President Bernardino Rivadavia of Argentina. In 1826, during war between Argentina and Brazil over the territorial control of Uruguay, Rivadavia's government officially asked United States chargé d'affaires, John Forbes, two leading questions.

Since the Emperor of Brazil was a relative of the Austrian Hapsburgs and Austria a leader in the European Holy Alliance, would not the United States, under the Monroe Doctrine, consider a Brazilian attack on Buenos Aires an effort on the part of the Alliance to interfere in the affairs of the Western Hemisphere? And further, if Portugal should send help to Brazil, would not Washington send out an army to defend Buenos Aires? Mr Clay was slightly firmer than Mr Adams had been with Senhor Rebello. The war in the South, he declared with definitely dead-pan emphasis, was "strictly American in its origin and its object" and there was no occasion for United States intervention.

Indeed, much of the century-old controversy between Latin America and the United States over the Monroe Doctrine has grown out of basically antipathetic mental outlooks. To the United States, the Doctrine has afforded simply a convenient formula for a long series of highly pragmatic "muddling through" policies. It was not invoked in the numerous wars which Spain, between the 1830s and the 1860s, waged against her former colonies. The primary aim in all of them was doubtless to "feel out" the possibilities of reconquest. But Washington took the view that Spain's efforts to reclaim former subjects were hardly in a class with colonization ventures by powers which had had no previous stake in the Western Hemisphere, and anyway that the Latin-American states could probably defeat the mother country alone—as the event proved. Again, Great Britain was permitted to take the Falkland Islands away from Argentina in the 1830s and to separate British Honduras from Honduras in the 1860s. Such minor seizures, the State Department held, did not represent a serious movement to extend European "systems" to the Americas and were not worth a clash with a major power.

Much later, after the turn of the century, however, the United States faced the question of invoking the Doctrine in the name of the weaker Caribbean republics threatened by debt-collection demonstrations of the principal European navies. Then Washington—via President Theodore Roosevelt—decided that it would be cheaper and less dangerous to step in and reorganize the finances of the debtors by collecting their customs. When this pragmatic solution had involved us, by 1933, in the embarrassments of several military interventions and an uncomfortable series of "dollar diplomacy" scandals, Roosevelt II—though quiet supervision of the customs remains a Yankee prerogative in half a dozen republics—finally eased the tension by calling home the Marines and proclaiming the Good Neighbor policy.

Yet, in concrete practice, the Monroe Doctrine achieved its major objectives. The mere insinuation that it might be called on, in the 1860s, had driven the French out of Mexico and crumbled Maximilian's empire. Spain was induced to withdraw from a reoccupation of the Dominican republic in the same decade by hardly more than the lifting of a diplomatic eyebrow. If Great Britain had any intention of bullying the Western republics into territorial cessions by her Venezuelan boundary claim of 1895, President Cleveland's explosion on that issue permanently blew it out of the realm of practical international politics.

From the North American point of view, the supreme test of the Monroe Doctrine's efficacy is pragmatic. Although most of the Latin-American states have had serious disputes and several of them have even gone to war with European powers since 1823, not a single republic's sovereignty has been permanently infringed by a European government. Since the Emperor Napoleon III's Mexican venture, no state's territorial integrity has even been endangered.

The Latin-American mind, however, with a few notable exceptions, judges the Doctrine on an entirely different basis. Because it has failed to implement an idyllic relationship between twenty-one republics and has often fallen considerably short of demonstrating Uncle Sam's infallible generosity, the whole principle of Monroeism has come to signify to many of its Latin critics a policy of deliberate and hypocritical international diabolism.

Thus as far back as 1905 a Venezuelan publicist lashed us for our sins in the dark affair of the Dominican customs. He wrote:

According to the latest interpretations given to the elastic Monroe Doctrine, the New World is the property of the United States. . . . The new interpreters of Monroeism . . . move toward the realization of their ideal with the tenacity of their race without considering the rights of another race or the violence that would be necessary to consummate their colossal ambitions.

Thus Manoel de Oliveira Lima, a Brazilian diplomat attached to the Washington legation at the turn of the century, and considerably more friendly to the United States than the Latin-American average, later wrote that—

with or without reason our people see in intervention a road leading to annexation. . . . If you continue to annex isles near the Caribbean Sea and to take possession of canal zones as you have done in the last twenty years, how can you abstain from securing land upon the northern coast of South America? . . . The small nations of the New World . . . are the Belgiums, the Montenegros and the Serbias of our continent, although indeed without the political progress of the first, or the picturesque history of the second, or the tragic memories of the third.

"For," De Oliveira Lima adds in characteristically Latin moral comparison, "if dictators have been assassinated in Hispanic America, yet their wives have been spared."

On the other hand, at least one Latin-American seeker for perfect intrahemisphere understanding saw merit in a kind of round-robin system of intervention itself. Carlos Tobar, a former Foreign Minister of Ecuador, urged in an open letter to a Bolivian diplomat in 1907 that—

the American republics, for the good name and credit of them all . . . ought to intervene, at least in a mediatory and indirect manner, in the internal dissensions of the republics of the continent. Such intervention could at least refuse recognition to de-facto governments which had been established by revolutions against the constitutional regime.

And Tobar's doctrine was essentially incorporated in the short-lived Central American Union Treaty of 1907 in a provision pledging the five republics not to recognize governments in their circle which came into authority by the revolutionary route.

When President Wilson, however, sought to discourage revolutions by withholding recognition from successful *caudillos,* philosophers, politicians and publicists screamed from the Rio Grande to Cape Horn that the dignities of sovereign nations were being infringed and imperialism was on the march again. What seemed perfection in a Latin-American blueprint of international policy became, when translated by a Yankee president into a specific program, an abomination of the infidels.

The yearning for absolutes cluttered up, too, the tangled eighty-year course of our Panama Canal diplomacy. As far back as 1846 when both countries were still shockingly inexperienced in practical diplomacy, the United States and Colombia, then called New Granada, made an almost perfect treaty covering canal-building rights on the Isthmus. The United States was granted permission to do the construction, when technology and her finances were ripe for it, but over Panama she was to guarantee forever, among other things, New Granada's "rights of sovereignty and property."

It was a charming ideological arrangement. But when, after the Spanish-American War, the United States took up the project of building the canal seriously, it was quickly obvious that a Canal Zone over which a treaty partner's economic and political authority was unrestricted was less than strictly practical. The Washington diplomats, accordingly, went to work, under President Theodore Roosevelt's and Secretary of State John Hay's instructions, to obtain a more serviceable agreement. Eventually they induced the Colombian minister in Washington to sign a treaty granting the United States a five-mile strip across the Isthmus for which the United States was to pay $10,000,000 cash and after ten years an annual rental of $150,000.

When the treaty reached the Colombian Senate, however, the patriotic furies were unloosed. This wasn't the original treaty at all, the Colombian statesmen complained in several days of outraged oratory. In that provision for ceding the five-mile strip of territory the United States had dishonored its signature to the ideal diplomatic instrument. "The Government of Colombia," declared Luis Rico, the Bogotá Foreign Minister, "has proceeded in this transcendental negotiation with the loftiest aims and inspired by the most refined patriotism," but . . . "the other high contracting party did not yield to the proposal to improve . . . the conditions of the pact." Besides, the senators argued, $10,000,000 in lump and $150,000 a year were not enough.

It was a tight box for Washington diplomacy. The Colombians quite plainly wanted more money. And by insisting on the literal application of the "property and sovereignty" provisions of the 1846 treaty, they could continue indefinitely to raise the ante on a Canal concession without seeming too vulgarly to ask for money. In any event the stand for perfectionism won the first round of the 1903 negotiations hands down. The Colombian Senate rejected the Hay-Herran treaty unanimously.

Washington slipped out of the stranglehold by the flamboyantly pragmatic device of encouraging a secessionist revolution in Panama and instantly recognizing the somewhat synthetic new republic's government. Colombia, on sheer form, had made a perfect stand for her sovereignty and treaty rights; but Uncle Sam, for once more expert in revolutionary technique than the Latin Americans, got the Canal Zone.

The perfectionists' field day, however, went on for years. As her sister republics saw it, Colombia was simply the victim of her idealistic patriotism. In all the volumes of literary and editorial indignation which erupted over the Panama rape in Latin America between 1903 and the mid-1920s, not a baker's dozen recognized that Colombia might have been obstructing an international enterprise of vast economic benefit to all of the twenty republics, that Colonel Roosevelt faced serious provocations, or that his action could be anything but a prelude to a general annexation program covering the whole hemisphere.

Since the United States had behaved badly in Panama, the dialecticians deduced, in all our future Latin-American relations, we would behave villainously. Since we had taken the Canal Zone, nothing was safe. We were aiming, as Manuel Ugarte, the Argentine publicist, charged, at establishing a new Roman Empire of which the Caribbean was to be our Mediterranean. We would seize, without warning, any port of any strategic area that might be useful to us. We would destroy the sovereignty of any nation that dared oppose us. International law meant no more to us than it did to Genghis Khan or Attila.

Ismael Enrique Artigas wrote in *El Nuevo Tiempo* of Bogotá at the time of the U.S. entrance into the first World War in 1917:

Our pro-Ally sentiments are so well known that it might be believed that the attitude of this journal would be definitely in favor of the United States in its contention with Germany. But—higher than these opinions—first in our minds is the sentiment of love for our country, and that love will never allow us to forget the offenses which the Anglo-Saxon republic has committed against us. . . . When that nation invokes the principles of international law to induce us to join her protest against Germany, she is engaged in a mockery . . . With what authority, after events like those of November 3, 1903, can a nation speak in the name of international law?

It is Manuel Ugarte, incidentally the most realistic of the Latin-American critics of the United States, who gives us, on the other hand, the soundest explanation of the psychology behind these slightly extravagant judgments. During General Pershing's "punitive expedition" into Mexico in 1916 on the trail of the revolutionary leader Pancho Villa, a detachment of American cavalry was rounded up by Carranza regulars at Carrizal and virtually annihilated. Writing of Carrizal, Ugarte in *The Destiny of a Continent* defines the essential differences in Latin-American and gringo thinking processes:

After Carrizal, Ugarte declared—

it would have been easy for the United States to have launched 200,000 men across the border, and within fifteen days to have been in the [Mexican] capital. Why did they not do this? According to Latin-American conceptions, their gesture was far from brilliant. We [the Latin Americans] would have gone forward, invoking military honor and all such principles.

The psychology of the great northern nation is different. In the face of the resistance which was developing . . . in the mountains . . . they made a calculation of advantages and disadvantages, posed the problem in practical terms, taking account of the time element, the sacrifices which the enterprise required, the benefits which it could pro-

duce and the possibilities of achieving the same ends by other means.
. . . An expert general put down the cost of the proposed invasion in
concrete figures. The gains to be made appeared insufficient compared
with the risks. . . . Finally, from the economic viewpoint, did not the
United States hold the future of Mexico in its hands already?

The contrast between mental processes described here hardly
requires explanation. In the Yankee scale of values, the Carrizal
engagement was merely a surprise attack by overwhelming forces
on a lonely detachment—a piece of bad military luck for the
soldiers concerned. But it changed nothing in the basic balances
of Mexican-American relations. To the Latin-American mind,
Carrizal was a piece of sheer emotional drama—a Mexican Lex-
ington and Concord wiping out old scores from the Mexican War
and the battles which won Texas. Even the shrewd and realistic
Ugarte feels himself obliged to go into elaborate detail to describe
the thought processes of a nation capable of suffering such a defeat and not feeling disgraced by it. He can barely delete the ironi-
cal sneer from his style in confessing that such a nation exists.

☆   ☆   ☆

However, to call Latin Americans self-centered, provincial and
perfectionist in their attitude toward Yankee imperialist gestures
is not, I trust, on a par with accusing a lady of losing her critical
integrity while being ravished.

Obviously, there is plenty to be said for Latin-American distrust.
In their home-front republics, Latin Americans come almost
exclusively into contact with North Americans who in one way
or another are the exponents of economic imperialism—and even
talk political imperialism with a somewhat scandalous looseness.
When the Latins travel in the United States, they seldom mingle
with the immense masses of Americans, who—whatever their
ignorance of Latin-American conditions and their lack of concern
for the issues of our Latin-American policy—look with acute disrelish on the idea of subjugating independent republics for the
benefit of powerful oil, mining, power and banking interests.

Moreover, in the declarations of numerous responsible statesmen during the "dollar diplomacy" era, Latin-American suspicion of our rapacious intentions had something to go on. It was not easy, after the Panama Canal difficulty, to accept Theodore Roosevelt's "We have begun to take possession of the continent," as a simple expression of a big brother's rough good will; or Secretary of War Taft's "The hemisphere is ours de facto, as already, by virtue of racial superiority, it is ours de jure." In Secretary of State Philander Knox's recommendation, to the Senate Foreign Relations Committee in 1911, that, besides collecting the customs of debt-harassed republics, the customs of Latin America in general should be supervised by the United States to keep them "from being seized as the means of carrying on devastating and unprincipled revolutions," Latin Americans quite naturally could see only the Marines and the smile of an insincerely paternal tiger.

The highlight in the Latin-American reaction was not that they protested against the stronger neighbor's conduct and suspected his intentions. The key to the Latin mental process is that the spokesman for the indignant republics recognized no imperfections or provocations in the conduct of their own governments, that they dramatized themselves as the victims of a wholesale outrage before the outrage itself had developed beyond a local basis, and shrieked against the imperialism of the "new Rome" without making the slightest effort to arouse, or co-operate with, the vast, latent forces in the northern republics which were opposed to imperialism.

Establishing its superiority to the enemy by branding him as a villain comes more easily to the Latin psyche than checking the villainy. Indeed, the swing of this effort has often carried Latin-American diplomacy into positions inconsistent with its own advantage and interests.

After the Woodrow Wilson administration, for instance, had done all in its power and seriously risked its political popularity at home to oust Victoriano Huerta, the puppet of the true Yankee imperialistic faction, from the Mexican presidency, Venustiano Carranza, his successor, maintained an almost openly pro-German attitude during the United States participation in the first World War. He conducted his correspondence with Washington on a plane of bicker and billingsgate, and in general treated the Wilson regime a good deal as Poland and Czechoslovakia, given a new chance, would doubtless like to treat the Hitler regime.

The Latin-American mind in Carranza simply could not face realistically either the fact of the obligation or the implications of Washington's friendliness. To put the stronger state in the wrong, to maintain the thesis of a perilous Yankee imperialism, and, above all, to keep his prestige as a leader independent of the help of outsiders, Carranza must be more anti-American than the politicos whom Yankee imperialism had actually injured; more anti-Wilsonian than the Yankee Republicans of Wall Street.

It is a simple matter, of course, to dismiss Carranza as a spiteful and self-seeking ingrate. But most of these questions of the Latin-American mind and temperament boil themselves down to questions of practical politics; and there is a lesson to be learned in Carranza if anyone cares to read it.

There are times in every Latin-American politician's life when the perfect attitude of dramatic defiance toward the superior strength of the United States is more useful than the practical utilities of Uncle Sam's friendship. At a period when defiance inevitably gives aid and comfort to dangerous enemies, a practical Latin-American policy would so frame its methods that the choice between prestige and the open admission of obligations would rarely have to be made.

CHAPTER IX

Conditioned Politics

In a pleasant andean cantina in Ecuador I heard one night the story of the honest *interventor*. There may have been an element of the fabulous in so tightly constructed a tragedy, but for whatever allegorical worth it may have, I give it.

There had been revolution, wholesale graft and finally a complete breakdown of public order in a certain down-at-the-heels coastal province. So the ruling statesmen in the capital removed the governor and sent the honest *interventor* down with drastic powers to make things reasonably right again.

Being intelligent as well as honest, he began by making a comprehensive survey of conditions. It showed him that he stood in the exact center of a vicious circle.

The people were ripe for revolution because they were illiterate and starving. They were starving—and suffering, incidentally, from most of the known malnutritional diseases—because there was a blight on their bananas, weevils in their cotton, and their cattle were dying of tick infections. The food which they grew reached them half poisonous, and their excess crop was unsalable. Totally lacking the money to buy anything better, they ate what they had and sickened of it. They were illiterate because even the small revenues which the province produced in its poverty had been stolen. No schools could be built or teachers' wages paid.

The honest *interventor* had a bright idea. He would establish a general-welfare department in his little government, put it in

[*137*]

charge of educational, public-health and agricultural improvement services—thereby saving the cost of an extremely topheavy provincial bureaucracy—feed practically all his revenues into operations, and grapple with trouble at its roots.

So he fired all the useless drones and the common grafters he could lay his hands on from the public pay roll, improvised an efficient espionage system to watch the others, and set to work. To save still more money on an expensive functionary's salary, he took over the duties of director of the Department of Public Welfare himself.

But the honest *interventor* had a brother-in-law. And when the *interventor* moved into his new post, the brother-in-law, together with his nine children, his aged parents and various aunts and servants, followed along. Worse still, from the moment the job of director of the public welfare was created, he claimed it for himself as his rightful share of the family patronage.

There was a big row about it, but the honest *interventor* won Round One. He told the suppliant that he was down there to straighten out the affairs of a province, not to keep a boarding-house. If relatives did not like starving in the provinces, they could go back to the capital and get themselves jobs.

The brother-in-law sulked. But he sulked with carefully planned exhibitionism. Day by day his linen suits grew shabbier and more studiedly unlaundered. One by one his children's once modish garments were withdrawn from circulation until by the end of a month they were appearing on the streets virtually in rags. When invited to an official reception at the residence of the *interventor,* as family etiquette required, the tribe appeared in unpressed clothes of vanished fashion eras and wolfed their refreshments in the public gaze like creatures momentarily released from an almshouse.

"Ah, *caballeros,*" the brother-in-law would sigh when he met enemies of the new *interventor* in the coffeehouses—particularly the bright young politicians who had been dropped from the provincial bureaucracy—"to think of the sacrifices I have made for that little autocrat's career! His plans sound beautiful now, but one day you will learn that you are being ruled by a man with a cold and vengeful heart. I know, for he has taught me to know ingratitude."

It went on until even the friends of the *interventor* and his program were shocked at such lack of family feeling. With the scandal to work on that the province was at the mercy of a miser who would let his relatives starve, the lately ousted young officials were seriously planning a revolution.

As if this were not enough, every night the honest *interventor* had to go to sleep against wife trouble. For the subjection of Latin-American wives seldoms extends to the boudoir. Hour after hour the lady reproached him with insulting her brother's pride, disgracing the honored estate of her aged parents, keeping her nieces and nephews in misery.

At the end of three months, the *interventor* abandoned virtue. If there was a revolution, he realized, he would lose his job and his chance to be useful anyhow. If he gave his brother-in-law the job, he would remove a focus of revolutionary infection and by constant watchfulness and doing most of the work himself see that the Public Welfare Department functioned. For a while the system worked. Then the *interventor* was called to the capital to report on his stewardship. It took several weeks to be received by the proper supervisors, as is customary in Latin-American official business. While he was gone, the long-frustrated brother-in-law spent the money for two public-health demonstration trucks on three private automobiles, gave five key school-inspection jobs to a pleasant coterie of mistresses, and devoted the school-construction fund to buying himself a country estate. Hostile politicians in the capital got wind of the scandal, and utilizing the disgrace of one *interventor* as a means of copping off an inter-ventorship for themselves, had our honest friend fired.

Another *interventor* was appointed to straighten out the affairs of the province, and, since he appeared with the usual consign-ment of relatives and reward-seeking political henchmen, things went on much as before.

Politics in Latin America, in a word, is not so much the art of the possible as a discriminating submission to its opposite. As a device for improving society anywhere, government is seldom much stronger than the social forces of its environment. In the twenty republics the social forces to which government must adjust itself are, to the Anglo-Saxon mind, almost unbelievably obstructive and conservative.

Our honest *interventor,* for example, was not defeated by a wicked brother-in-law. He was defeated by the ancient and honorable tradition of clan loyalty which prescribes that a man's good fortune should be shared by his relatives. Nor was the brother-in-law himself a horrible example of unique depravity. Unquestionably he was generous to his wife and children. Quite possibly, he paid his gambling debts promptly and—with due time allowance—his bills. In his way he was a gentleman hagridden by a sense of responsibility. As a high servant of the State, he realized that he must live as grand-ducally as possible in order to maintain his prestige. With his personal finances arranged, he might even have settled down as a fairly average administrator.

☆　　　　☆　　　　☆

The difficulty is that these or similarly obstructive forces are constantly in play against government in Latin America.

Let us consider for a moment the fundamental problem of all the republics. In the broad view it is the same as ours—to adjust their people to twentieth-century economics.

But most, if not all, of the crucial factors are different. We begin with an enormous educational plant which has overcome illiteracy as a general social handicap, a high general health and efficiency average, an aptitude for technical skills developed from generations of practice, and almost boundless resources for technological research and training. To maintain these standards and improve them, we can look to the revenues produced from several hundred billions in taxable property and a $65,000,000,000 national income.

On the other hand, the Latin republics, with one or two exceptions, need vast educational campaigns to overcome the illiteracy of between 20 and 80 per cent of their masses. They need billions of dollars' worth of technical equipment and facilities for training millions of young men and women in the skills of mechanized industry and agriculture. They need far-flung campaigns of sanitation and primary health instruction, extending to frontiers where travel is both more difficult and vastly more expensive than in the United States.

Our job in all these activities is to carry on with a going concern and make it more efficient. Latin America's job is to organize the activities from the bottom and, with all the duplications of effort and expense involved in the existence of twenty separate governments, put them on a rudimentary operating basis. To do all this, Latin America never saw an income of more than $20,000,000,000 and has only a few dozen billions on her tax roll where we have hundreds. If the job is to be accomplished at all, it must be done with the narrowest sort of penny-pinching economy and heroic devotion to the public service.

Yet both economics and social values in Latin America are unfavorable to these rarefied virtues. In most of the republics, for one thing, there is a shortage of business and professional openings for young men of talent and ambition. They seek political jobs in the government service because few other jobs with comparable chances of advancement are to be had.

Nor do they go into the public service because they are interested in ascetism. They are interested in getting ahead, in winning affluence for themselves—if possible, in establishing fortunes. So far as go-getting motivation is concerned, they are a good deal like the young men in the United States who rush directly from the universities to jobs with Wall Street brokerage houses, the big motor and oil companies—entrepreneurs, not idealists. Much of the best—and most ruthless—entrepreneur blood in Latin America, in fact, is fed into the government service for lack of opportunities elsewhere.

Furthermore, once he gets it, public office confers on the young entrepreneur a kind of patent of local nobility. He has acquired "rank" and must look to the government to maintain the living standard which goes with it. His colleagues and superiors expect him to put up something of a social front if only to enhance the dignity of their own stations. Now that he is a man well placed in the world, his friends look to him for lavish entertainment and often more solid favors. His wife nags him for more modish clothes and a house in a better neighborhood. His relatives, having a powerful friend at court, expect their—and their bosses'—business deals with the government to be looked after, not to mention their personal job needs.

If our young man fails to deliver in all these directions, his natural boosters feel that he has let them down. His superiors wonder whether he is an innocent too naïve to know what public office is for, or a dangerous reformer showing off his virtues to embarrass them. If he does deliver, he is trapped in a squirrel cage of lavish expenditure, and the government must help him solve his perennial problem of making ends meet.

The chances are that he will keep his skirts clear of straight embezzlement. But when he has supplies to buy, he will buy shoddy goods for phony prices—and a rake-off on the side. When he has regulations to enforce, he may add to his income whatever he can collect by winking at violations. When he travels, or conducts negotiations, his expense accounts will suggest both a romantic imagination and a passion for details. To business houses which have important favors to ask of his office, he will seldom pay his bills.

All this is part of the custom of the country, and it is only by observing its customs that our young man manages to live as his position demands. Meanwhile he must spend an inordinate amount of time feeling the pulse of office politics, building himself up as a worthy and charming character with the bigwigs in national affairs, and keeping himself in subtle touch with all prospective and potential coups and revolutions. If he neglects these highly interesting operations—and since the society around him regards them as absorbing, our young man is likely to lead a painfully cloistered life if he shuts himself away from them—the quality of his official record is not likely to save him when the next upheaval comes.

Between all these exciting extracurricular activities, some of the work of the young man's bureau—educational, sanitary, technical or what have you—manages to get itself done. But it is done at reckless cost per unit of accomplishment when what the republics need is a pared-to-the-bone fiscal economy in all their operations. It is done to the accompaniment of a vast time wastage, when to get broad national programs organized at all requires the drive and devotion of zealots. Hence, while practically without exceptions the republics have maintained ambitious bureaucracies to cure themselves of intellectual and technological backwardness and to end their poverty and its diseases, most of their work never gets done. There are plenty of impressive little demonstration projects dotted over the map from Chihuahua to Patagonia, but the business of adjusting the peoples of the twenty nations to contemporary economics has been applied in most cases only to minute fractions of the populations.

It is easy, of course, to scold the Latin Americans for these failures and shortcomings. They ought to see their problems with clear eyes, we can say, and attack them with the earnestness of Iowa schoolmarms. They ought to be galvanized with the sense of their necessities and make themselves over into the self-denying and passionately achieving kind of persons that our pioneer ancestors were supposed to be and as our captains of industry were depicted in the old-fashioned success magazines. They ought to get themselves a few moral Titans like Franklin and John D. Rockefeller Sr to beat the doctrines of hard work and self-sacrifice into them.

But, unfortunately, the Latin Americans are galvanized by wholly different social appetites and values, wholly different problems of self-preservation and career-making—all of them historic and inherited and heavy with the compulsive weight of folkways. Their public officials have to operate in a civilization where, for better or worse, if you lose your prestige you lose your opportunity to be useful. In such a situation moral Titans do not count for much. They are fighting against the strength of the inherited prejudices and appetites of society. Latin America has bred moral Titans in reasonably impressive numbers, it is true. But some of them have faced firing squads, while others have ended less romantically merely by losing their jobs and their political sex appeal.

The young men who weaken and fail at their task of lifting the twenty republics by their bootstraps, at any rate, are not so much intrinsically vicious characters as victims of a system—a system of conditioned politics.

☆   ☆   ☆

Let us see, in a somewhat classical instance, how the system works.

The great 1911–20 Mexican revolution was waged on the slogan, "Land for the peons." It was a sound idea. Mexico, like so many other Latin-American nations, was bogged down by the abject poverty of her rural proletariat. If her peons could be made over into enterprising, independent small farmers, self-sustaining and producing a little on the side for world markets, Mexico could rationally hope to develop purchasing power, a sizable tax roll, the elements of prosperity on which a modern state operates.

Mexico's population today is hitting around twenty millions; her oil and mineral wealth is enormous. If she could raise her rural masses to a decent standard of living, she could afford schools, public-health campaigns, armies and navies—a whole galaxy of modern public services. She could not only make her people happier, but she would even have a chance to establish herself in the hemisphere as a vastly stronger power than Argentina.

Mexico was aiming straight at the root of her problems. For all their military deficiencies and the sins they committed, the armies of Villa, Zapata and Carranza, ramping through the republic in the second decade of the century, were roaring economic horse sense.

As soon, then, as General Alvaro Obregón was more or less firmly seated in the presidency in 1920, the business of apportioning the lands started. The government had ample authority. Its expropriation laws gave it the legal power to break up the estates of the great landholders practically without redress. Many of the estates, due to the fact that the owners had taken the wrong side in the revolution, were already confiscated.

So a vast bureaucracy was recruited in Mexico City and the provincial centers, and the noble work begun. There were generals retiring from the wars and thousands of young civilian leaders temporarily discharged from revolutionary politics. Nothing could be simpler than to enlist the personnel.

But the bureaucracy had to live in a style which cast the proper glamor on their official status. And this automatically threw them into a friendly working alliance with rich landowners. To a land-distribution agent, trying to make ends meet on a meager and often unpaid salary (the revolutions had emptied the treasury), what could be more natural than to accept an occasional friendly present from members of the local landed gentry, and thereupon proceed to forget about initiating the legal red tape of expropria-tion proceedings? Or see to it that only the alkali desert acres of the Croesus were taken when expropriation could no longer be staved off?

Against these internal handicaps the expropriation went for-ward with exasperating slowness. There were peons by millions, yet they got land in driblets of hundreds and thousands. The basic economic evil was being attacked not on the broad front, but in demonstration plots. And there were further interesting developments.

The peons who got land immediately developed a mild psycho-sis not unrelated to that of the bureaucrats. They were landown-ers now, so, in a small way, a cut above the neighbors. In order to do what the new prestige required of them, they must live a little above the neighborhood standards. The land-distribution agents fell in with this tendency enthusiastically. If the new pro-prietor could show a phonograph or a battered jalopy or a brass bedstead or a new plow on the place, it looked as if things were going prosperously and the agent was doing a magnificent job. But these signs of progress had also a practical advantage. The new member of the landed gentry was running into debt to show off his luxuries, and if he went far enough into debt, he would lose his land.

The distribution agents became expert in encouraging the ex-peons to contract these little obligations. Indeed, many of them

became, in a quiet way, some of the shrewdest real-estate opera-
tors in Mexico. As, one after another, little proprietorships faded
out into bankruptcy, they bought them out piecemeal for the few
pesos which the bankruptcy victim's poverty required, and merged
them together into fairly considerable small estates of their own.
Or they collected titles to ownership and quietly traded them in,
for commissions or favors or promotions, to some political bigwig
in Mexico City who was going in for landed proprietorship in a
really large way. Or, after expropriating the local landlord's holdings with impressive thoroughness, the distribution agents decided
in their wisdom that the peons on the estate could better be accommodated on somebody's alkali lands elsewhere; so they turned
the main property in to the big politico's hands intact—for appropriate brokerage fees.

For all these reasons the project of turning peons into independent small farmers did not work very well. The land-distribution bureaucracy lived rather better than the average of Mexican
bureaucracies, but Mexico, in the large view, was simply exchanging new landlords for old. The peons were getting new bosses,
and the old Diaz land barons were being replaced by parvenu
Obregón-Calles land barons. The peons were practically as numerous as ever and just as abjectly poor. Everything seemed to be
working against transformation, including the peon's own social
appetites.

So the Cárdenas administration in the mid-1930s launched off
on another tack. Since the ex-peon, alone and poor on the few
acres which expropriation had brought him, could not cope with
the politicians sent out to safeguard his interests, the Cárdenas
program would attempt his economic enfranchisement en masse.
It would stop trying to create independent farmers against such
powerful obstacles and see what could be done to restore the old
Aztec and early colonial system of communal farms—or *ejidos*.

Under the *ejidos* whole farming communities are organized into
producing, selling and buying co-operatives. Presumably, with
help from government credits and management by expert government economists, they should be able to carry on. In any case,
the Indian would not stand alone against government agents

functioning as agricultural realtors. He would have his *ejido* behind him.

The *ejido,* however, also requires a bureaucracy. And to see that bureaucracy in action is not always encouraging. There are *ejidos,* like the coffee co-operatives in the state of Vera Cruz and the cotton co-operatives in the Laguna region near Torreón, which, according to the first few years' figures, are impressively successful. But even when they win through they have to carry a disturbing amount of overhead weight on their backs.

Early in April 1938, for instance, I visited the sugar *ejido* at Zacatapec in the state of Guerrero. In the hot valley between the mountains stretched away mile after mile of sugar fields. In the exact center, bold as a grain elevator on the Dakota prairies, stood the white upright bulk of an immense sugar mill. That sugar mill had cost close to $1,000,000 in hard-won Mexican revenues, and in technical equipment there are few plants that could match it anywhere in the world.

I was to meet there an executive of one of the Mexico City government land banks, who was to show me over its magnificence. But as I approached the main entrance to make inquiries, at least half a dozen guards and watchmen leaped to attention to inform me that only technicians were to be found here. The main executive offices were in an old hacienda half a mile distant. Their air suggested that merely asking for a financial official in such a temple of mechanical gadgetry smacked of social error.

So, between track spurs crowded with trainloads of sun-cooking sugar cane, I drove over to the hacienda. At the main gate I was stopped by a file of highly ferocious-looking little Indian soldiers. "You can't go in by this gate," they said, brandishing businesslike bayonets toward my chin. "You have to go in by the other gate."

So I went in by a smaller doorway ten feet away, where there were no guards at all. Obviously no one was trying to keep the public out of the executive offices. The army simply was there to see that nobody used the more convenient gate.

In the main hacienda courtyard my troubles began in earnest. The old mansion was less office building than labyrinth. The entrances that I tried were locked, or they led into cul-de-sacs of masonry where one stood in huge, empty *salas* and confronted blank walls. Or they led up fire-blackened stairways to galleries overlooking mysterious patios where clerks were working behind barred windows. But there were no descending staircases, and apparently the personnel was unreachable from the outside world. I pounded on doorways where no one answered, and I walked through corridors which tunnel-like ran the whole length of the household, with no doorways at all.

Hundreds of Indians in their pajamalike cotton drawer suits and sandals milled about in the courtyard. I asked them where my friend Don Fernando, the banking *gerente* (manager) from Mexico City, might be found. They stared at me with blank politeness. I might as well have asked for the equations governing the transit of Jupiter.

Finally, at a far corner of the mansion I came on a row of barred windows, behind which in a dim parlor numerous clerks stretched away in a heaving forest of white papers. There was no door to their retreat in sight, so I shouted through the bars. At length, with an air of sorrowful condescension, a young man arose and consented to parley with the madman who insisted on disturbing his routine.

Where would I find Don Fernando's office?

"I am sorry," the young man answered, "you must be mistaken. I know of no such person."

"But he is the *gerente* from the bank of the *ejidos* in Mexico City," I insisted. Thereupon the young man entered upon a series of conferences with his colleagues and eventually came back with three sub-*gerentes* of his own.

"Don Fernando's office is in Mexico City," they informed me. "You will find him there."

"But he made an appointment to meet me here this morning," I protested.

"In that case," the delegation informed me, "you will have to ask the fiscal office." And with immense diagramming of the labyrinth, they showed me where the fiscal office was. Half an hour later (their directions were wrong) I found it. There another huddle of clerks and sub-*gerentes* informed me severally—and with much side argument among themselves—that:

1. Don Fernando was in Mexico City.
2. He would be at the *ejido* next month.
3. He was expected that very afternoon.
4. He had come already and at this very moment was inspecting the sugar mill.

I took the last advice as the most promising and bumped back through the glaring tropical noon to the plant. I talked my way past the suspicious guardians with the news that I bore an important message for the banking *gerente;* and suddenly I was in the midst of the technicians.

The mill, in fact, frothed with technicians. And most of the technicians were accompanied by their best girls—not to mention the best girls' parents and relatives.

It was a Saturday noon, and the sugar-refining business was in the grip of the festive Mexican week end. So from Cuernavaca and Taxco, and even from more distant Mexico City and Acapulco, the young staff engineers had assembled the best that their taste could afford in fashion and pulchritude to show them the huge, span-clean vats and the bright new machinery.

But everybody at last agreed that there was such a person as Don Fernando; that he was either on the premises or had been there. And in the wake of a posse of technicians and an atmosphere of Cornell Junior Week, I dashed up the crazy spiral staircases, with which modern heavy machinery surrounds itself, on his trail.

On the topmost vat we came at last on the *jefe ingeniero* of all the *ingenieros.*

"It is a pity," he said. "Don Fernando left two hours ago. He did not come this time on a mission of inspection. He came merely to felicitate his nephew, the chief of the agricultural science section, on his birthday."

That I did not find Don Fernando was, of course, unimportant. There can be no reasonable doubt that I saw more of the *ejido* and its operating methods by looking for him than I would have seen under his agreeable chaperonage.

It was April when I visited it; the last bit of machinery had been installed and the plant wired for power in January. Enough cane stood on the rail sidings to keep it busy for a month. But no cane had been ground. The Indians milling by hundreds in the hacienda courtyard were waiting for land allotments and work assignments, yet three months after the mill—the central part of the project—was ready for operation, most assignments and allotments were still pending.

Back of the delay was the bureaucracy's insatiable appetite for paper work—and jobs. The mill could not operate until all the items in the construction account had been balanced. One regiment of clerks was busy winding up these. Work assignments and land allotments could not be made until base pay and ideally equitable sugar-patch divisions could be computed by higher mathematics; and another regiment of clerks was engaged in these researches. Nobody could speed the clerks at their labors because the two regiments of clerks were enormously valuable to certain politically important personages in the capital. And where but on a remote *ejido* at Zacatapec could two regiments of clerks so conveniently be given jobs?

The *ejido* was choking in its own bureaucracy.

☆   ☆   ☆

The incident, I suspect, gives a realistic sample view of the eternal conflict between economic progress in the twenty republics and the Latin-American version of practical politics. For the overweening ambition of practical politicians, despite many fair professions, is not to raise the general living standards or to organize governments in the interests of the public service. The ambition of practical politicians is to acquire mastery over men and enhance the politicians' personal prestige. The type politician is not so much interested in the job he has to do as in the opportunities which his public station gives him for the delicious pastime of self-dramatization. Sugar grinding for the masses leaves him, consequently, a little cold. But acquiring monumental pieces of glittering modern gadgetry which he can show off to admiring strangers and his best girl is one of the ultimate raptures which, as a careerist in self-dramatization, he lives for.

The over-all conditioning factor in Latin-American politics is —in short—the yearning for dramatic precedence over one's fellows. And being a careerist in self-dramatization, the politician is also a passionate patriot. Indeed, it would hardly be inaccurate, or unduly sententious, to describe several of the twenty brands of Latin-American nationalism as the pooled self-dramatization of the politicians.

CHAPTER X

Synthetic Nationalism

THERE IS NO QUESTION that the twenty republics are sold on nationalism.

At first, in your foreigner's ignorance, you may not quite realize this. Architecture may not differ from one land to its neighbor, cooking and customs and manners change no more than between counties in Iowa. Political behavior patterns may be the same. There may be no detectable variations in the local idioms. Latin-American nationalism, you conclude a little pompously, is an empty formality of flags, national anthems and customs examinations.

But sooner or later someone will enlighten your darkness. Each republic, you find, is a glorified demonstration plot of the special virtues it admires in itself. Each neighbor republic, it appears, is a poisonous distillation of the vices which your host republic of the moment peculiarly detests.

"Ah, señor," they told me in El Salvador, "we Salvadoreños are not perfect. We are a passionate people, and we massacre in war, and we kill when we are thwarted in love. But we do not kill in cold blood simply because we love cruelty like the Guatemaltecos. And we are hard workers. We support our families. We are good to our children. We are kind to our animals. We do not let our fields go back to the jungle and starve our families and abuse our stock like those lazy savages in Honduras."

Sure enough, on the town streets and the country roads in El Salvador the babies, the burros, the oxen are fat, the dogs and cats all but panting from overweight; while in Tegucigalpa family pets hairless from mange scrabble for offal between the cobblestones; and the sore-eyed, nearly naked urchins who beg the visitor for pennies are as skeleton-thin as famine victims.

But listen to the Hondurans in re the Salvadoreños. "We are a nation of poor but peaceable farmers," they say. "The Salvadoreños love bloodshed so much that they would rather kill their sweethearts than have them." The Hondurans, indeed, have made a—should I say pointed?—proverb about the neighbors. "To marry a Salvadorean husband," it runs, "is to marry the knife with the butcher."

Again, sure enough, the Salvadorean newspapers are crowded every day with enough accounts of knifings and shootings growing out of the dark triangles of love, jealousy and alcohol, to make blood run cold even in the Memphis levee district. If some Spanish equivalent of "Frankie and Johnnie" is not the national folksong of the republic, it is because matters like passional murder are much too casual to require commemoration.

Yet for hardly less striking reasons the Hondurans also hold themselves above their southeastern neighbors, the Nicaraguans. "We are a simple, hard-working country folk," they say. "The Nicaraguans are city loafers and clever cheats who wish to live by stealing honest people's land." And in the everlasting boundary dispute between the republics, it is true that Nicaragua has won most of the verbal arguments. "What else would you expect?" reply the supercilious Nicaraguans. "The Hondurans are too primitive and disease-addled a race to argue with a people of culture and lineage."

So throughout Latin America it goes. To the Guatemalans, the Mexicans are Red terrorists—and imperialists, as well, who would like all Central America for a New World soviet empire. The Colombians, in pride of their relative liberalism, speak of the Venezuelans—with their long medical history of ruthless dictatorships—as a "semislave" race. The Ecuadoreans think of the Peruvians as snobs and international bullies, since the Lima aristocracy is cold to strangers and the Peruvian army from time to time has threatened to settle a perennial boundary dispute by invasion. The Lima gentry, on the other hand, customarily refer to Ecuador and Bolivia as "those peon republics."

Because the Brazilians love gaiety and social chatter, the dour Argentines call the northern neighbors *"los monos"*—the monkeys. The Brazilians reply in kind by calling the Argentines after the South American wood that is too solid to be cut with an axe and too heavy to float—*quebracho* heads. Even before the Chaco war, to the Bolivians all Paraguayans were savages from the plains. To the Paraguayans, the Bolivians—passively nonresistant to the tyranny of their upper classes and chewing their daily ration of coca leaves—are dope addicts and degenerates.

Once, too, in Ciudad Trujillo, I was given new light on the distinction between the Haitians and the Dominicans. As a guide about the town and its officialdom, the Foreign Office had assigned me a red-haired young man, grandnephew of a local archbishop, who claimed to have attended half the Catholic colleges in the United States, and who was the only person I have ever met outside a book who literally said, "f'r n'instance."

"The Haitians," he solemnly informed me, "are a people doomed to the jungle. The Dominicans are a people predestined to civilization and culture. Among the Haitian upper classes," he continued, "you find occasionally charming persons. But their masses are black savages relapsing into heathenism and cannibalism. . . . Now among the Dominicans, when a black man has a single drop of white blood in his veins, he considers himself white and behaves like a white."

☆   ☆   ☆

It goes without saying, to be sure, that both culturally and racially there are genuine differences between individual Latin republics. When you see an Argentine regiment march by in a street parade, some of your preconceptions of Argentina as a strictly all-white republic may vanish. Nevertheless, it is a far less Indian spectacle than a Mexican regiment. There may be plenty of quarter-breeds in a Costa Rican crowd, but in a Guatemalan or a Paraguayan market place you will look a long time before you find even a half-breed; and the white man, when you see

[154]

him at all, is generally there in his capacity of local aristocrat. There are enormous gaps between peoples like the Argentines and the Uruguayans, who have received most of their new blood from western Europe, and peoples like the Venezuelans and the northern Brazilians, where, among certain classes, there is a strong Negro strain.

Furthermore, in the predominantly Indian republics there are differences between the Indian stocks themselves quite as striking as between the ancient Greeks and the Scythians—far more marked even than those in modern Europe between the Balkan peoples and the Scandinavians.

The Guaranís of Paraguay, for instance, were living at the time of the Spanish conquest in a "hut culture" stage roughly equivalent to that of the Creeks and the Cherokees. The Bolivian Indians were living under the stable and civilized empire of the Incas, whose art forms were in most respects as advanced as those of pre-Renaissance Europe and whose elaborately communistic arrangements for distributing the physical necessities and the basic comforts of life among the masses have never been duplicated by a white society at any cultural stage. Yet the Bolivians, gentled by centuries of discipline and used to being cared for by the State, yielded to the conquerors almost without a struggle. Since the republic was founded, they have permitted a small aristocracy of white and mestizo landowners and mining tycoons to hold them in virtual slavery. The Guaranís, on the other hand, though ruled for the first sixty years after independence by three of the most ferocious dictators of Latin America on record, have remained fighting men. In the broad sense they have run their republic and still run it. At the worst their dictators were the kinds of chiefs Guaraní Indians wanted.

To this extent, then, the intense feeling the Paraguayans and the Bolivians have of belonging to separate breeds is justified—if not the faces that they make at each other. When a tough little Guaraní soldier in the national police office at Asunción growls at you to take your hands out of your pockets while waiting for tourist clearance, you may not like his manners but you recognize that his virility means business. When a Bolivian Indian drops his glance to the ground rather than face a white man in roadside traffic, you know you are meeting a fellow creature who does not fight back against the beating he is taking from life.

Only once in either Bolivian or Peruvian history since the conquest, in fact—in the Tupac Amaru insurrection of 1780–83—has the ancient Inca population revolted against white oppression in mass. When their altars were overthrown and their god-emperors dishonored, for the Incas a world order perished.

By contrast, in Mexico—after Cortez—resistance simply went underground. The Indians of the Toltec and Aztec stock, shedders of blood and rulers by violence, accepted the white man, not with fatalistic lethargy but with a sullen resentment. A dozen bloody rebellions had to be quelled by the Spanish authorities during the colonial period. And all of the serious wars in Mexico under the republic—the independence struggle itself, the anticlerical wars under Benito Juarez, the great "land for the peons" revolution of the twentieth century—have been essentially wars for Indian emancipation from white supremacy.

In Central America, on the other hand, it has not been so much a question of wars for emancipation as of persistence of Indian and mestizo autonomy in the face of white overlordship. Especially in Guatemala, the white man since the earliest colonial times has been able to commandeer for a pittance the Indian's labor on his plantations and in his mines. But he arranges these matters with the head men of the Indian communities, and within the highland villages the basic forces, political and religious, of a more ancient tribal life go on much as before the conquest. Apart from Costa Rica, which has largely exterminated its Indians, Central America has preserved its indigenous culture more nearly intact than either the Andean republics or Mexico.

One could go on with these contrasts interminably. The gentle, if culturally savage, Indians of the Brazilian coastal regions have merged almost entirely with the white and Negro population. In Chile, on the other hand, the Araucanians, unconquered by the arms of either Spain or the republic, maintain autonomous tribal rights within the Chilean state a good deal as we might imagine the Iroquois doing if they had never been subdued in New York.

In the Dominican Republic black blood denies itself, while Haiti strives desperately—and with a gradual success in spite of her difficulties—for a conscious Negro nationalism.

Between the larger divisions of the Latin-American populations there are without doubt differences in physical inheritance, in temperamental characteristics and cultural backgrounds sufficient to account for the development of nationalism anywhere. In spite of linguistic affinity between all the republics and the fact that eighteen of them speak the same language—in spite of the obvious similarities between their social and cultural inheritances from Europe—there is no more reason to suspect that a United States of Latin America could become an effective governing unit than to assume that the Far Eastern problem could be solved by giving the Chinese representation in the Japanese parliament.

But this does not mean that the legitimate cleavages of racial and cultural inheritance and economic interest, in any realistic sense, follow the actual national boundaries of the twenty republics. Indeed, if one had dictatorial powers to impose a common-sense pattern of nationalism on the Latin-American world, the boundaries might run about as follows:

1. Argentine, Chile and Uruguay, the three predominantly white countries of the far Southern Hemisphere, would form one power.

2. Bolivia, Peru and Ecuador could be amalgamated. For the relative homogeneity of their predominant Indian populations, the similarity of their resources, and the "mountain economy" which conditions their export, import and self-provision problems provide a basic unity as obvious as that of the Mississippi valley.

3. Venezuela, Colombia and Panama would make another unit. The three are maritime nations of approximately the same racial composition, specializing in the same type of tropical and mineral products. Panama's cultural and historical affinities are with Colombia, and if its Canal involvements could be satisfactorily arranged, it would gain by union with the stronger state.

4. Brazil would stand intact. Both its racial composition and its inheritance from Portugal rather than Spain entitle it to the separatism which it demands.

5. Mexico and the Central American republics would be com-

bined; with the possible exception that Costa Rica, on the score of racial and cultural bonds, could go over to the Venezuela-Colombia-Panama combination. The differences between the Mexican and Central American Indian stocks are largely moonshine. The net product of a union would be more efficient economy for the region and a less expensive government.

6. Cuba and the Dominican Republic are close enough together in blood ties and historical background to merge their affairs conveniently. For that matter, if administrative costs and other difficulties did not forbid, a good case might be made out for adding the two island republics to the Venezuela-Colombia group.

This would leave only two smaller powers, Haiti and Paraguay, outside the scheme of large federations. But French-speaking, black-skinned Haiti genuinely lacks affinity with its neighbors. And the Paraguayans differ quite as much from their white neighbors in Uruguay and the Argentine as from the Indians of the Andes republics. In any rearrangement which fully recognized the individuality of distinct racial groups and their rights to self-determination, the title of these small states to separate existence would not be questioned.

Yet despite the poverty of the peoples, the extravagance and waste administrative motion involved in the existence of the twenty republics, in spite of the enormous cost of rival armies and navies, of diplomatic, fiscal and frontier establishments, no movement toward amalgamation is being made anywhere in Latin America. Instead, the general trend over nearly a century and a quarter of Latin-American history since independence has been toward greater separatism.

There were, for instance, when the Monroe Doctrine was promulgated in 1823, not twenty strictly independent governments but eight. Cuba was destined to seventy-five years more as a Spanish province. Haiti and the Dominican Republic were still one nation. Uruguay's formal independence was not established until 1828. The Central American states formed a single federation. Panama was a part of Colombia, and so were Venezuela and Ecuador. Bolivia and Peru, under the rule of Bolívar and his lieutenants, were the "Gran Colombia's" satellites.

Nor can it be predicted today with absolute certainty that the subdividing process will stop with twenty republics. There is a strong secessionist sentiment in southern Brazil which conceivably, given certain twists in national political developments, may ripen into some future secession crisis. Yucatán, which seceded in the 1840s from Mexico and maintained its independence for several years—incidentally offering itself to the United States as an annexation prize—furnishes an interesting potential precedent. Granted strong sectional divisions on the leftist and rightest issues which bedevil Mexican politics, the future secession of some disaffected region of the Mexican republic is definitely not inconceivable.

The whole Latin-American scene, in short, is brooded over by the passions of an intense and potentially explosive local patriotism. The United States is the "Colossus of the North" to all the republics. But Mexico is also a special "Colossus of the North" in Central America; while both Peru and Bolivia cherish dark suspicions of an even greater "Colossus" in Chile. Argentina and Brazil are engaged in a devious underground struggle for "spheres of influence" in their continent. Venezuela and Colombia are pitted against each other in bitter economic competition. Haiti and the Dominican Republic are divided by racial prejudices far more than by the differences of their racial and cultural inheritances.

Year by year the leaders in the twenty republics harp on the petty variations of traits and customs which differentiate their peoples. Year after year from the jungles they rattle the big and little drums of nationalism, while the advantages of union and the bonds which might unite are neglected.

It is as if in the United States Bostonians spent so much of their time brooding on the points in which they were superior to New Yorkers, and Ohioans so much time contemplating the defects of civilization in Iowa that they had no time left to remember that they are one people.

So, it may be a fair question to ask—how does this intense passion for nationalism come about?

☆   ☆   ☆

[*159*]

The answer begins with geography. And through a few layers of strikingly human psychology it leads very shortly into practical politics.

The lonely Spanish colonial frontiers which became the eight republics of 1823, and eventually the twenty republics of the 1930s, were peopled exclusively, as we have seen, by passionate provincials. Probably not one of a thousand of the Spanish king's subjects in the Argentine, before the wars of independence, ever saw a royal subject from Peru. It is unlikely that one Argentine colonist in fifty thousand ever saw a fellow colonial from Mexico. The wars of liberation, when Venezuelan armies roamed as far afield as Bolivia, and Argentine soldiers campaigned in Ecuador, broke down these barriers a little, but not enough. In their isolation all brands of the New Freemen of the 1820s were unsure of themselves and proportionately mistrustful of strangers. The stranger might know more than you and therefore look down on you. Certainly, if he was wiser in the ways of the world, he would take advantage of you.

So the last thing in the world that the residents of any fairly cohesive regional settlement wanted at the time of independence was to be linked with strangers. The little separate provincial areas filed their separate declarations of independence from Spain as instinctively as they recruited their armies on regional bases. They simply did not think of themselves as Latin Americans or South Americans. They thought of themselves as Chilean or Peruvian or Mexican colonists in rebellion. Furthermore, there were other practical obstacles to wider union—some physical and some psychological. Into the heart of the revolting Spanish colonies was plunged the vast bulk of Portuguese and royalist Brazil. Though Brazil also felt the independence urge, and in 1822 achieved her separation from Portugal, her Portuguese quality and her monarchism remained as barriers to political co-ordination with the rest of the continent. And a United States of Spanish America stretching in a shadowy arc around Brazil from Venezuela to Buenos Aires would have been both a geographic and an administrative monstrosity.

But Brazil's embarrassing bulk explains only a part of the

tendency to separatism. Under the Spanish colonial system, the viceroyalty of Buenos Aires ruled over the future Argentina, Uruguay, Paraguay and eastern Bolivia. The Lima viceroyalty had authority from Chile to the Ecuadorean border. The viceroyalty of New Granada covered Venezuela, Colombia and Ecuador. The Mexico City viceroyalty had jurisdiction over Central America as well as Mexico. All of the governing units set up under the emancipated republics were smaller than these. For the outlying regions in each viceregal area had already been ruled by strangers, and they did not like it. They were as anxious to throw off the authority of the great colonial capitals as they were to be rid of the King of Spain. The same centrifugal forces which broke up the Spanish Empire also broke up the viceroyalties.

Thus Central America tore away from Mexico the moment the Iturbide empire was finished. During this brief year and a half of union, no special abuses seem to have occurred—certainly none which have not been matched or exceeded by subsequent native dictators. But Central Americans still look back on the period with horror.

Thus, although parts of Bolivia had been ruled both from Buenos Aires and Lima, the politicians of the region, yearning for a field free from both sets of masters, created a new republic where no very clear administrative unit had existed before. Venezuela and Ecuador disentangled themselves from the coast-to-coast "Gran Colombia" republic as soon as Bolívar's health failed and his political potency weakened. Uruguay—with considerable diplomatic help from the British, who preferred to see the South American coast line politically divided—struggled free from both Argentine and Brazilian invaders. In Paraguay, the grim dictator Dr Francia kept his Guaranís armed to the teeth to fight off the imperialism of the larger neighbors.

In its mainsprings the independence movement was a struggle of local and regional politicians for self-expression and self-fulfillment. They were not going to see their dearly bought new prestige belittled, the dignities of their new offices sullied, their chances for power and gain destroyed by subjecting themselves to the rule of faraway strangers. Why fight a war of liberation merely

[*161*]

to replace the viceroys in Lima and Buenos Aires and Bogotá with a set of semicontinental dictators? Why not keep the new governmental units small enough so that every active and resourceful politician would have a chance to become a dictator himself?

The provincial vanity of the liberating patriots was beguiled with instinctive visions of themselves functioning as international statesmen and flaunting before the world the delicious attributes of semiroyal sovereignty. On their subconscious yearnings for this type of aggrandizement the separatism and petty nationalism of the republics were founded.

☆   ☆   ☆

To this day the charms of office and the powers and perquisites that go with office are the mainstay of nationalism in Latin America.

Let us, as an illuminating case study, take Uruguay. Geographically, climatically, economically, Uruguay and the Argentine are as nearly one land as Kansas and Nebraska. The pampas are the same, the products are the same. The pioneers of both republics were, to a large extent, drawn from the same Spanish provinces and today speak a Spanish with the same curious local accents. Their later immigration has been largely of the same Italian peasant stock. Incorporated with Argentina, Uruguay would be able to draw on the larger Argentine revenues for its public works and social programs, would have the benefit of Argentine military protection, would be able to cut off the entire cost of its diplomatic corps and frontier guard and collections establishments.

But Uruguay, incorporated in Argentina, would at most consist of two or three Argentine provinces. No one could be president of the republic again, or enjoy the honors and dignities extended to those ranking archdukes of practical politics, the cabinet ministers. Uruguayans could be governors and state department heads only, and in Buenos Aires governors and state officials rank only a little above the swankier night clubs' headwaiters. The whole galaxy of Uruguayan senators and congressmen and supreme justices would be demoted to provincial legislators and rustic judges. Worse still, most of the really interesting favors a sovereign republic has to pass around among the friends of its rulers would be dispensed in Buenos Aires, not Montevideo.

To the Latin-American—or indeed to any—political mind such tragedies are unthinkable. You might as well suggest that Nebraska deflate itself into three Kansas counties. So if any Uruguayan statesman proposed so much as even a harmless customs union with the Argentine, the opposition would immediately shriek that he was selling out the fatherland. His own followers could escape the contamination only by publicly disowning him. If a dictator proposed it, Uruguay would simply, in the next few hours, have another dictator. All parties and factions, revolutionary or otherwise, would be one in a passionate conviction that their offices and their future chances for office were being tampered with, and that the tampering involved the direst of crimes against patriotism itself. Whatever the arguments for union, against such instinctive resistance Argentina could win Uruguay only by military conquest.

There is, to be sure, the record of almost a century of effort, in at least one Latin-American area, to overcome the evils of excessive local patriotism. The five Central American republics were originally five small administrative units—called *audiencias*—in the Spanish colonial system, under the immediate authority of the captain-generalcy of Guatemala and more remotely under the viceroy at Mexico City. In actual fact the whole captain-generalcy, on September 15, 1821, declared its independence from Spain as a unit. As a unit it joined, more or less voluntarily, the Mexican imperial state under Iturbide, and as a unit it peaceably seceded when Iturbide fell in 1823. From then on for fifteen years it functioned as a single republic under the name of the United Provinces of Central America, under a federal constitution in which the five former *audiencias* and future republics appeared as states.

But though no distances are tremendous in Central America, the settled portion of each of the provinces was separated from the others—and still is—by stretches of difficult mountains and jungle penetrated only by decidedly sketchy mule trails. Consequently the isolation of the various brands of Central Americans from each other was almost as great as that of the Andean valleys. And the provincial prejudices which isolation fosters soon began to make trouble.

One Manuel José Arce, the federation's first president, proceeded to make a political alliance with the conservative party in Guatemala. The Salvadoreans promptly launched a revolution with the cry that the Guatemalans were running the federal government. In the melee which followed, the presidency was seized by Francisco Morazán, an able statesman from Honduras. As terminology went in contemporary Central American politics, Morazán was a liberal. So the practical politicians in the various states immediately raised the alarm that a foreign radical was enslaving the rest of the federation for the benefit of Honduras. The terrified states countered by electing conservative governors and legislatures, and shortly confronted Morazán with a conservative federal Congress.

Obviously, then, the federation plan would not work. The states could automatically elect a Congress hostile to the president simply on the grounds that, to four out of five of them at least, any president was a dangerous "foreigner." The helpless Congress ended the deadlock in July 1838 by proclaiming the five states sovereign and independent bodies, and Morazán was driven into exile. Local nationalism had won.

It was not, however, the end of federation projects. Morazán tried to restore the old republic by revolution in 1842. He was captured and shot for his pains by patriotic Costa Ricans. Honduras, Nicaragua, El Salvador and Guatemala, nevertheless, carried out his plans to the extent of forming a loose union which was supposed to become a functioning republic when Costa Rica had been forced to join it. Instead, the Guatemala conservatives revolted again and ousted the "foreign oppressors" by the effective expedient of making war on El Salvador. The three remaining states clung to their pact until 1845, when Honduras and El Salvador turned on Nicaragua on the grounds that she was threatening their autonomy by giving shelter to their political exiles. Once again, in 1850, the central trio attempted to impose federation by force. The Guatemalan despot, Rafael Carrera, raised the cry of nationalism and destroyed the movement by crushing its armies.

So the business of federalist project and nationalist counterstroke went on. In 1885 it was a Guatemalan federalist, J. Rufino Barrios, who tried to achieve union by conquest. The Salvadoreans killed him in battle. In 1898 the Nicaragua-Honduras-El Salvador combination once more established a republic and got as far as adopting a constitution. A nationalist revolution in El Salvador kept the government from being inaugurated. In 1921 a joint republic, proclaimed between Guatemala, El Salvador and Honduras, located its capital at Tegucigalpa and even elected a president. But before he could be seated the nationalists revolted in Guatemala and drove out their own president, mainly on the grounds that he had agreed to the federation. President Herrera may have been willing to demote himself to a provincial governor, but the practical politicians both of the opposition and his own following did not propose that he should demote *them*. So Guatemala resounded with the usual outcry: Will the strongest people in Central America submit to being ruled by the bloody Salvadoreños, the savage Hondurans and the wily Nicaraguans?

So much blood has been shed and so many hatreds and suspicions engendered in outbreaks of this character, in fact, that it is doubtful if the prospects of federation in Central America are as good today as they were a hundred years ago. Since 1923 the five republics have tried to better their relations through a series of treaties pledging each other to armament limitations, to noninterference in each other's civil wars, the nonrecognition of revolutionary governments and to the maintenance of a Central American Court of Justice for the arbitration of disputes between them. But the instant one of the stronger republics develops an acute self-interest in the discord of its neighbors, these agreements, too, will be in serious danger of being thrown overboard. There is practically no chance at all that the old United Provinces of Central America will be restored except by conquest, and for that no individual republic is strong enough.

[*165*]

Conquest, moreover, has its drawbacks on other counts. As an instrument both of sensible federation projects and of power politics it has been tried in Latin America and found wanting.

In the early brash days of independence, both Brazil and Argentina tried to conquer Uruguay. It involved the stronger powers in wars with each other which lasted for the greater part of fifteen years. Today the Argentine could overwhelm Uruguay much more easily, no doubt, than she could in the 1830s. But it would involve her instantly in conflict with Brazil, with Chile almost certainly attacking on her rear to weaken her for any potential future westward expansions.

Peru, with vastly greater wealth, population and armaments, unquestionably could overwhelm the impoverished two and a half millions in Ecuador, and a chronic boundary dispute between the republics would afford an aggressive administration in Lima a plausible pretext for taking off. But the moment the Peruvians occupied Ecuador, they would find themselves up against Colombia's greater population and stronger resources. The little nationalisms in Latin America, in a word, are usually buttressed by stronger nationalisms. Even if the Ecuadoreans, in some incredible seizure of self-immolation, went pro-Peruvian and voted unanimously for annexation to the larger republic, the Colombians would probably march in to spank them and show them their patriotic duty again.

Indeed, the South American West Coast already has a case history to serve as a solemn warning against such adventures. In 1835 the Bolivian dictator, Andres Santa Cruz, conquered Peru. But before he could finish the work of incorporating its provinces in the new federated republic, the Chileans attacked him. When they had driven him out of Peru after the battle of Yungay in 1839, the Bolivians also deposed him. What did the ambitious Bolivian politicians want with a *conquistador* who could not hold his empire? The leader who had promised them the offices of a bigger and richer republic, and failed to deliver, had obviously let them down.

Yet there is more to nationalism than an obstacle to the establishment of more efficient governing units. Both in the diplomacy of Latin America and in the domestic politics of the republics it is a constant irritant.

Everlastingly, Peru must watch Chile, Bolivia and Colombia; Brazil must watch Argentina; Ecuador must watch her stronger neighbors, and the five Central American states must watch each other, to see that the rival gains no advantages in armaments, in diplomatic understandings and alliances, in favors from foreign powers.

Out of this situation grows an endless round of difficulties for Washington's Latin-American policy. The moment a concession is made to Brazil or Honduras, say, an equal and opposite concession must be made to Argentina or El Salvador, or the touchy nationalism of Argentina or El Salvador will flare into tantrums of patriotic jealousy.

Almost equal difficulties are created for the traveling stranger. The foreigner must be watched everlastingly to see that he casts no slurs on the dignity of the republic; that he appreciates the peculiar villainy of the neighbors and takes them no secret information of any conceivable military value. Hence his camera is taken away from him for large sectors of his Latin-American journey, and not in military areas only. In Paraguay, for example, he can be sent to jail for photographing the colorful Asunción market place, and often, to the embarrassment of his home country's diplomatic representatives, is. His pictures might suggest to alien critics somewhere that Paraguayan peasant costumes are cruder than peasant costumes elsewhere and Paraguayan markets fully as dirty as Bolivian markets. And in Rio de Janeiro his Brazilian friends whisper a barrage of dark doubts concerning their beautiful harbor-front airport. "Shouldn't it be back in the hills?" they say. "If war comes, think how easily the Argentines could attack it."

The war never comes—or at least this one hasn't—but in the rich Latin-American imagination, nationalism incessantly dramatizes it.

In Paraguay, again, has occurred the most recent classic example of the potency of nationalism as an issue in domestic politics. Between the armistice which closed the Chaco war in 1935 and the

Buenos Aires treaty of 1938 which settled it, the little river republic saw exactly three revolutions—all of them for the same cause. Each separate government came into power on a platform of superpatriotism. Each one, that is to say, solemnly pledged itself not to yield an inch of territory occupied during the war by Paraguayan soldiers and eternally to refuse the Bolivians port or navigation rights on the Paraguay River. Paraguay won the war, was their slogan. She could not abandon the fruits of victory without dishonoring her heroes.

The difficulty was that each administration—after it had been in power for a short time—began to learn certain things. The Paraguayan military lines were overextended, for example. If Bolivia chose to renew the war, they probably could not be held. And Bolivia, though definitely worsted in the first encounters, manifestly could fight again. If she did, she had, in her mining and oil wealth, the economic resources to last out a longer struggle than Paraguay. Worse still, if Paraguayan stubbornness forced a renewal, stronger powers might be driven to intervene, either with military or diplomatic pressure, on the Bolivian side. Finally, even if she got all the territory she demanded, it was extremely doubtful if Paraguay had either population or money enough to administer it. On the other hand, by letting approximately a third of the occupied territory go back to the Bolivians and giving them a minor up-river port, the Paraguayans would be confining their gains to lands they could actually hope to use and making a peace that had some chance of lasting.

As these realities dawned, the natural tendency of each administration in Asunción was to become reasonable. But the moment reasonableness showed its effete head in the presidential palace, and the Foreign Office began dickering for a practicable peace with Bolivia, something happened in Paraguayan politics.

The opposition raised the "Who won the war?" banner, and ambitious young garrison officers turned loose the troops with pronunciamentos that the traitors were selling the blood of the martyrs.

Peace in the Chaco war could not be made for three years because every time an administration in Asunción came to the point of understanding how a practicable peace must be made, there was another nationalist revolution—and another administration which had to be taught from the beginning the terms on which peace could be had.

At length the late General José Estigarribia, the great Paraguayan war hero, was summoned home from his post as minister to Washington. He managed, with his extraordinary prestige, to dramatize a realistic settlement as Paraguay's contribution to the peace of the continent; and the job was done.

☆　　　　☆　　　　☆

Not all of the countries of Latin America are, like Paraguay and Bolivia, in the grip of war and postwar passions. But the jittery tensions of the same emotional nationalism run through them all, like the delirious phase of a chronic fever. With the passion for prestige and mastery, with the historical inheritance of violence and the chronic economic unsettlement of the lands, nationalism, too, is one of the uncontrollable forces in Latin America which help to explain—and even to a degree to justify—the dictators.

CHAPTER XI

Inevitable Dictators

I HAVE AN IDEA that the shortest way into the subject of dictators is through a backdoor entrance.

Let's postpone talking about dictators at all, for the moment. Imagine, instead, that you have been chosen president of the mythical but typical republic of Contra Costa, and are determined to govern it strictly by its constitution and the principles of liberal democracy.

Since the constitution is practically a replica of the one in the United States, you will have to operate through a government of balanced powers. You will let Congress do the legislating, then; keep your hands off the judiciary except for the proper use of your appointive powers, and confine yourself to enforcing the laws which your congressional majority in its wisdom enacts for you.

Also, you have a bill of rights in your constitution. So you will permit freedom of speech, press and assembly and maintain the right of the citizens to organize in as many different political parties, labor unions, employers' associations, secret societies, religious, reform and cultural bodies as pleases them.

You are, of course, commander-in-chief of the armies and navies. But as a liberal executive you would not dream of using the armed forces to enforce your political views. On the contrary, you will turn over the actual command to the generals and admirals, on the theory that they will conduct the army and navy as strictly professional services.

The population of your republic is 55 per cent illiterate. Ninety per cent own nothing beyond their meager household furniture and are struggling against odds of desperate poverty and poverty's diseases. So you set up a network of government departments, necessarily bureaucratic in organization and operating methods, to spread education abroad in the land and promote the general welfare.

Finally, your constitution guarantees free elections. So you make it plain both through public pledges and your treatment of opponents that next time a congressional or presidential election rolls around, the government will keep its hands off.

Then, having restored to the people their liberties and given back to the various branches and departments of the government their proper constitutional powers, you sit back and wait for Contra Costa to proceed to the business of governing itself.

Nothing about your experiment is beyond the bounds of imagination or even unprecedented. Almost every one of the twenty republics in its history has had one or more presidents who have tried it. However, the question is not one of precedents. The question is—what happens next?

Your Congress, for instance, is full of energetic and plausible statesmen who want to be president themselves—or at least want to be close enough to the President in a political way to be paid for their support in cuts that go with the government business. Since your administration grants no such favors, you promptly have a congressional revolt on your hands. Your hurt supporters join with your enemies in using the newly restored powers of Congress to block all your bills and policies. If it obstructs your program and sufficiently humiliates you personally, Congress feels you will lose face with the public, and the time will shortly be ripe for a revolution which will make someone else president— someone who realizes that the first rule of Contra Costa politics is to give political friends the gravy.

Next, your judiciary goes overboard. No suggestions come down from the presidential palace as to what is wanted in the way of decisions. Hence your venerable justices conclude that the State is masterless. Since being mastered is its normal condition, the eminent legalitarians try to put themselves on a friendly footing with the masters-to-be and begin taking their orders from the leaders of your opposition in Congress. Suddenly, despite urgency of the questions in litigation and the weight of the arguments, all the court decisions in the land begin running against your government.

Meanwhile conditions are rapidly veering toward the madhouse stage in the country at large. The press celebrates the freedom you have just restored to it by making up interesting and damaging, if wholly unsubstantiated, stories that you and your cabinet are robbers of the public till, traitors in the pay of Contra Costa's worst international enemies, and degenerates in your private lives.

The freedom of assembly you have guaranteed is used by your political enemies to stir up a succession of mob scenes, several of them involving damage to foreign property, and hence highly embarrassing to your international relations. The labor unions you have sanctioned proceed to spice their legitimate activities with a few deplorable acts of public terrorism. In the rural districts agitators raise up bands of illiterate peons who go about proclaiming that the time of the equal division of wealth has come and imagining that their economic ills can be cured by murdering hacienda proprietors and burning their mansions.

When you send the army out to put down these insurrections, you find the generals in charge of the disciplinary detachments either going over to the insurrectionists or issuing plausible pronunciamentos that, since a military emergency exists, one of their number ought to succeed you.

All these disturbances—and their costs—have naturally shot your educational and social welfare projects to hell. But they were not getting along too well in any case. The eminent scholar whom you appointed Minister of Education has spent the price of several gunboats on journeys to imposing intellectual congresses in the United States and Europe. His speeches have won flattering international kudos for Contra Costa, but meanwhile he has left the task of reorganizing the department to subordinates who have monumentally overstaffed it with political henchmen of the opposition in Congress.

The Public Health and the Agricultural departments have labored under similar handicaps, and in addition have been starved by the refusal of the hostile Congress to make appropriations. Your Resettlement Administration—a carefully thought-out, long-term project for slowly buying up the unused land of the great estates and assisting the peons to purchase it—seemed to be working well until, in midcareer, it developed a crucial scandal. A ring of brilliant young economists and soil experts, hand-picked for their competence, are being bribed by the rich estate proprietors to buy in huge tracts of jungle and swamp land for the about-to-be-emancipated farmers. Your government prosecutes, but somehow, in the politically hostile courts, despite the glaring evidence no one's guilt can be proved.

And if, by some political miracle, you serve out your term in spite of all these disturbances, and election day comes around again, what happens? You find on election morning that the troops of your rival candidate, General Barbosa, have surrounded the polls while your own supporters are quietly going about their business on the theory that voting is unhealthy.

But the chances are several thousand to one that you will not survive until election. Long before your term is half over you will either have been ousted by a revolution, or you will have become a dictator yourself in order to keep Contra Costa from being ruled by a worse dictator.

Graft, ignorance, ambition, military insubordination, the habits of being bullied and of looking on any statesman who fails to rule with an iron hand as a weakling—there are too many of these forces and traditions abroad in the politics of most of the twenty republics to be controlled by the democratic processes. Even by ruling as a dictator you cannot completely master them. Hence, a little while back I called them—and meant it—the uncontrollable forces. At least, however, by exercising the supreme power, you can ride herd on them and keep your country from drifting into chronic anarchy.

Whether you preserve the forms of the constitution and even manage to salvage a good many shadowy individual liberties for your citizens in the process, or whether you frankly suspend the

[*173*]

organic law and rule as an admitted local sultan, is not very important. You will make your choice, no doubt, on the basis of which of these methods is more efficacious and which will go down best with the Contra Costa public. It is largely a matter of balancing political expedients.

In any case, your brief Contra Costa experience gives you an insight into the pathology of Latin-American dictatorships. Scolding the "sister republics" for putting up with dictators, you perhaps begin to realize, is a good deal like scolding a man with malaria germs in his blood for having chills and fever.

☆   ☆   ☆

Still, when we are talking of dictatorships and of ruling republics through the supreme political power of an individual, just what is it that we mean? It is a painfully complicated question, since there are almost as many different brands of dictatorships as there are republics, and within the republics themselves the dictatorships often differ from one to another with the individual dictator's methods and political talents. So let's begin close to home base in Mexico.

Many of my Mexican friends have sat up long hours arguing with me that there is no dictatorship in Mexico at all. Look at the press carping at President Cárdenas' policies like Wall Street brokers ganging on President Roosevelt, they say. Look at the way the opposition parties are allowed to hold their meetings—including even the frankly revolutionary Fascists. You don't hear of leaders who are unfriendly to the President disappearing for mysterious jail terms or going before the firing squad. There hasn't even been an exile since ex-President Calles was run out years ago. And Calles was run out only because he was trying to be a dictator-behind-the-scenes himself. What more have you got in the United States than that? What more have they got in England?

But the situation isn't as simple as that.

President Cárdenas, for instance, controls his Congress in a way that no American president has ever controlled his legislative department. It would be unthinkable for a member of the overwhelming Cárdenas majorities in either house to stand up and oppose an important administration measure in debate or vote against it on roll call, as members of President Roosevelt's party do by scores in Washington. If he so much as flirted with such tactical imbecility, his political career would be finished.

For the president of Mexico absolutely controls the congressional elections. The gentleman who has chosen to break with the administration on the floor of Congress could not get to first base on a renomination campaign. The congressional candidates are hand-picked in star-chamber sessions of the president and his intimate political advisers. If, lacking renomination, he chose to run as an opposition candidate or an independent, every force element in his district—state government, police, the army garrison—would make it plain to the voters, in subtle ways which the Latin-American public understands, that it would be "unhealthy" to cast their ballots for him. If they voted for him anyway, the president's fellow party members would do the final counting of the poll boxes.

In Mexico, then, the president holds his Congress in the hollow of his hand. There can be no more back talk in ranks than there is in a crack regiment being inspected by a field marshal.

But this is only the beginning. The Mexican president also controls his courts. He controls them through the power of appointment, in a sense, but his power of appointment has numerous stronger intimations than the United States president's. A controlled Mexican Congress would pack a court against a dissident majority without a sign of a political tremor. It would impeach a justice who stood out against a major administration policy at a drop of the presidential eyelash.

Again, the Mexican president has a whip hand over the state governments. He can remove a state governor for anything from treasury shortages to seditious political activity, and in cases of public disorder suspend state legislatures. It is not difficult to find errors in a state's account books to warrant gubernatorial ousters, and there are precedents in Mexico for treating practically all the known forms of political opposition as seditious. Though President Cárdenas has hardly been guilty of such an adroit form of skulduggery, public disorder, in a pinch, can be fomented by presidential provocative agents; and every Mexican governor tempted to oppose the national administration is well aware of this.

Finally, the Mexican president can regulate—and for that matter practically abolish—mass political action throughout the republic. At the slightest hint of a threat to the public order, he can suspend civil rights, impose censorships, disband political parties, labor unions, secret societies, in local areas or everywhere. Provided the pretexts can be found—and pretexts come easy to politicians—not a wheel can turn in the whole machinery of organized democratic politics unless the President wills it.

It is true that in fairly calm times a president as levelheaded and temperamentally undespotic as General Cárdenas uses comparatively few of these powers. By keeping his courts and his congressional majority in order, by seeing to it that key posts in the army go to friends of the government, and by very occasionally disciplining a governor who develops delusions of independence, General Cárdenas gets along very well. So newspapers can sound off against the government, opposition parties can hold meetings and organize and a few remote districts may even be permitted to return antigovernment statesmen to Congress. The administration does not need their votes, and by giving his enemies this much headway, the president shuts off the charge that he is conducting a tyranny.

The dictatorship exists, however, because the powers are there, and every Mexican with the slightest intimation of what his national politics are all about—and this includes several millions of illiterate citizens who know nothing else whatever about politics—knows that they are dangerous. Mexican politics is controlled politics in the sense that, from top to bottom of the nation's political activities, the politicians are guarding their conduct and stepping warily to see that the President is given no provocation to put his extraordinary powers to use. The politicians —including his opponents—normally hand over to General Cárdenas the essential dictatorial privilege of one-man control over the government's policies in order to restrain him from functioning openly as a dictator.

And Mexico should be described as a dictatorship for one more reason. President Cárdenas holds a combination of political advantages, through control of Congress, the states and party nominating machinery, which makes it virtually impossible for his opponents, or any hostile faction in his own party, to choose his successor.

True, the Cárdenas administration represents the virtuously progressive elements as against the vested interests of his most vociferous opponents. Moreover, in the July, 1940, elections Almazán, in opposition to the Cárdenas-chosen successor Camacho, received what was described as unparalleled opportunity for expression. Nevertheless, the opportunity resulted in riots and struggles whose toll, when the smoke at the polls cleared away, amounted to hundreds of dead and wounded. As this is written there are even intimations of a potential civil war.

☆　　　☆　　　☆

The pattern of the modified dictatorship has a good many imitators. Panama, for example, is seemingly even more easygoing than Mexico and certainly has less trouble-inciting problems. The presidential palace is as approachable by day as the city hall in a Missouri county seat. The Panamanian Congress yawns and sprawls through its occasional debates as if the public business were an undue interference with the inalienable right of tropical Latin Americans to siestas. Except for counting them out at elections and occasionally appointing them to distant diplomatic posts, the presidential party never dreams of disciplining its enemies.

But if you happen to be kept out at a late party in Panama City, and come home through the velvety tropical dark after midnight, you notice something. There are more traffic officers on duty at the empty street corners than there are in the rush hours. And all of the traffic officers are soldiers. Incidentally, if you happen to pass close to any of the important government buildings, you will see soldiers on guard in platoons and even companies. If you stop in a favorite cantina for a final rum Collins, a soldier is likely to poke his head in at the doorway and, with a smiling greeting to the bartender, look you over.

Panama's last successful revolution, as it happened, was put over by a rush of not many more than a hundred dissident gentlemen on the practically unguarded presidential palace after midnight. So Panama administrations take no chances. If a noticeably large group passes the corner traffic sentry, its members, in consequence, are likely to be conspicuously shadowed by a detachment of night guardsmen until they disperse peaceably and go to their homes. If you are a native son and happen, over your nightcap, to be speaking uncharitably of the government, you may go to a comfortable detention room in the local barracks on the totally unwarranted charge of being drunk and disorderly. In the morning there may be due apologies, and the offending guardsman even nominally "punished." But meanwhile the safety of the State would be just that much more secure.

Panama, of course, is not a dictatorship in the opinion of its local apologists, any more than Mexico. It just happens that you cannot successfully oppose the government at the polls and that if you are at all outspoken as an administration critic you are watched as a potential revolutionist.

More or less similar situations prevail in Cuba, Nicaragua and Haiti. The chief difference is that the rulers in these republics are somewhat more capricious in their methods. In Cuba, for instance, Colonel Fulgencio Batista, who, on the way to his own presidential election, has pulled the strings for a series of puppet presidents since 1933, has switched back and forth from leftist to rightist politics and from liberal to despotic methods with the agility of the man on the flying trapeze.

At times he has governed under practical martial law with a censorship so severe as to convert the newspapers into virtual government house organs. In his darker moods he has employed a castor-oil squad of soldiers in the best early Mussolini manner to minister to his political enemies. At other times he has launched out into interesting social-welfare projects, such as putting the army to work investigating drug monopolies, and taken the brakes off the press to the point of permitting it to indulge in its favorite sport of political scandalmongering. Again, during 1939, he went to the incredible lengths—incredible for a Latin-American dictator —of allowing the Communist party to register itself as a legal political organization. Batista, in a word, governs by the usual methods of the modified dictators, plus a knack for glittering and varied showmanship.

In consequence of these gifts, it was unwise to exult unnecessarily—as certain sanguine editorial writers did at the time—over the election of a technical anti-Batista majority for the Cuban constitutional convention in November 1939. When a dictator is "defeated" at the polls in Latin-American politics, it is always a question of several strategic items: whether the opposition is divided, for instance, as it definitely was in the Cuban stroke for freedom; what *el caudillo's* ties may be with the controlling bloc of his nominal opponents, how much "arranging" he has done behind the scenes with his adversaries, what motives or plans for vengeance he may have for disciplining his ostensible supporters. When a Latin-American dictator permits his caudilloship's "opposition" to triumph, it is always a fair assumption, until factual developments disprove it, that he has found a new and slicker way of taking the opposition into camp.

Nicaragua, under General Anastasio Somoza, rocks along without these exotic touches, yet hardly on an even keel. For General Somoza recently wrung from his disciplined Congress a constitutional amendment permitting him to succeed himself. And in Latin America a dictator's repeal of an anti-reëlection statute usually can be taken as a warning symptom of a harsher dictatorship.

Haiti, on the other hand, is a bit more uneasy. Stories come regularly that President Sténio Vincent is being subjected to demands from the army, the Garde Nationale, for a larger share in the government, with the possibility of military insurrection in the background. If this gossip materializes, Haiti may drop out of the modified-dictatorship class into the more primitive pattern of the military dictatorships.

☆   ☆   ☆

This is the pattern which definitely prevails in Honduras, Ecuador and Paraguay, and, with certain reservations, Bolivia.

The distinguishing trait of the presidents in these republics is that they would like to rule like the modified dictators but are not strong enough. The sophistication of their civilian politicians is so slight and the ignorance and poverty of their masses so deep-seated that they cannot even improvise the methods of machine control through which the modified dictators function. In result, they are almost wholly dependent on their armies for authority and tenure of office. And the army officers, skittering back and forth between rival cliques and factions according to their stakes of the moment in national politics, make and unmake presidents more or less at will. The presidents whom they create by these confused tactics of garrison revolts, capital "putsches," palace revolutions and provincial uprisings are not by any means all military men. Often the "front" of a military coup looks better if a time-saving congressional statesman or a harmless intellectual is nominally selected to lead it. At other times the personal rivalry between the big generals is so acute that none of them cares to risk putting himself on the spot of the presidency. But regardless of who sits in the presidential palace and issues pronunciamentos to the country under these conditions, it is the army's ruling clique of the moment which really runs it.

Under this interesting method Ecuador has had 13 presidents since 1931—three of them in 1938 alone. And nearly three times as many attempts have been made at revolutionary coups which did not quite come off. Paraguay, as already described, has had four changes of administration since the 1935 Chaco war armistice. Before the conflict, the military adventurers had run the show in Asunción since 1870. In August 1939 her "war hero" and strongest practical statesman, General Estigarribia, was seated as president after being chosen through the forms, at least, of a constitutional election. But an air of impermanence clings to the effort. After a period of dictatorship followed by a successful plebiscite on a new constitution in the summer of 1940, Estigarribia was killed in a tragic airplane accident leaving Paraguay possibly at the mercy of new and less competent dictators.

Honduras of late years has had a less disturbed period. General Tiburcio Carias Andino, its huge, taciturn, 300-pound Indian president, was even legally elected in 1933, and since then has managed to keep the lesser generals in order by a variety of adroit stratagems. He keeps them constantly on the move, for one thing, from the capital barracks assignments to the provinces and from one provincial post to another. Thus, none of them stays in one place long enough to build up a local following or to establish working junta arrangements with the brother officers. Carias also feeds the rank and file sufficiently—it takes quantity rather than quality to satisfy a Honduran private—and makes it plain that the soldiers are directly indebted for their provisions to *el presidente*. And finally he buys airplanes.

The Honduran air force is a job-lot aggregation of between fifteen and twenty nondescript flying machines, some of which date back to the immediately postwar training ships. But for its purpose it is highly efficient. Along toward the middle of 1938, when General Carias heard that one of his *comandantes* in a province two or three mountain ranges away from Tegucigalpa was planning to raise a revolt standard, he simply sent his air fleet cruising over the region. In a preview of bigger *Blitzkriegs,* it sprayed machine-gun bullets more or less harmlessly over the countryside, especially in the neighborhood of the military outposts.

Feeling the hot breath of aerial warfare down its neck, the revolt collapsed before it started.

It is fairly rare, however, for the tactics of the military dictatorships to be as decisive as that. Though there is sometimes a good deal of fatal shooting in their battles for capitals and presidential palaces, many of their coups have been executed by simple barracks insurrections without any bloodletting at all.

As a rule, too, there is a touching mildness about their sequels. Revolutionary presidents may send their predecessors and their cabinet ministers abroad for brief periods of exile, and victorious generals may take the juicier commands away from deposed generals and even confine them under nominal arrest on pleasant haciendas. But everyone realizes that in the next shuffle of the cards of army factional politics the help of the lately ousted warriors and statesmen may be desperately needed, and that at worst, in standing out against one's side, they were merely being loyal to the factions where momentarily their bread-and-butter interest was centered. So there are seldom any firing-squad orgies, and even the leaders of unsuccessful attempts at revolution are rarely more than gently disciplined. Quito and Guayaquil, for example, are so full of former Ecuadorean presidents living in agreeable retirement that a mild gag man in the group once suggested that they form a national association and hold annual conventions. If they were a little younger, he frequently assures members of the American colony, they could make it two baseball teams.

The difficulty with the military dictatorships is, of course, that few of them dictate long enough to settle anything. With the constant changes in ruling cliques and policies, the governments are in a constant stage of disorganization ranging from minor confusion to shambles, and none of the uncontrollable forces that dictatorship is supposed to master are more than coped with in passing. In fact, under the generals, one of the worst of the uncontrollable forces, military insubordination, is precisely the power which governs—and chronically unsettles—the republics.

☆   ☆   ☆

Nevertheless there are in Latin America rulers who have licked the army cabalists and managed their countries for years at a time —sometimes for a full generation—without resort to the more or less delicate artifices of the modified dictators. They are the personal despots by whom, at one time or another, every Latin-American republic—with the possible exception of Chile and Costa Rica—has been ruled.

Mexico had Porfirio Diaz. Argentina, from 1835 to 1852, had Juan Manuel de Rosas, who, Mussolini-style, forced the churches to display his portrait and disciplined his opponents with the aid of an oath-bound band of professional assassins. Yet in his quiet old age, tending his garden in philosophical exile in England, Rosas boasted, not unjustifiably, that he had kept Argentina from falling apart into half a dozen Uruguays.

Paraguay had Dr José Gaspar Rodríguez de Francia, the tyrant of Edward Lucas White's curious novel, *El Supremo,* who with his terrible secret service ruled without courts and virtually without a legal code by the simple device of imprisoning—and frequently torturing or shooting—everyone who was heard to whisper against the government. And after Francia came the Lopezes—Carlos and Francisco Solano—who converted the country into a Spartan hierarchy of soldiers.

Ecuador had Gabriel García Moreno who, past the middle of the nineteenth century, restored the Holy Inquisition as a mode of popular discipline. Venezuela had José Antonio Paez, the terrible cowboy lieutenant of Bolívar, and after him Guzmán Blanco, Cipriano Castro, and, for twenty-eight years in the twentieth century, the notorious Juan Vincente Gómez.

For a contemporary instance, however, consider Guatemala's present Jorge Ubico. Guatemala during the 1920s went through a troubled period. Its presidents tried to rule as modified dictators, but none of them could hold the power long enough to make the system function. The republic appeared to be drifting into a cycle of military adventurers' revolutions when, out of the turmoil of 1930, came Ubico.

The new president broke the cycle by returning to older precedents. Guatemala, as he saw it, was not ripe for control by mere machine politics. Its history was that of a succession of despots, broken by interludes of disorder. From the 1840s to the 1860s, Rafael Carrera, an illiterate, superstitious Indian, had ruled it by sheer terror. Rufino Barrios, enlightened and progressive, had controlled it in the 1880s by making the army the core of the government. From the turn of the century to the end of the World War, Estrada Cabrera kept order by torture and espionage. Ubico came of a long lineage, and his way was cut out for him.

So Ubico went to work. He did not abolish Congress. He simply made it clear, by a few mysterious arrests and disappearances, that no one who was not hand-picked by the President would be permitted to serve in Congress. He maintained the courts. But every judge is still his personal appointee, and the President himself often steps in to dispose of political offenses by secret executive order. The army, as always, was potentially dangerous. But the army shortly—as generals suspected of plotting or even whispering against the President began going into exile or before the firing squad without benefit of court-martial—found out who its master was.

The picture of despotism in Guatemala, then, is somewhat like this: If the Ubico subject confines his political activities to praising the regime, he will not be molested. But his mail is read by censors and his private conversations are watched—so, for that matter, are the foreign visitor's. At all meetings, public or private, the chances are many to one that the spy is present. Even the Rotary Club of Guatemala City, to be on the safe side, for years has practically omitted all discussions of public problems from its programs and confines itself to harmless jocosities.

On the other hand, the Guatemalan who is even vaguely suspected of agitating or whispering against the government can be imprisoned, shot, exiled or have his property expropriated, by simple executive verbal order and without trial.

Naturally, all these powers imply enforcements in extraordinary fields. Both the press and the mails, for instance, are under a hogtight censorship. Nothing can come in or go out of Guatemala, either for publication or private circulation, that in any way reflects on the regime's merits.

Labor unions come under the ban, more or less inevitably. By an exquisite extension of the Ubico logic, all gatherings of workers are regarded as union agitations and all labor unions are branded as Communist.

I sat up one evening discussing this question with an intelligent Guatemala City newspaperman—necessarily, of course, an Ubico apologist.

"The President's attitude is not as unreasonable as it seems," he argued. "After all, except for the workmen in two or three of the larger cities, our people are too much out of the world to go about organizing labor unions on their own. Consequently, the only pressure they get for labor organization comes from Mexico. And the Mexican unions are Communist—or Socialistic enough so that it amounts to the same thing."

"But suppose," I suggested, "that some original organizer really did try to form a strictly conservative union—one that accepted the social organization as much as the older A. F. of L. craft unions do in the United States. What would happen to him?"

"In the first place," he answered, "he could not accept the social organization as it is in Guatemala and form a union at all. In the second place," he went on without batting an eye, "he would be shot as a Communist."

And Guatemala chronically throbs with whispers of these mysterious shootings. There is the legend, for example, of the general to whom the dictator, in gratitude for some delicate personal service, gave a horse. A few months later the general was caught in a revolutionary plot. Both he and the horse faced the next morning's firing squad.

There is the legend of the special Ubico way with labor agitators. Men accused of fomenting "Communist" activities are not dispatched by the guns of trained soldiers. The dictator picks for their executioners his latest consignment of rookies—Indians brought in from the hills yesterday who have never seen a machine gun before. And it is with machine guns that he turns them loose on his helpless prisoners. It is messy, but the general—or so "they" say—smilingly comments that it is good for the rookies' marksmanship and for properly inuring a soldier to violence.

Such tales, as I say, are legends. And in Guatemala one lacks facilities for tracking down legends. They are significant, in any event, as part of the folklore of terrorism in which the regime wishes its public to believe.

For the rest, there are things to be said on Ubico's side—or at least for his better achievements. The despot controls the forces of disorder which split so wide apart the life of certain other republics. His generals obey orders as humbly as Prussian corporals and start no revolutionary ructions in the provinces. The country is policed with impressive diligence. Life and property—provided the citizen keeps out of forbidden political paths—are as safe as anywhere in the world.

The dictator has gone further than probably any Latin-American ruler on record in eliminating graft. Some of his own relatives are in his crowded penitentiaries for indulging in this favorite enterprise of Latin-American presidential families. Guatemala's neat and efficient new customs house—a handsome but curiously unpretentious building for a despot's capital—was built for the rock-bottom construction-cost price of $350,000.

And there are more specifically progressive points in the record. In a 50,000-square-mile land, which geographically is little more than a wild rubble of swampy jungle and volcanic mountain chains, Ubico has brought all but a handful of villages into touch with civilization by motor roads or motorcycle trails. He has upped school attendance by 25 per cent and put all Guatemala under Central America's—if not Latin America's—most efficient national public-health department.

Although Ubico fights labor unions with the methods of Chicago gangsters, he has put a stop to a centuries-old custom which is one of the most abominable of all Central American labor abuses. No longer can the coffee-*finca* owners and the banana planters fill up their labor rolls for the working seasons by the simple expedient of dickering with the head men of the Indian mountain villages for the "hire" of their "prisoners." On the contrary, various *jefes politicos* who have tried the old trick of arresting half the village just before the picking season and selling the "prisoners'" services down the valley to the nearest planter have sometimes paid for their enterprise before Don Jorge's firing squads. Today the poorest Indian in the republic can take the plantation capitalist's job if he wants it—or he can loaf over his corn patch or looms in his native village, and leave it.

Thus, political and social agitations apart, there is a kind of rough potentate's justice in Don Jorge. Unquestionably, too, he works at his job. Nearly half his time he spends scouring about the country by car and motorcycle inspecting conditions at first hand. And more than once—and this is not legend—he has returned from forays into the mountain villages with a local judge or two or a little collection of *jefes politicos* in his train as captives. For when Don Jorge calls a village council, the local officials can be complained against as well as the local malefactors. When graft or oppression can be proved, Ubico takes his usual shortest ways of dealing with it.

Don Jorge, in short, undoubtedly considers himself a model ruler. His cruelty and his harshness keep almost perfect order, and the results that he gets from order justify—as he sees it—his ruthlessness.

Ubico's formula, too, has plenty of imitators, though not all of the imitators are such authentic iron men. General Maximiliano Hernandez Martinez runs El Salvador on straight Ubico principles. He came in in 1931 when a president named Araujo fancied that El Salvador was ripe for the democratic processes, and shortly, for his indiscretions, serious agrarian revolt was rolling up. The uprising was conveniently labeled "Communist" by the propertied classes, and Martinez, the vice-president who belligerently shouldered his way into the startled liberal's job just before the storm broke, was hailed as the "savior of the republic." Several thousand —some Salvadorean estate proprietors boast as many as twelve thousand—agrarian peons were slaughtered by the troops, and Martinez, with a brief interregnum, has held on ever since as a kind of perennial savior of the republic.

But El Salvador's is a definitely sloppier despotism than Guatemala's. It has not relieved the peons of labor abuses—though it has experimented with a somewhat graft-tainted estate-partitioning program. Its road-building program is less successful, for it has made no very serious efforts to check the political passions for graft and nepotism. The Salvadorean mestizos are fiercer—or at any rate harder-drinking—than the Guatemaltecos, and the country holds something like the all-Latin-American record for its daily grist of murders and highway robberies.

All the Ubico machinery of oppression is present and active, but the Salvadoreans get few corresponding benefits.

In Peru, on the other hand, we get another variant. General Oscar Benavides, 1933-to-1939 dictator, ruled without benefit of Congress—although to the general surprise late in 1939 he permitted the election of Manuel Prado as a successor. But the Benavides system, though it has suspended for nearly four years even the surface properties of a democratic regime, positively oozes concern for the Peruvian proletariat. It has introduced a roads-and-public-works program to give jobs to the unemployed and raise living standards. In the cities it feeds the jobless five-cent meals at public soup kitchens which, one of its Lima apologists earnestly insisted to me, are the best meals the Peruvian lower classes have enjoyed since the days of the Incas.

Benavides justice, too, metes out less firing-squad discipline to dissenters than the Central American contemporaries. Secret arrests and long sentences to remote Andean work gangs, sudden and swift orders into exile—these, together with a rigid censorship of the press and a ban on all public discussions, are the means through which it suppresses a powerful opposition party. In office Benavides is thus a more suave and possibly a more self-seeking despot than Ubico. For Lima is waiting, with a somewhat humorous curiosity—having seen others of the type—to learn what the extent of the treasury shortages will be when, if ever, the Benavides controls are removed.

Far over on the other side of the Latin-American world is the Dominican despot, General Rafael Leonidas Trujillo. General Trujillo—who since August 1938 has controlled through a puppet president—has ruled also with a certain surface geniality, at least for the last seven of his nine years of service. He shot, or by other means disposed of, practically all serious rivals to his prestige in the first two years. Otherwise, it is a sufficient commentary on General Trujillo's political quality that he encouraged his Congress to build an imitation Washington Monument to him in the capital, describing him as the "preserver of the republic"; and that, when the Dominican Republic was assessed a $750,000 indemnity for the slaughter of some twelve thousand Haitians in the massacres of 1937, *el presidente* paid the first instalment of $250,000 out of his own pocket—the treasury being, at the time, without sufficient funds.

For more than two years in the late 1930s there were indications that Bolivia, too, was enrolling itself among the personally conducted autocracies. Lieutenant Colonel Germán Busch, a thirty-three-year-old Paraguayan war hero, who seized the presidency in July, 1937, had the authentic Ubico touch. Plotters and agitators against the regime were liquidated by the firing squad. Malcontents and verbal critics, if prominent enough to be dangerous, often found themselves locked up for months in four-foot-high cells, not quite long enough for a man to lie down in. Disagreeing cabinet ministers occasionally emerged from the presidential presence with their eyes blacked.

Then, in the early summer of 1939, Despot Busch abolished Congress and proclaimed that henceforth his republic would be "totalitarian." North Americans who shivered in their beds at the thought that a definite Fascist conquest had come at last, seem, however, to have been in error. "Totalitarian," in the Busch semantics, turned out to be merely a modish way of expressing the idea that one man was boss.

In any event, there was nothing "totalitarian" about the Busch life span. In August 1939 the dictator was found dead in his private apartments in the presidential palace at La Paz with a bullet in his temple. Officially, the government pronounced it suicide, due to the strain of excessive patriotic labors. But successful Latin-American politicians seldom commit suicide, vital statistics suggesting that they are more likely to die of rival trouble. When *el caudillo's* first elected successor, Enrique Panaranda, announced the "restoration of democracy" it seemed that Bolivia was, officially at least, pointed back toward modified dictatorship.

☆   ☆   ☆

There is one more type of dictatorship to deal with—perhaps as a harbinger of future developments. This is the streamlined, European-simonized model which General Getulio Vargas in November 1937 instituted in Brazil.

Vargas came into power by injecting a revolution into the presidential campaign of 1930. Later he regularized his position by holding an administration-controlled election. Until 1937 he governed through a well-chastened Congress and the gadgetries of machine politics a good deal after the manner of the modified dictators elsewhere.

But Vargas had unusual troubles. In 1932 he had to crush a rebellion in the powerful state of São Paulo, the wealthiest and most populous commonwealth in the Brazilian confederacy, which aimed either at seating a São Paulo man in the presidential palace at Rio de Janeiro or at secession. In 1935 he faced a widespread revolt of leftist labor unions, the rank and file of several army divisions and scattered bands of the agrarian proletariat, outraged at generations of starvation wages and mistreatment. Though hardly authentically Marxian in its aims, the movement was unquestionably backed by Communist organizers. Vargas suppressed it, but confidence in his ability to hold the aristocratically-topped Brazilian social structure together was seriously shaken.

Then, no sooner were his leftist troubles shelved than he had a rising Fascist movement on his hands. Local politicians, making an emotional racket out of the "Communist" menace, started it, but before long German money and Italian moral support—there are several million Italians in Brazil, so this was not a strictly academic contribution—were pouring into its war chest. With an enrollment rising toward two hundred thousand, the Integralistas, as they called themselves, became, by 1937, the biggest political-action group ever assembled in Brazil.

Meanwhile the 1938 elections were coming along, and it seemed fairly plain that the Vargas group, in the face of all its troubles with rebellious states and with the leftist and rightist factions, would not, by the usual modified dictatorial artifices, be able to control the nominating or the electing machinery. Another ruling clique would take control, and Vargas (according to his apologists) did not feel that he could trust any other clique to control the Fascists. Neither did he believe that the Integralistas, at least without civil war and bloodshed, would be able to control the leftists.

So Vargas—a little five-foot-three dumpling of a man whose slightly buck teeth wear the half-amused, half-leering smile of a profound political cynic—acted with amazing suddenness. On November 10, 1937—first having planted the federal troops at all strategic stations—the President issued a proclamation abolishing the constitution, discontinuing both houses of Congress, putting courts under strictly executive jurisdiction, imposing censorships and indefinitely suspending civil liberties, and announcing that the 1938 presidential election was off.

As a momentary sop to the Integralistas, who were supposedly spoiling for trouble, he announced that a new "corporative constitution," hastily modeled after the one under which Portugal is governed by the Salazar dictatorship and giving labor and industrial groups the right of representation in the law-making machinery of the government, would shortly be offered to the country in a plebiscite. But within a few months the Integralistas' organization was outlawed, and since then nothing has been heard of the "corporative constitution" or any other.

Today Vargas—ruling by "decree-laws," decided upon in intimate conferences of his cabinet and inner circles of political advisers—governs Brazil with a power as autocratic as that of the Romanoffs over prewar Russia. Oswaldo Aranha, the autocrat's foreign minister, once euphoniously described the regime to me as "a leadership for the preservation of democracy." But there are no suggestions whatever within the Vargas governing circle as to when the preserved democracy will be permitted to resume its functions as the partner of its autocrats.

At the same time the Vargas autocracy is far less rigorous in many respects than many of the dictatorships which cling to the color of constitutionalism. The press censorship is sometimes harsh and often capricious—once Pimentel Brandão, Aranha's predecessor in the Foreign Office, called Rio de Janeiro's foreign correspondents' corps into his office and flatly announced that dispatches which reflected adversely on Brazil were not "news"—yet "constructive criticism" of government policies is tolerated now and then in amazing profusion. There are dark tales about barbers and small shopkeepers spending days in jail for the indiscretion of not displaying Vargas' picture in their places of business, but on the other hand the average Brazilian citizen is free to speak his private political mind whenever and wherever he pleases.

Under the republican constitution, Brazil had adopted one of the best labor codes in the world, and it was carried over intact—"by decree" of course—into the autocratic regime. It is not enforced to the letter by any means, but neither was it enforced very ardently under the republic. Strikes, however, have been prohibited, and the once growing labor unions have been tied to the government by an insistent chaperonage. Their only hope of progress is through the government's labor bureaucracy.

Vargas, in fact, has concentrated chiefly on the more strictly utilitarian problems of the State: on striking a balance between Brazil's vast excess export surpluses and the tangled condition of her foreign exchange and debt structure, on breaking down the intense separatist tendencies of the states, which with their quarrels and their jealousies, their separate armies and internecine tax and tariff wars, have made the integration of the republic into a modern national economic unit all but impossible.

The main point about Vargas' singular adventure in open autocracy, however, is that he feels that it is only by absolutist methods that the evils which lie at the root of all Latin America's disturbances can be overcome.

☆   ☆   ☆

So here are the dictators in their various degrees of harshness and mildness, of self-seeking and statesmanship—begotten less of Fascist imitations or impulses than of the practicalities of Latin-American politics as control stations for the uncontrollable forces.

The problem of the development of democracy in their republics thus reduces itself to a paradox:

When will the dictators sufficiently master the uncontrollable forces so that they themselves can be dispensed with?

CHAPTER XII

The Outlook for Democracy

IF ONLY TO CALM our nerves against the world crises of 1940, it would be delightful to report that Latin America's prognosis for democracy is favorable. Indeed, on superficial evidence, many optimistic observers of the political panorama below the Rio Grande have managed to persuade themselves that it is.

The bases of their hopes might be expressed substantially as follows:

1. Six Latin-American republics—Costa Rica and Colombia, Venezuela and Chile, Argentina and Uruguay—have more or less a toe hold on the democratic processes. By and large, though with here and there an exception on one point or another, they are the most prosperous and progressive of the twenty republics, as well as the ones with the best mass educational facilities. Hence, if only because life in these important respects seems to go better in the more liberal republics, their example is bound to spread.

2. The United States can help democracy spread by high-pressure diplomatic policies: putting the dictators in the doghouse, say; refusing them loans, favorable economic treatment, and in some cases diplomatic recognition; giving its moral blessing, or even direct financial or diplomatic assistance, to political leaders fighting the battles of liberalism. Or perhaps it can increase its "liberalizing" influence by drawing Latin America closer to it as a "good provider" of its second World War needs.

3. Or, by sterner means, the more disorderly dictatorships can be restrained in their iniquities. For instance, a sadistically inclined

tyrant can be ousted now and then by force, for the moral example, as has been done in Haiti and Nicaragua. The election of a presumably more liberal successor can be arranged if United States agents—backed by the military arm when necessary—are on the ground to see that voting is honest and free to all.

Such hopes and projects, however, when we look at the problem realistically, develop certain cloudy surfaces.

There is the primary question, for example, of how democratic *are* Latin America's six democracies. Let's investigate.

In the Argentine the press is undoubtedly free except in grave—and usually brief—periods of disturbances. Furious political activities against the government are permitted. Yet there are certain strongly plausible indications that the Radical party won the 1937 presidential elections in the republic and was counted out by the sitting Conservative party's polls officials. Also the Argentine president pulls the ultimate strings in state politics by his power to remove displeasing governors from office and rule through federally appointed *interventors*. A Radical landslide would no doubt be accepted by the losers, but the Argentine constitutional system is adroitly rigged to keep opposition landslides from occurring. Argentina, then, might be described as a modified democracy, flavored with a Chinaman's chance for overwhelming opposition majorities.

Uruguay, on the other hand, boasts of having held in 1938 one of the fairest and most untrammeled elections in Latin-American history. But the background of the contest somewhat qualifies this idyllic picture. Uruguay through the 1920s had a series of decidedly leftist administrations, until one Gabriel Terra came into the presidency in 1931—partly by Fascist tactics at the polls. Terra decided to change all that. He reigned for seven years as a dictator almost in the Ubico style, and drove the leaders of his leftist opposition either into exile or under cover. Consequently, when the 1938 election rolled around, the situation was distinctly under control. The platforms of the republic's two effective political parties were marked by vivid Tweedledum and Tweedledee resemblances to each other, especially in their straddlings between liberalism and conservatism—and both of the candidates were Señor Terra's in-laws. Largely, it is supposed, because the women of his vast family circle were making life miserable for him, Terra *did* keep his hands off the election. As things turned out, General Alfredo Baldomir, the in-law who nominally belonged to the "opposite" party from Terra, was elected. Whether a "fair" election would have been permitted if a straight left-right issue had arisen, is better left to the imagination.

Chile has had a unique—for Latin America—political development. Down to the post-1918 period the republic was ruled—with comparatively few revolutionary disorders—by a close little oligarchy of bankers, merchants and big landowners who rotated the presidency and the cabinet offices and controlled the seats in Congress a good deal as the landed aristocracy did in England during the eighteenth century. Within this charmed circle there was plenty of genuine conflict over policies and a fairly free party life. But the masses of the voters, the agrarian peons and the unskilled city workers—though eventually given the ballot—for years were regimented to the polls and voted by their bosses much as blocks of proxy stock are voted at a niftily managed corporation stockholders' meeting. Chile, in fact, was the sort of a republic some of the more conservative Federalists hoped to make of the United States at the time of the Constitutional Convention of 1787. But it was hardly a democracy.

Then, in the 1920s, this condition changed. The end of the World War collapsed Chile's nitrate industry, put her copper mines on fractional production, and ruined the export market for her fruits and farm products. Unemployment prevailed everywhere, and the distressed masses, who had enjoyed a taste of relative prosperity during the war boom, demanded that something be done.

President Arturo Alessandri attempted to meet the situation with heavy income-tax levies and curtailments of the aristocracy's economic privileges, but eventually was driven out of power by a group of army officers angered at pay cuts and delayed salary remittances. Army cabals in due course tossed one General Carlos Ibañez into the presidency. Ibañez began his administration with an impressive series of leftist and pro-labor broadsides, but shortly showed symptoms of degenerating into an old-fashioned military despot.

Chile, which considered itself finished generations ago with the Ecuadorean brand of political leadership, got rid of Ibañez when the deterioration became too obvious. Then—in 1932—Alessandri came back. But it was an Alessandri changed by years of exposure to the "discipline and order" formulas of Fascism in Italy. The restored president sought to re-establish the old oligarchy's governing system with the conservatives on top, aided in their hold on authority by various economic and social control devices borrowed from Signor Mussolini.

Evidently, however, the Conservatives neglected to tighten all the washers on their election-control machinery. For in September 1938, despite their cordons of polls officials, the candidate of a coalition of radical and leftist parties, Pedro Aguirre Cerda, a "radical" with a few moderate Socialist leanings, won the presidency by a hairline majority.

Chile, then, is a democracy to the extent that a "popular front" —in opposition to the administration—has actually been permitted to win an election. But the question remains: how long as a democracy will Chile stay put?

Aguirre Cerda has a congressional majority against him in both houses. His government's credit, already strained by the Alessandri regime's operations, has faced a drain, fatal to his economic reform projects, since the southern provinces were devastated by the great January 1939 earthquake. Furthermore, at a time when money trouble has forced him to disappoint his own followers, the opposition has rallied. There have even been numerous indications, emphasized by an abortive Santiago garrison revolt in August 1939, that its extremists are organizing for a genuine rightist putsch on the model of the 1936 rebellion of the Spanish army officers. If anything of this sort happens, Chile may be the first republic in Latin America to undergo a left-right civil war on the Spanish scale of virulence. On the other hand, if Aguirre Cerda can hold onto his authority without war and without resort to dictatorship, Chile may become the first Latin-American republic to attempt to solve its problems realistically by the democratic processes.

Colombia's democracy, again, brings us closer to the Argentine model. There are no restrictions on the press or on political activity, but the vote-counting machinery runs amazingly in favor of the party in power. Before Liberal Enrique Olaya Herrera was elected president in 1930, for instance, the Conservatives had been in control for more than fifty years. Yet by the 1938 elections, the Conservatives—between recognition of the Liberals' popularity and fear of their vote-counting technique—were so discouraged over the prospects of making a showing at the polls that they did not even put up a candidate.

On the other hand, Liberal administrations since 1930 have lived up to their name in several practical directions. President Alfonso Lopez Pumarejo, 1934–8, against the scandalized protest of the Conservatives, adroitly managed to bring about the separation of Church and State in the constitution of the republic and to hand over the direction of the school system to the secular authorities. Labor unions have been provided with a legal code giving them rather more freedom of action and protection than they enjoy in the United States. Although enormous problems of poverty and illiteracy and virtual agrarian serfdom still confront Colombia, free institutional life for the people is perhaps more advanced than anywhere else in Latin America. It might not continue to be so, however, if the Conservatives returned to power. For the Conservatives, like other similar groups in the twenty republics, were, down to the great disillusionment over the Hitler-Stalin surgical puncture of Fascist fronts, developing a Falangista "Catholic Action" fringe in accordance with the best Franco-Spanish precedents.

Costa Rica's democratic pattern differs from Colombia's in that it is slanted in a laissez-faire rather than a mildly leftist direction. Yet in many respects—and with that limitation—it approaches the classical ideal of democracy more nearly than any of the other republics.

With the exception of a bloodless revolution during the World War, its parties have rotated the presidency back and forth between them for half a century, with a minimum of skulduggery even at elections. It is the only republic which points with pride to the fact that there are more school teachers on the national pay roll than soldiers. Costa Rica's liberalism is so easygoing, in fact, that in some respects its tolerances leave the visitor faintly jittery. The large German colony in the republic, for example, is restrained neither by law nor by local convention from displaying its enthusiasms, and down to the war on the business streets of San José, the capital, one saw more swastika flags than in several of the capitals whose bonds with European Fascism are closer. Small Falangist and Catholic Action groups flourish their "Viva Cristo Rey" signs without let or hindrance.

"These things are not important," your Costa Rican friends assure you pleasantly. "Costa Rica has been a liberal democracy for so long that the democratic methods are second nature to our people. Isn't it better to let a few extremists have their say in their own peculiar ways than to do away with any of our democratic liberties?"

Venezuela, by contrast, might be described for the present as enjoying democracy in an experimental stage. For twenty-eight years of this century, 1908–35, Venezuela was ruled in and out of the actual presidency by Juan Vincente Gómez, the most ferociously tyrannous of all the despots. Gómez exiled his opponents in thousands; but mainly he crushed opposition by imprisonment and torture. Men who whispered, not necessarily against the government, but merely expressed ideas which the despot disapproved of, were confined for years in medieval dungeons for their indiscretion, with daily or weekly torture exercises—such as hanging by the testicles—to test their powers of resistance.

Gómez, to be sure, put the finances of the republic on an even keel—Venezuela is the only country of its size in the world without a national debt today—by arranging a smart pro-rata taxation plan with the American and British oil interests. But he used the revenues of the state to support the families of his eighty-odd illegitimate children in luxury. He built a few modern highways in the republic, but most of them ran to the Gómez family ranches. An almost illiterate cattle rancher, the most characteristic things about Gómez, perhaps, were that during his twenty-eight years he blocked all improvements to the Venezuelan public-education system, and even—to isolate his people still further from new ideas—refused to allow the city of Caracas to import motor-driven fire apparatus.

Gómez died on the job, and curiously enough the return toward democracy has been accomplished under General Eleazar Lopez-Contreras, his former War Minister. Although for years a dutiful Gómez subordinate, Lopez-Contreras from the first has made obvious efforts to function as a democratic administrator. Many of the exiles were called back, and some of them were put in crucial administrative posts. The jails were emptied of political prisoners. The notorious one in Caracas was destroyed by an otherwise orderly mob in celebration of the despot's obsequies. Freedom was restored to the press and freedom of action to dissenting political groups. To suggest how liberal the regime is, during 1938 a newspaper campaign was permitted which eventually forced Lopez-Contreras to remodel his entire cabinet. The government has organized and is spending a part of its huge oil revenues on a three-year plan of school building, national sanitation and public-works construction activities. It is giving every proof of an earnest intention to take up the slack in social progress which the Gómez regime left behind.

But the real test of Venezuela's democracy will come with the elections of 1941. If the republic can turn that corner without revolution or relapsing into modified dictatorship through machine control by the majority party, it will definitely establish its claim to be counted among the progressive Latin-American states. If the Lopez-Contreras faction perpetuates itself in power by the usual methods of the machine dictators, Venezuela will have to be "put back" into the class with Cuba and Nicaragua, and perhaps, given time, may even get another Gómez.

☆   ☆   ☆

All this description of the democracies and fractional democracies does not, however, clear away the cloudy surfaces from the problem of democratic development in Latin America as a whole. To get nearer to fundamentals, what factors have aided six of the republics in improvising a more or less democratic political life for their peoples which are absent in the others?

Here, of course, the answers can only be summarized. But even in brief they throw into strong relief certain vital Latin-American forces.

Four of the more liberal republics—Argentina, Uruguay, Chile and Costa Rica—for years have been considerably ahead of the others in economic progress. In the case of the first three there has been a steady, and at times a boom, demand in Europe for their products. As a result, a little of the prosperity has drifted down from the top in the form of wages, opportunities for advancement, etc. For the better part of two generations, and in some local areas for considerably longer, standards of living and literacy have been well above the Latin-American average. Their masses have been informed enough and sufficiently aware of what has been going on in their world to sense a few of their basic needs and rights and possibilities as citizens.

In Costa Rica the economic foundation for democracy is even stronger. Costa Rica, in fact, enjoys something closely approximating democratic equality. Its land was not greatly prized by the nabobs of the colonial era, so it came into independence without the problem of liquidating the great landed estates to bedevil its politics. Today the country is a republic of small, independent farmers. Though living standards are frugal according to North American averages, there are no great extremes of wealth or poverty, and it is the only Latin-American republic without a vast landless peon class to cause trouble.

Again, the same four republics are untroubled by racial divisions. Argentina, Uruguay and Costa Rica exterminated the wild Indian tribes of the settling period a good deal as the Indians were exterminated in the United States. The surviving elements merged in the white population without producing a racial chasm in the body politic. Chile made an honorable peace with the Araucanians; and in their own localities today the Araucanians, not the whites, are masters. In result, the four republics are without a vast servile population to drag politics down into a kind of perpetual master-slave relationship.

Finally, at least two of the republics, Chile and Colombia, have been governed by exceptionally competent and soundly educated aristocracies, with some rudimentary inclination—at least on the Liberal side—toward the noblesse-oblige attitude.

None of these background influences adequately explains the case of Venezuela, of course; but for the present, no doubt, Venezuela should be regarded as an essentially synthetic democracy—a state in which the democratic processes are being initiated and encouraged from above rather than by widespread popular demand. If the oil wealth of the state, however, is sufficiently spread around in the republic in the form of wages and higher living standards through the operations of the government's program of spending and public construction, the economic foundations for a genuine democratic society should soon begin to appear.

Democracy, in a word, does not "spread" from one republic to its neighbors like a disease or a fashion in wallpaper. Where it appears at all, it grows from roots which can take hold of something tangible in the social situation and draw nourishment from its surroundings.

For all such reasons there is a distinctly illusory quality about the hopes of certain cheerful political philosophers that Latin-American democracy can be ushered in by the moral suasion or *force majeure* of mere diplomatic policies in Washington. Washington, indeed, for causes native to Latin-American practical politics, is, if possible, even more helpless to promote democratic progress where soil is unprepared than are the idealists in the dictator-ridden republics themselves. In result, the case histories of elaborate North American programs for curing Latin America of dictator addiction are punctuated with tragic and sardonic failures.

For, invariably, the first effect of a thrust from Washington at a dictator's power is to strengthen his political grip on life. If diplomatic recognition has been taken away from him, his loans curtailed, or favorable trade arrangements canceled, he is a beleaguered patriot where, before, he was simply one of a succession of petty tyrants. Now he can checkmate the machinations of his natural enemies in domestic politics and rally the passionate nationalism of his people by posing as the victim of the imperialist Northern colossus. "The gringo is trying to steal the fatherland," he can maintain through several sixteen-hour days of patriotic speechmaking. "The time has come to march behind the leader who can save you from slavery to the foreign barbarians."

Eventually, of course, if Washington is stern enough, he may succumb to his economic—or Marine—embarrassments. But meanwhile, by a logical development of tensions in practical politics, he has committed his successor to even stronger methods of dictatorship. For the successor enters office under the stigma, right or wrong, of being Uncle Sam's chosen protégé. His prestige, then, is roughly equivalent to that of "teacher's pet" in a schoolroom, while his political enemies—skilled revolutionists all—begin their campaign to undermine him by adopting the role of superpatriots. Because the opposition is so much the stronger through its appeal to nationalism, Uncle Sam's new "liberal" protégé, if he is to last, must rule with an even heavier hand than the dictator he has supplanted.

Nor is there likely to be any comfort to Washington in the new dictator's grateful friendship. To take the sting off his enemies' challenge that he is the State Department's puppet, the "protégé" must go out of his way to think up new anti-American agitations and policies which will advertise his proper independence.

Washington's record of Latin-American relations is full of these instances in which interferences with the natural course of practical politics in the neighbor republics has either sharpened anti-American agitations, or increased the rigors of dictatorships—or both. Pure and undefiled elections of presumably democratic regimes have twice been brought about by direct intervention in Cuba, for instance. But out of the first experiment—an occupation of the republic by the United States Army from 1906–9, and rule by an American provisional governor—came eventually the Menocal dictatorship which led to a second intervention by a "special commissioner" in 1921. And out of the "special commissioner's" services came the Machado regime which in 1933 culminated in Cuba's bloodiest revolutionary period. Finally, after the State Department rather reluctantly pulled the props of military support out from under the Machado dictatorship, it was succeeded by the Batista dictatorship, which has gone further than any previous Cuban regime in the restrictions it has placed on United States economic activities and exploitations within the republic.

In the Dominican Republic, the withdrawal of Marine-chaperoned government led to the rise of the Marine-trained—and notorious—General Trujillo, who disposed of his supernationalist domestic opponents by the firing squad and assassination.

In Nicaragua, in 1927, the Marines supervised an election so conscientiously that they actually stained the fingers of voters with indelible ink to prevent repeating. But the democratic tradition which this heroic device was expected to foster was upset in 1936, when General Anastasio Somoza ousted the liberal President Sacasa by revolution and established Central America's most competent modified dictatorship.

In Mexico, of course, all practical political appeals have had an anti-American theme song since President Wilson's diplomatic treaties and arms embargoes of twenty-five years ago enabled General Venustiano Carranza to triumph over General Victoriano Huerta.

Quite possibly, if the Marines or judicious arms embargoes could be maintained indefinitely at all focal points in the struggle for political power in the twenty republics, a nominal and protected hothouse form of democracy might be imposed everywhere. But it would be our democracy, not theirs. No matter how much personal liberty and freedom from oppression the inhabitants gained under it, it would be a foreign imperialist regime rather than a chosen way of life or a normal habit of political conduct.

The more we look at this problem of democratic progress in Latin America, in fact, the more it appears that democracy, if it is to come at all and develop political functioning capacity below the Rio Grande, must grow out of the economic and social soil of the twenty republics themselves.

☆　　　☆　　　☆

Then how fast may we expect it to grow, and by what methods may we rationally hope to hasten its development?

As to Question No. 1, it must be frankly confessed that the current omens are definitely unpropitious.

The Latin-American republics are going through a phase of history—along with the rest of us, it should be added—in which autocratic methods in government have fascinated nations of vastly greater resources and considerably more political experience. Faced with the problem of gearing their fully developed technical plants to the economy of the power age, the United States, Great Britain and France—since the first World War—have immensely enlarged the power of their central governments, while Germany has not only reverted from democracy to absolutism, but has combined it with a regimentation of the intellectual, emotional and economic life of the populace such as no Latin-American despot ever dreamed of. Italy, with a weaker educational background and less technical development, has copied the German example in all except the last thumbscrews of thoroughness. Spain and Portugal, whose examples are at least as potent in Latin America as British political conduct is with us, are following the same path. So is Greece, and Poland was. Hungary, Rumania and the other Balkan states, until overshadowed by totalitarian might, were rough equivalents in Europe of "modified dictatorships."

Also, in many ways, the problems of the Latin-American republics are, if possible, more complicated than those of the European nations and ourselves.

In addition to the difficulties of adjusting their economies to the ebb and flow of power-age forces, the ups and downs of currency values and foreign exchange and of world-wide technological unemployment, the twenty republics have on their hands the tasks of pioneering and settling new lands, of creating self-dependent industrial economies in the midst of primitive pastoral and agricultural societies, and of working out some solution that will be both economically profitable and socially tolerable of the master-and-serf relationship between the races. For behind the façades of its modernized cities there lurk in Latin America vast pockets of living conditions as crude as those of the less favored frontier regions of the United States in the 1830s; and further dark expanses where the individual's economic and social facilities for "the good life" are hardly better than they were in medieval Europe.

To ask that all these problems be solved and all these maladjustments corrected by the democratic processes is hardly less quixotic than to demand that the Republican National Committee establish a branch in Germany and defeat Hitler at the polls. For as many decades as we can see ahead, if not for many generations, the dictators will have on their side the arguments used to justify the autocracy of Brazil's Getulio Vargas: that the job of organizing Latin America to play its part in the modern world is too great and too complex to be performed by any agency except a one-man government with supreme powers.

☆ ☆ ☆

But dictator appeal is not only inherent in the basic problems of the republics. The practical prospects of the indefinite survival of the autocrats have been immensely increased by modern military gadgetry. Every dictator's government today, for example, is investing as heavily as its finances will permit in super-machine guns, armored cars, late-model artillery and, above all, airplanes.

The effects of this concentration of shooting power, even on the minor scale in which it is being brought about in republics like Honduras and Ecuador, are easily apparent. The old-fashioned Latin-American revolutions of the classical nineteenth-century form were of two types. They either started with an uprising of a few hundred Indians in a distant province several mountain ranges away from the capital, with machetes and a few old muskets or rifles, and perhaps a company or two of soldiers under some rebellious local *comandante* to act as a vanguard. Or they started with mobs in the capital streets whose members were plentifully armed with pistols, hunting rifles and knives from the domestic arsenal. In the former case, as the revolutionary "army" rolled on toward the capital it gradually attracted to itself a following of dissatisfied peons and ambitious *comandantes,* so that when it came to the capital's strategic defenses it frequently outnumbered the national army both in numbers and munitions. Or

[205]

if it were a question of street fighting, the ramping mobs in the capital had as many and as good weapons as the soldiers. At the worst, almost any revolution had a fighting chance.

But what can street mobs today do against machine guns, tanks and armored cars? As we saw a few pages back, Honduras' latest potential revolution in the provinces was deflated by a squadron of antiquated airplanes doing a little target practice above the corn patches. There is scarcely a republic today where army planes cannot begin strafing a revolution within half a day after its leaders first raise the cry of "down with the government!" Yet twenty years ago it often took weeks of mountain and jungle campaigning merely to establish fighting contact with a first-class provincial uprising.

Furthermore, the modern war tools are, in practice, something that revolutionists cannot get hold of. It costs too much for most revolutionary treasuries. And if now and then this obstacle can be overcome by interested outside assistance, how can private citizens run tanks and armored cars and artillery past the customs service? A revolutionary conspiracy, no doubt, could fly airplanes into the country, but how could it establish military airports and service facilities without unfortunate publicity? Here and there, perhaps, a disaffected general in the provinces could rake together a small stock of modern fighting implements, but by keeping its bigger guns and better planes in the capital's defense the government would still be safe.

By the old procedures, too, much could be done by an adroit conspiring group to seduce the officers in charge of the gadgetry into joining the revolution. But the air corps, tank squadrons and the heavy artillery commands in most Latin-American armies today are extremely small groups of technicians. They can be pampered as a corps d'élite with higher pay, brevet ranks and special privileges—to say nothing of the extra social swank that goes with their glamorous specialties—and practically without exception the dictators make it their business to pamper them.

In Guatemala and Honduras, for instance, the young air officers practically have the run of the presidential household. They are nearer to the sources of power—and favors—than many of the ranking political advisers. The masters of the gadgetry may in time become a new type of mechanized praetorian guard which will make and unmake presidents a good deal as the old-fashioned orthodox generals have been doing for a century in the military-dictatorship republics. But so far they have apparently failed to recognize these potential opportunities, and remain tied to the regimes by bonds of acute self-interest.

All these factors have gone a long way toward ruling out revolutions as mass movements. In so far as revolutions, like the great Mexican civil war of 1911–20, have brought on new orientations of the social policy of republics, or in so far as they have served now and then as crude but partially effective "substitutes for elections," their day appears to be almost over. For nearly ten years a succession of Peruvian dictators from Leguia to Benavides has kept the powerfully organized and politically conscious Aprista movement in check by mastery of the killing gadgetry. There were no symptoms of an uprising in the Argentine in the 1937 elections even when the Radicals had good reason to believe that they had been "robbed."

A civil war on the Spanish model would no doubt be possible through a split in the army on ideological grounds in a country situated politically as Chile is. But otherwise the only kind of revolution with a remotely rational chance to succeed in the better munitioned republics is the "palace revolt"—a quick stroke at the president's person or the capture of the strategic public buildings by a band of intimate conspirators. And this method—tried out in a midnight attack on President Vargas in Rio de Janeiro in May 1938 by a palace-guard squad which had been "reached" by the Integralistas, as well as in an attempted "putsch" of the Chilean Nazis in the government plaza at Santiago in September of the same year—failed miserably on both occasions.

Democratic hopes for Latin America, then, can hardly be built up with any realistic plausibility on any lessening of the background stresses and strains in government and politics which have produced the dictators, or on any decline in the dictators' power to hold on. There is a fairly strong possibility during the rest of the century, in fact, that the twenty republics, with or without European pressure, may see more dictators rather than less.

☆   ☆   ☆

The facts to be faced, therefore, are that most of our theories that Latin America is on the brink of a democratic awakening are sentimental moonshine, and most of our quick-trick recipes for expediting the democratic progress of the republics are narcotically tinctured with wishful thinking. Except in particularly favored areas and political circumstances, the forces propitious for the growth of democracy must be built up under the dictators, and, in most cases, against their shrewd and powerful opposition.

The task, however, is not so hopeless as it sounds. For one thing, the dictators themselves are increasingly forced to improve the soil in which democracy normally grows and flourishes.

All of them today, for instance, including the most despotic, are working with more or less vigor to overcome illiteracy in their republics. Even if their motives are only to increase the wealth of their privileged classes, they are finding out that it is impossible for them to conduct their national economies successfully in the power age while vast segments of their populations are too uninformed and sunk in ignorance to be taught anything but the simplest manual-labor processes. Mere literacy does not make nations democratic, to be sure, but at least it increases their comprehension of, and appetite for, ideas of social progress.

Most of the current dictators, too, if only for practical financial reasons, are seeking improvement of mass living standards. The State today, even the most primitive of Central American states, requires vast amounts of money to attack its complex social-adjustment problems. It is only by creating greater purchasing power and broader general prosperity—and incidentally greater tax resources—that the money can be had. For that matter, the idea is beginning to penetrate into certain dictatorial circles that without something better than absolute penury at the bottom of the society, there cannot be anything very lavish in the way of riches and great fortunes at the top. Thus the dictators are being forced to give somewhat more than passing attention to the problem of mass poverty by the very self-interest of the exploiting classes for whose benefit they are expected to rule.

All this is not saying, of course, that Latin-American dictators are singularly enlightened despots or that they are working wholeheartedly for the economic advancement of their peoples by methods of which progressive sociologists—much less people of acute social conscience—would approve. There is an enormous amount of backing and filling, of political exhibitionism and plain fakery in their efforts.

The best of them are enormously handicapped by entrenched habits of corruption in all their political services. Nevertheless, Despot Ubico's Guatemalan Indians are considerably better off, in their right to take plantation work or leave it, than they were a few years ago when their local jefes politicos could march them down from the mountains to their jobs—and incidentally collect anywhere from 20 to 90 per cent of their wages. Brazilian workmen are better off under a Vargas "model" labor code which is insufficiently enforced than they were in a society which looked with the shocked horror of Portuguese medieval aristocrats on any labor codes whatever.

Again, and for similar reasons, most of the dictators are striving seriously to improve the quality of their republics' products, to increase outputs, to introduce better agricultural and mechanical processes, to widen the scope of industrial activities and technological development in their countries. These objectives, too, can hardly be realized without a considerable development of both primary and secondary education among the masses, or without materially increasing the number of relatively well-paid semi-skilled and skilled workers and technicians in the republics.

☆   ☆   ☆

So, over against the increased political appeal and physical strength of the dictators, you have to place the slow but inevitable progress of all these basic social conditions, favorable, in the long view, to the growth of more democratic organization of society. For it is hardly reasonable to expect that populations in touch, even if dimly, with the world stream of ideas, and working groups conscious of their numbers and their technical proficiencies, will be willing to accept indefinitely the economy of the master-serf relationship under which the societies of the republics have endured since the colonial period.

Dictators may be harder to overthrow than formerly, but there will be other dictators who will cement themselves in power by responding, in one degree or another, to the mass demands for better social and economic arrangements. Democracy may not come to Latin America through the classical laissez-faire processes of the North American frontier, or be laden down, when it arrives, with the typically North American clutter of laissez-faire institutions and inhibitions. But this is not saying that it cannot arrive, or that new forms of democratic social organization may not be wrung, eventually, from the dictators.

Not even the epic success of the European totalitarian regimes in their wars and domestic bullying operations need be taken as absolute evidence that new millenniums of authority stretch ahead for the Latin-American dictators. Despite the charms which the nationalism and pseudo-nationalism of the patrioteers of the twenty republics may find in the fascist pageantry it still remains to be proved that the nightmare melodrama of the Hitler and Mussolini establishments can be repeated in settings so different from Europe's as those of the pampas and the cordilleras. For few conditions in Latin America today encourage even the more despotically inclined dictators to experiment with strictly orthodox Fascism. Latin America is fretted with plenty of minor dislikes and jealousies and prejudices, but hardly with the background of the intense popular hatreds and war fears which have led great nations to fly off into dictator worship as a refuge from greater terrors. There are passionate boundary disputes among the twenty republics, but not the overcrowding of peoples which leads to the desperate tensions of hate for "living room's" sake. There is still plenty of land in the 8,000,000 square miles below the Rio Grande for their 120,000,000 people to expand in.

☆   ☆   ☆

In the meantime, problems of controlling or progressively reforming the dictators from Washington are badly muddled by the
world crisis. For the duration of the hemisphere defense emergency
the United States is scarcely in a position to pick and choose
among rulers of neighbor states or to distribute its favors as rewards for imitating gringo virtues. The emergency requires us to
act as a recruiting station for whatever dictators will join us rather
than as a chaperone of hemisphere morals.

Nevertheless, from the broadly practical viewpoint, the very
policy best calculated to hold Latin America to us during the crisis
is one which over the years is most likely to prepare the ground for
democracy and thus render the dictators dispensable.

This policy would support movements toward better wages and
living standards throughout Latin America with the same adroit-
ness and determination with which "dollar diplomacy" once supported the sanctity of its Latin-American investments. As under
the cartel system proposed as an economic defense measure in the
summer of 1940, it would make clear that Uncle Sam's loans and
economic favors would be available to the republics in proportion
to the genuine efforts they were making, or were willing to make,
to conserve their resources and essentially to increase mass purchasing power.

There would be nothing quixotic about such an attitude, for the
trade of prosperous Latin-American populations would be worth
many times the dividends which flowed into the bank accounts of
a few rich Americans through the exploitation of Latin-American
cheap labor during the "dollar diplomacy" era.

It would be a policy, again, which would strengthen the social-
service departments of the Latin-American governments with
expert U.S. advisers—agricultural and industrial technicians, experts on sanitation, on labor relations, on public school methods
and organization, etc. A good beginning has been made in this
direction by the Agricultural and other Federal Departments' programs in "loaning" experts to Latin governments anxious to
develop their resources and improve their crop technique. Enormously more of this type of "penetration," however, is needed,
and much could be arranged, doubtless, even with the more re-

actionary dictators. Promoting universal literacy in Latin America, improving health standards and teaching skills to the rank and file of the peoples are activities which fertilize the very soil of democracy.

Such a policy would also pull no punches in supporting progressive governments wherever in Latin America they come into power. It would see to it, for instance, that the Aguirre Cerda regime in Chile enjoyed the strongest possible diplomatic support and exceptionally generous consideration of its fiscal and economic needs. It would take, as the Roosevelt administration has done in the face of tremendous obstacles, the long view of difficulties with leftist regimes, such as the ones in Mexico which chronically strain our relations with that country: realizing that, although President Cárdenas has maintained a dictatorship and the oil-expropriations crisis represents the climax of a long history of "anti-American" gestures, the statesman who has put land in the hands of 750,000 peons and their families—with whatever accompaniments of corruption and inefficiency—has made a profound base contribution to the cause of democratic progress.

Finally, such a policy would be long-suffering in its patience with the local frustrations of its aims, with defeats and with tragic disappointments. It would take this attitude because against the menace of totalitarian pressure from Europe the preservation of even the pseudo democracies of Latin America are of definite strategic value. But in a still longer view, our policy would also realize that the economic, the social, the political and the psychological factors unfavorable to the development of democracy have been built up through the conditioning processes of centuries; that other centuries of labor at the roots of the evils of Latin-American society may be required to condition them away.

CHAPTER XIII

Certain Life Forces Confront a World

For a good many more or less tedious chapters we have been talking about forces whose play is felt chiefly under the surface of Latin America's consciousness.

This is not to say, of course, that no Latin Americans are aware of them. Among intellectual upper-crusts in the twenty republics, and among philosophically inclined lay citizens—including some politicians—there is probably as large a proportion of informed scholars, scientists and psychologists, and of discriminating intro-verts, as you would find in similar groups anywhere. These people know what geography and history and economic forces, social and cultural inheritances have done to condition life and its values for them, in their minds as well as in their bones.

But Latin America is so largely illiterate, or barely literate, that these rare exotics have an almost insuperable task on their hands in putting over to the masses an awareness of these basic factors. To Latin Americans in general the impulses which they get out of the soil of their environment are as instinctive, as unassayable and as unrealized as the obscure forces of gland and bloodstream chemistry which make certain women—or men, for one's women readers—alluring to us, while others are mere passing shadows who happen to have epidermis and avoirdupois. Like the over-whelming majority in most racial groups and civilizations, the bulk of the Latin Americans neither know *that* they are that way nor why.

Yet these subcutaneous conditioning factors are amazingly important. We have seen, not far from the beginning of this book, how the very isolation and proud provincialism of the Latin-American settlements turn their faces toward Europe with a kind of unsure and nostalgic craving for an Older World's accolades. They are a long way off, so they want to be patted on the back and told that they have preserved the old values and *mores* like ladies and gentlemen. And there is nothing that the conditioning factors condition more compulsively than the twenty republics' responses to the flux and riot of the world balance of power struggle and to the psychological forces involved in it.

Volumes would be required to plumb this subject with self-respecting profundity. Here the facts can only be hinted at.

The Latin Americans, for instance, have been reared by history to the politics of violence. What happens, then, in Europe, in the way of ravished nationalisms and overthrown sovereignties, shocks them definitely less than it does United States opinion. United States mass opinion, after all, was brought up in the slightly naïve belief that nations expand because, after the Indians have magnanimously retired to less happy hunting grounds, the founding fathers found Keokuk.

Latin-American sentiment has intimations of grosser procedures. Herr Hitler has become overlord of Europe by methods not wholly unrelated, let us say, to the methods by which less flamboyant statesmen become presidents of Paraguay. To this extent Latin-American politics is nearer in bloodstream sympathies to Hitlerite politics than is the United States Senate. To this extent the twenty republics are not quite so horrified at Herr Hitler as democracy's Antichrist as are United States citizens—(it is almost impossible in these comparative passages to avoid using the clipped Spanish nickname *"Unistadenses"* which the Argentine newspapers have invented for us).

This does not mean, of course, that Latin Americans as a class —or of any class—are, in any conclusive sense, "pro" Hitler. They simply regard Hitler as a not quite incredible fact in human nature: an emotionally lush Teutonic Ubico, galvanized with *Weltmacht* aspirations, sketchily rinsed in *Gemütlichkeit*.

Nor is historical adjustment to violence the sole influential factor in Latin America's orientations to the diabolisms overseas. Fascism's domination of its masses, economic and ideological, hardly rate as major crimes against nature in most of the republics. A society which for four hundred years has subsisted, with casual and fatalistic acceptance of the necessity of class control in a well-ordered economy, on the labor of several score million peons, is instinctively inclined to regard the Nazi world's mass-herding processes as a technique of discipline—an excessively "dynamic" technique, perhaps, but still just a method. It is not, in the sense that it is above the Rio Grande, an assault on a body of moral doctrine.

Again, the Nazi world's tendency toward public orgasms of exhibitionism and self-praise in its *"Kultur"* propaganda may not sit well with the Latin Americans as an appeal to gentility. But at least it rides better with stallion-mounted military statues in a hundred ornate plazas than the stinging—and not always quite sober—wisecracks of the Contra Costa "American colony" at the expense of Latin-American culture in general. The strut and yammer—not to mention the plain brutality—of Nazi *Weltmacht* manners scarcely chimes with the Latin-American technique of subtle ingratiations. Still, to people who spend their social lives and their psychic energies seeking mastery over their fellows, it is not wholly unintelligible.

Yet the mere fact that, on points of economic and cultural values and historical inheritance, little in the Nazi outlook awakens chills in the Latin-American bloodstream, does not justify us in assuming that none of the basic conditioning forces in the twenty republics is in resistance to Nazi pressures. One form of resistance, indeed, is on a point of incompatibility between Nazi and Latin-American "under-the-skin" philosophies which a great many *"Unistadenses"* may find more difficult to understand than these foregoing relative "compatibilities."

On the point, in fact, of religion. And to make clear the impingements of the twenty republics' religious addictions upon world political balances, we have for a moment to consider the differences between Latin and North American Catholicism.

Somewhat over 20,000,000 United States citizens are convinced

Catholics. But virtually all of Latin America's 120,000,000 are what we might call "instinctive" Catholics. North America's twenty millions are confident, no doubt, that they possess the ultimate absolute in spiritual truth and theological revelation, but at the same time they are conscious that they are competitors in a kind of nation-wide appeal to faith and conscience with Methodists, Holy Rollers and Christian Scientists. Latin Americans in mass are scarcely conscious that Methodists are different from Mohammedans, or that Holy Rollers and Christian Scientists are human beings.

It is not a question of the Latin Americans being more devout Catholics than the North Americans—often they are not!—or of their being less tolerant. Total lack of competition, it sometimes appears, can actually lubricate tolerance. What is important is that North American Catholics, on the whole, tend to regard their Catholicism as an unshakable religious conviction. Latin Americans regard it—and, with due respect for convictions regarding unseen worlds, swim in it—as a way of life.

In consequence, an affront or a menace to a North American's Catholicism is an insult to a passionate certainty about what life and God mean. A menace to a Latin American's Catholicism is an axe laid upon a root of life itself.

Hence the twenty republics' policies, alliances and antipathies in a wicked world and their reactions to the political forces at play in it—including, most specifically, the reactions of two or three "anticlerical" republics which customarily and exhibitionally react in reverse—are controlled to an almost incalculable degree by a universal abomination of the authentically anti-religious. It is hardly putting it too strongly to say that the twenty republics would regard a world campaign for the obliteration of Catholicism with as much horror as twenty republics of hedonists would regard a world campaign for totalitarian castration.

So over against the instinctive feeling of Latin Americans that, as a menace to manners and culture, democratic freedom and "the economic man's" laissez-faire ease on his acres, Nazism and its Führer may have been blown up into somewhat fantastic bogies, you get a strong and vigilant opposite feeling:

[*216*]

The suspicion that Herr Hitler, having entered into the curiously opportunist partnership with the state atheism of Stalinist Russia, may one day come into the garden of the Lord as an axe wielder: corrupter and slayer of a root of life itself.

This reaction is, to be sure, no guaranteed safety device. It was strongest at the September, 1939, Panama Conference when the shock of the Russian alliance was new and when vast Polish populations of Catholics were being turned over to the missionaries of godlessness from Moscow.

In the war's later stages, however, terror of the Soviet anti-Christ has definitely weakened. The Latin-American statesmen approached the Havana conference in the summer of 1940 with the comfortable feeling that since Catholic Italy had found Nazi Germany a fit war associate and clerically reactionary Spain had adopted a practically benevolent neutrality toward the axis, there could be little immediate danger of abominations in the holy places. Meanwhile, events in Rumania and the Balkans were suggesting that Herr Hitler's bonds with the atheist statecraft themselves may be due for a speedy fracture.

More expertly than seemed possible in September, in other words, the Führer has rebuilt his natural emotional corridor into Latin America's practical politics: The corridor which runs through Italy and Catholic-Franco-Fascist Spain. For quite apart from the question of how atheist is Russia and how fit atheism may be as a civilizing instrument, a great deal of the twenty republics' attitude toward the world march of totalitarianism may be determined by subtle emotional responses on the religious front.

Yet neither religion nor the other under-the-surface forces which we have followed through so many chapters are the final orientating factors. Above them are forces of which the twenty republics are sleeplessly conscious—often bitterly and belligerently conscious.

The behavior of the Latin-American world as player on the stage of the larger world's politics is directly determined by these conscious forces, and the rest of the book will be about them.

CHAPTER XIV

The Semi-Colonials

In THE FAT, GREEN, mile-high valley of Antioquía about the Colombian city of Medellín, one of my Colombian friends was taking me for a motor drive. Sleek Holstein and Hereford cows, with thousands of lively calves at their sides, munched the thick grass in pleasant landscapes of rain-rich pasture. Beyond lay indefinite stretches of corn, grain and cotton fields. Coffee climbed in easy rows over the nearer hills. Now and then an ore truck rumbled past with a load from some mine in the mountains.

I said something casually complimentary about how charming it looked and what a sensibly balanced local economy it seemed after the overspecialized coffee and banana regions of Central America.

"Yes," Don Alfredo agreed, "it would be a nice country if we owned it."

"What do you mean?" I demanded.

"Simply," he answered, "that all our mines are either owned or financed by foreign money and that all these farms and plantations you see are mortgaged to foreign banking interests. Also, they would be taxed even more ruinously than they are at the moment if the republic were keeping up to the minute in the payments of its foreign loans. There isn't a calf in these fields, I imagine, out of which either you Norte Americanos or the British, if you insisted on your literal pound of flesh, couldn't cut the choicest veal steak.

"You foreign landlords fail to realize," he went on with amiable

[218]

cynicism, "that we Antioquians are some of the best tenants you have anywhere. Or what is that short and ugly phrase you Norte Americanos have for it?"

"Share croppers," I offered.

"Precisely," said Don Alfredo. "But it sounds much more dignified to call us what we really are—semi-colonials."

It was not the first time I had heard the expression. It was invented by the Peruvian publicist, García Calderón, almost a full generation ago. Indeed, in Latin America you hear it in practically every conversation with people who are conscious of economic forces. For "semi-colonial" expresses a factor which crucially affects practically every phase of Latin America's problems of internal development and international relationships: the fact that the twenty republics do not own their own homes.

They have nominal title to their territorial possessions, it is true. Ostensibly, they enjoy the full rights of independent political sovereignty. In representing the situation as a parallel of the landlord-share-cropper relationship, my Colombian friend was amusing himself with a slight distortion of the technical realities. But not a very serious distortion. A more exact comparison could put it, perhaps, that most of the republics are in the position—in respect to their foreign creditors—of the businessman in the United States of whom we say, "Sure, he's got title to the property, but the banks own it."

☆   ☆   ☆

In the cloudy arithmetic of international finance, the situation can only be hinted at. According to the best figures available, those of the United States Department of Commerce, the sum of foreign investments in the twenty republics somewhat past the middle 1930s approached a grand astronomical total of more than $11,000,000,000. Possibly, if all loans from government to government were included, it would top $13,000,000,000.

Such a sum, of course, bears only the shadowiest relation to the fiscal realities. In it are included all the "owned property" and commercial securities of foreign interests in Latin America, all bank loans on Latin-American property and enterprises, and all Latin-American bonds and loan securities held in foreigners' portfolios.

Inevitably, the round-up cannot be complete—especially now, with the whole question of foreign finance further scrambled by was dislocations. Many holdings tend to be overvalued by owners who compute their interest not by current market prices but by the original investments. The eleven-to-thirteen-billions figure represents the nominal grand total of the twenty republics' obligations to foreign claimants rather than any one's rational "balance due" or collectible assets.

Also, one is painfully handicapped by the lack of figures indicating with even impressionistic accuracy how large such a sum bulks in Latin America's basic fiscal economy. No statistics have been compiled even roughly to suggest what may be the aggregate national wealth of the twenty republics. We not only do not know what the eleven-to-thirteen billions means in terms of negotiable holdings. We have not even an approximate idea of how large a fraction it represents of Latin America's total resources. Whether "outsiders'" equity represents a little less than a fourth or well over half of Latin America, considered as a unit business enterprise—whether the nominal owner of the house can be regarded as a reasonably independent freeholder, or simply as the tenant of the banks and the first, second and third mortgagees—is as hard to decide on the basis of the available arithmetic as it would be to make a diagram of the Martian breathing apparatus from what we know of the Martian stratosphere.

There are, however, certain helpful clew figures in the madhouse equation. We can be reasonably certain, for example, that the total annual income of the twenty republics can never have gone above twenty billion dollars, and that in the years of nominal peace between the century's two general wars it probably hovered between ten and fifteen billions. Foreigners own, then, or have a mortgage on, a share of Latin America's wealth that is nominally nearly as great as the republics' total annual production of purchasing power. It is somewhat as if, with our present annual income of approximately $65,000,000,000, more than

$50,000,000,000 of United States government obligations and corporation securities were held in Europe.

In addition, we know positively that Latin America's total exports seldom run above $2,000,000,000 and generally run considerably below it. So the overseas sales operations of the republics—viewed again as a gigantic unified business enterprise—are less than a fifth of the grand total of indebtedness.

For a more specific example of the sheer bulk of the foreign interest, look at the most prosperous and economically best organized of the twenty republics—Argentina. The total value of movable-goods production in Argentina in 1937, as calculated by the able economist Dr Alejandro E. Bungé, was $2,141,000,000. Yet the amount of foreign credit and investment in Argentina, as indicated by the U. S. Department of Commerce surveys, is, in round numbers, $4,432,000,000. Argentina's total movable-goods production could, in other words, have been sold for 1937's best market prices without paying off half the principal. And it should be considered that credit and investment figures for the Argentine are far more realistically computed than in the case of the less orderly republics.

Moreover, far beyond the mere size of the foreigners' stake in comparison with the aggregate wealth of the twenty republics, the alien's command of the fiscal control points gives him a power over the life of their peoples singularly inconsistent with the twenty governments' passionate claims of technical political sovereignty.

In the relatively prosperous Argentine the citizen either rides on a British railroad or on a government line which is financed, in the last analysis, by British loans to the Buenos Aires treasury. The estancia proprietor may go to his republic's national land bank to get a credit extension for pay rolls or a new land purchase, but the bank has the resources to meet his needs because credit has been provided to it from London. Brazil and Chile boast of imposing nationally owned railway systems, but construction and maintenance are financed by government bonds, and the bonds are held in London and New York.

United States interests finance the banks and the currencies, not to mention the planters, the mines and the local industrial activities of the whole Caribbean area. American and British capital controls the oil of Venezuela and Colombia and will dominate in Ecuador if the fields under exploration begin producing commercially. Americans own the choicest mines of Peru, and an Italian does the banking for the republic's commerce.

Down to the Cárdenas administration, Americans and British owned the Mexican oil and the railways. They still own most of the mines, and, through their control of credit and the United States Treasury's control of silver prices, the power to make or break the Mexican currency. Cuba's railways are British owned, but Americans do the banking, and, by control of the credit machinery, dominate the vast sugar industry. Brazil's gigantic coffee agriculture would collapse with the withdrawal of New York and London loans to the Brazilian banking system.

In the same sense in which discriminating modern economists speak of Birmingham and Seattle, the Iowa corn belt and the Southern share-cropper area, as being "colonies" of the New York banking interests, the twenty republics are economic "colonies" of the older and richer nations. To the North American public, being New York's colonials means that you do not ride on a street car or go to a movie on any normal Main Street, or plant a field of wheat or hire a Negro to pick a row of cotton, without participating in an arrangement for paying an ultimate—and fairly considerable—tribute to some banker on Manhattan island.

The estimate that sixty families own the United States of America lock, stock and barrel may be melodrama mathematics, but it advertises the fundamental truth that very few people anywhere in the United States can make plans for their economic future without the approval of a small group who exercise control over the money economy of the nation—or even enjoy their economic present until this same group has been cut in on the profits.

A similar truth prevails throughout Latin America. Above the most primitive subsistence and distribution activities, no economic enterprise can be launched in the twenty republics, no government can initiate new economic programs or policies, without considering the attitude—and the "take"—of the sources of credit abroad. To an even greater extent than the famous "sixty families" own the United States, London and New York and Paris (until recently)—with small "cuts" for Rome and Berlin—"own" the Rio Grande-to-Cape Horn layout.

Yet in two or three aspects the spirit of the "owning" groups is different. Whatever may be said against the economic morals of the "sixty families," most of the tribute they collect remains in the United States to enlarge and freshen the general stream of investment and economic progress. From Latin America the funds due the banker on his mortgage on the old homestead drain away—to freshen the stream of some other country's economic progress.

Also, the fiscal heads of the "sixty families" have not quite the same set of aims in their domestic investments that the capitalists in the world financial centers have in respect to their investments abroad. They realize, for instance, that a generally prosperous United States means bigger profits and larger fortune accumulations for themselves, while an excessively niggardly attitude may actually curtail their operations and privileges by arousing powerful political forces against them. Most of them, besides, are motivated, to some degree, by patriotic pride. They like to see their country "get ahead," achieve things and outshine its rivals in enterprise and prosperity. Within the limitations of their operating methods and their personal vision, they frame their investment policies to this end.

In reality, of course, the banker who is funding a loan for the Brazilian railroads has precisely as much profit interest in better living standards and higher per-capita purchasing power for Brazilians. But, separated from Brazil by thousands of miles and free from any very definite acquaintance with Brazilian poverty, he is likely to view this angle of self-interest with considerable fuzziness—an astigmatism immensely assisted by the fact that his personal milieu is composed almost entirely of individuals who have no interest whatever in Brazil except what can be got out of it. Obviously, too, the motive of patriotic pride in Brazilian prosperity and achievements is altogether absent. On the contrary, the natural human vanity of a foreign banker normally

[223]

prompts him to imagine that the Brazilians could not get along without him if they tried.

In result of all these psychological and economic factors, the feeling of the foreign investing groups toward Latin America tends to drift into a general attitude of—"To hell with general conditions in these republics. We want our dividends and our interest now, and the bigger the better."

There are, of course, virtuous exceptions to this viewpoint, for corporations and credit agencies exist which have made Latin America's interests their own interests, and there are frequently cross currents in the policies of even the most rapacious investment groups. But, by and large, there is even less of the *noblesse oblige* spirit in international "colonialism" than there is in the type of domestic "colonialism" to which Birmingham and Seattle are subject.

☆   ☆   ☆

The effects of this situation on Latin-American economy are prodigious, and, for the individual Latin American in almost any walk of life, inescapable. For one thing, the new "colonial authorities"—it was no mere quip on the part of the Colombian labor leader who told me that the chief effect of the Wars of Liberation was to replace the Spanish viceroys with London and New York bankers—have done, and are doing, all in their power to condemn the 120,000,000 from the Rio Grande to Cape Horn to permanent sweatshoppery.

From the foreign investors' viewpoint, the reasons for pressure in this direction are logical and realistic. To do business in Latin America is extraordinarily risky and expensive. Most of the tropical products are highly speculative commodities, and mining products are often subject to even more startling fluctuations than coffee and bananas. Industries in the Latin countries are generally feeble both in their technical efficiency and in the strength of the domestic markets. And beyond this, all economic activity must be conducted in an environment where political changes are swift and often destructive; where currencies and credit institutions are unstable and operating concessions likely to be terminated with little or no notice. The one constant factor in the future calculations is that labor is cheap, and if it can be kept cheap long enough, it may be made to pay the differential for the losses on all these other accounts.

In the first World War, for instance, dividends in some of the Latin-American "strategic raw materials" industries multiplied themselves ten and twenty and even thirty times without producing any significant raise in "real wages" on the labor front. The masses in the twenty republics today have that record to stir into the decision pot before letting themselves be emotionally carried away by their "democratic sympathies."

Furthermore, being so enthusiastically for low labor costs, the financial forces which hold the ultimate economic power in most, if not all, of the republics tend to range themselves in a kind of malevolent phalanx against all mass efforts of the Latin Americans to raise their own living standards. Although the investment interests are hardly passionate partisans of labor movements in their own countries, at least they usually recognize unions as inevitable evils and their spokesmen as fellow creatures using the same language. In Latin America, however, to the branch managers and subexecutives of the foreign "interests," the labor union is a kind of superanathema of all that infuriates in a strange environment.

There are no words to express the contempt with which the aims, methods, ideas, personnel and medical histories of labor organizations are discussed in the intimate *causeries* of these cheerful "economic ambassadors." As their talk goes, all unions are artificially fomented by the personal viciousness or corrupt ambitions of their leaders. Their objectives are theft, murder, rapine and the reduction of civilization in the republics to peon standards. All the errors of union tactics; all of the petty blackmail operations which crop out on labor fronts everywhere—and are not unprecedented in the operations of the "captains of industry"; all of the unreasonable demands, such as the insistence of a Mexican mining union a few years ago that syphilis in the camps be compensated as an occupational disease—are advertised

[225]

as final proofs of the labor movement's total and vicious incompetence.

The mere fact that a labor movement assumes that peon living standards can be changed for the better is hailed by the "colonial bosses" as evidence that it must be led exclusively by crooks and maniacs. Objections that there might be something in higher Latin-American purchasing power even for entrepreneurs are met, in the twenty republics' "foreign colonies," with perpetual growls of—"If you doubled their wages, they'd only work half the week." Wherever the alien lords and masters have gone in for paternalism and built somewhat better housing accommodations in the oil and mine settlements, their cocktail hours are brightened with tropical equivalents of the "damned if they didn't put the coal in the bathtub" saga.

Where the laws of the more progressive republics demand it, the alien entrepreneurs deal with the labor unions, inevitably. But they do so in the mood of men facing criminal enemies, who feel that any stratagem of force they can introduce into the negotiations, any corrupt influence they can procure or exert, is justified as a measure of warfare against savages. Often, too, at the bottom of the mood is a persisting and unlovely vengefulness.

"One of these days," an internationally known mining engineer of more than thirty years' Latin-American experience said to me in Mexico City, "you and I are going to have a field day. *Our* kind of a revolution is going to happen in this republic. And you and I are going up to our hotel room, order a few drinks, and shoot labor leaders from the windows."

"When you mention labor leaders to me," another mining Croesus warned me acidly, "say bastards."

There is a degree of conscious overstatement in such witticisms, but it is scarcely the humor of exuberant jocosity.

In their less aggressive moods, it is true, the "new colonial" satraps often boast with bland self-admiration of the contributions which they are making to civilized progress in the republics. They are introducing better technical processes, they say—about which there is no argument. They pay slightly better wages than the local averages, they insist—which is often true to the extent that they find it helpful in procuring the best groups of workers. They cite the sanitary improvements they have made in their camps and settlements—which are distinctly more genuine, but which also have the advantage of keeping expensive field executives and their families from the home country safe from tropical diseases.

All of these meritorious services are mentioned, in any event, as still further reasons for freeing foreign-owned industries from all "truck" with native labor movements. Technical progress and sanitation and fractional wage improvements, runs the philosophy of the foreigners, should be offered by the beneficent overlords in accordance with their self-interest and caprices, and accepted by the native populace with beautiful gratitude. But that "native" masses should seek these same improvements—and sometimes more of the same—as matters of right on their own account, smacks of the horrors of servile revolution against the white man's proper mastery over congenital inferiors.

This is not a pretty background psychology for the day-by-day contacts of Latin Americans with the stronger powers' "economic ambassadors." Neither are the by-products of the aliens' cheap-labor yearnings impressively salubrious. Because the foreign colonies and the investment groups abroad regard low wages as their ace card in the play for Latin-American profits and labor unions as a threat to the foundations of their empire, the "colonies" and the investment groups are almost invariably passionate partisans of the dictators who can keep wages low and labor movements down.

Everywhere you go in the less liberal republics, for instance, club, bar and dinner-party conversations among entrepreneurs from "the States" buzz with admiring anecdotes of the local dictator's ruthlessness toward "labor agitators." If you cross a border into more liberal regions—or worse, into the realm of a dictator with taint of leftist sympathies—they buzz with nostalgic boasts of what a marvelous republic this was when it had the genuine article in despots.

Thus Venezuela's North American residents tenderly mourn for the vanished Gómez of the political torture chambers. He was a hard man to deal with, they admit regretfully, but once a deal was made, "his word was as good as a Standard Oil bond." Once you got to work on your concession, and anything remotely resembling labor difficulties appeared on the horizon, you simply told the local *jefe politico*, a group of bad *hombres* went to jail, and that was that.

"Today," the lament goes on, "you never know how your business stands with this wishy-washy liberal administration, and out in the field you find every Tuesday morning that you've broken the union rules again."

Tortures of the late despot's political critics are recounted with obvious admiration for the stamina of the victims, but with definite social sympathy for the despot's objectives. "The old man sure knew how to handle his people," is a stock concluding line in these symposiums. "And whatever you can say against his morals, he was one swell businessman."

Polite conversation in the Guatemala foreign colonies is similarly tinctured with Ubico worship. And on the whole the dictator's harsh anti-labor tactics come in for more praise than the few genuine social-service activities which go a certain slight distance toward justifying his regime.

"You can't take the chance," my American mentors in Guatemala insistently advised me, "of giving labor unions in a country like this the same kind of breaks that we give 'em back home. The moment you put a union card in the hands of one of these Indian bozos, he thinks it's a license to take down the old machete and carve up the first guy he meets who ever saw two dollars."

Even in countries like Peru and the Dominican Republic, where the local despots have established a routine of building up vast family fortunes on political corruption—and have been known to draw some highly profitable tribute from American sources—there are few very harshly critical comments on the side of the invading industrialists. "What if the big boss does get himself a few extra comforts at the expense of the taxpayers and the government contractors?" the worthy Generals Benavides and Trujillo are defended. "Maybe a fellow who knows how to keep the labor scum quiet in this republic deserves something in the way of an annual bonus."

Wherever the "new colonial authorities" dare throw their weight in local practical politics, moreover, it is thrown in the more ruthless dictators' favor. The American banking and sugar interests fought for the Machado regime in Cuba to the last two-dollar-word press agent release. For the quarter of a century from the Taft to the Hoover administrations inclusive, "dollar diplomacy," inspired in the State Department by the heavier investors and bondholders in the "banana republics," kept the Caribbean littoral a "free zone" for the harder-fisted petty dictators. In Mexico, in 1913, a cabal of American banking, mining and railway magnates supplied funds and arms and the strategic advice of the United States ambassador, Henry Lane Wilson, for the uprising in which Victoriano Huerta overthrew the first of Mexico's leftist governments. And subsequently it took the last ounce of Woodrow Wilson's political prestige to oust Huerta against the will of Mexico's economic overlords in New York and the oil and mining fastnesses.

There is little question, on the whole, in the minds of the overseas rulers that their interests give them the right to dictate the conditions of life for the masses in the "semi-colonial" republics, and that the power to dominate governments should be a natural appendage to their ownership.

Such convictions naturally color the attitude of the representatives of the "owners" in Latin America toward the society which surrounds them. It is fundamentally the attitude of colonial overlords toward subject populations everywhere. The branch-factory superintendents, the mine managers, the oil-field executives, the banking submagnates—and often surprisingly, too, the general sales managers—are not there to "grow up with the country" and merge themselves with its interests. They are there to rule possessions.

"We have found," the American manager of several Andean mining properties informed me, "that if we treat anyone besides the necessary public officials as equals, it has a bad effect on labor."

In Nicaragua a hard-boiled young building contractor proceeded to instruct me on the niceties of the linguistic situation.

"I speak bum Spanish," he boasted, "and I'm damned proud of it. I'd be a better gang boss if I made 'em speak my language or get along with signs. The English know their stuff on this business of dealing with inferior races. Let 'em come to you and ask for it—is their system. One of these days we'll take over these lousy republics and make 'em speak pidgin English or starve."

More picaresquely still, the infatuation with Latin America's harsher political institutions sometimes leads to unfavorable comparisons with conditions back home. At least a dozen times on my passage through the republics expatriate gringos argued with me that a taste of the hard-pan peon living conditions and strong-arm discipline of the dictators would be good for unrest on the North American labor front. Once when I protested to a coffee *finca* proprietor in El Salvador that turning Ubico firing squads loose on John Lewis's stalwarts might lead to widely bloody consequences, I was presumably stopped in my tracks by the answer. "When you've seen as much life go out as I have in this so-called struggle of inferiors to take what doesn't belong to them," he turned on me, "you may begin to realize that human life isn't quite so precious as our old-maid schoolteachers taught us back home."

At vast intervals, to be sure, there is an exception.

There was the veritable impresario of North American entrepreneurs who advised me in Buenos Aires, for instance: "Don't believe anything they tell you in any American colony anywhere. All they want is two-bits-a-day labor, no trouble, and nothing to interfere with the impression that they own the country. Then the dividends flow in regularly, and their bright reports from the field are praised by the big boss in the home office, and every year they get their bonus.

"When they find a dictator who's tough enough to give 'em these conditions, they'll tell you he's a combination of George Washington and Napoleon Bonaparte—and believe it."

He was an accurate forecaster. But even he did not advise me to count the number of times when a North American host would lead me to some view of goat-ranged mountainside or tropical seashore and muse: "My God, what a country this would be if Uncle Sam could only take it over!" It would buttress this discussion of control objectives in the republics to have that statistic in the record.

The more one studies the question on the ground, in any event, the more the expression "semi-colonial" seems a choice example of graceful Latin understatement.

☆   ☆   ☆

There is, of course, room for endless argument over the complex rights and wrongs involved in "semi-colonialism." Naturally, the question looks different to the bondholders of the twenty republics, the investors in Latin-American economic activities, and to the agents who manage their interests on the ground.

They own Latin America's railways, mines and industries, the investors' side goes, and have their crucial mortgages on Latin-American agriculture and the revenues of the governments, because Latin America didn't have the technical skills to get these activities going on her own account, or the resources to finance herself. It isn't the investors' fault that they command the control points in the republics' economies. The Latin Americans asked them to come and buy themselves into these strategic possessions. There is no law to prevent the Latin Americans from buying foreign "owners" out again—if they care to save their money and pay the market prices. There isn't even any absolute statute against an Ecuadorean capital consortium's coming to Pittsburgh and buying control of the U.S. Steel Corporation.

Neither do the investors consider it their fault that they contribute so little to raising Latin-American purchasing power. If the republics maintained better political order within their borders and were more "reliable" in their financial operations, investments would be rendered more secure and more money might be available for labor costs. As it is, when you get a "good thing" in Latin-American investments, you have to make your killing now, because you never can tell how the next revolution will affect your dividends.

Meanwhile, having been invited onto the ground and being

there with the full powers of owners and mortgage holders, the investors feel that their first duty to civilization and morals is to collect what is due them. If their rights to do this were abrogated, or their facilities for doing it destroyed, their world, as the investors see it, would collapse hardly less shockingly than the empire of the Incas.

Interesting, however, as are these theoretics of a "hardheaded" business group, more practical is the question of how the semi-colonial status looks to the Latin Americans mired in it.

Quite possibly the most graphic way of putting ourselves in the Latin Americans' place is to imagine for the moment that the war had not wrecked French finance and that the control points in the economy of the United States are similarly commanded by French investment interests.

French banks hold, let us say, or have disposed of, nine tenths of our government bonds. French capital owns the copper mines of Arizona, the gold mines of California and Alaska, the silver mines of Nevada and the iron mines of Minnesota. Frenchmen own our transcontinental railway system, the Detroit automobile industry, the Pittsburgh steel plants, the New England and Southern textile factories, the national network of power utilities.

French banking interests in the country are as big as the Federal Reserve system, and dominate the system, besides, through credit they have extended to it. Agriculture from the Maine potato fields to the fruit ranches of Florida and California is blanketed by French crop loans and mortgages, to say nothing of the fact that a considerable percentage of the national farming acreage is owned by Frenchmen outright.

Moreover, French branch managers and technicians—farms, to a certain extent, excepted—run all these enterprises. In every community of more than picayune industrial or financial importance there are lively little "colonies" of French bosses, keeping to their own customs, keeping themselves aloof from the local social life; obviously, even when polite about it, regarding us as somewhat amusing inferiors; insisting that our workmen are too barbarous to know what to do with more than a bare subsistence wage, and using their power behind the scenes to support reactionary governments which will keep down all movements for the improvement of living standards.

Better than three quarters of the profits of our industries drain away to France in the form of dividends. An appalling percentage of the national revenue is paid out in interest to Paris on the national securities. An indeterminate but certainly enormous share of our agricultural profits goes with it. Together, these forms of annual outflow make up a sum which is disturbingly close to what we have left for a national income. A part of it, to be sure, may flow back as reinvestment, but that merely means in future years that the "take" of the foreigner will be larger.

Although we are unquestionably a sovereign nation by all the respectable political theories, it looks very much to the practical sense as if we were just a crew of hired hands working on pittance wages for the bosses who really own the country. Meanwhile, too, it comes to us interestingly from time to time, from servants who have overheard the bosses' private meditations and from members of our own groups to whom they have unbuttoned their enthusiasms in confidence, that the "owners" are saying: *"Mon Dieu,* did you ever think what a swell country the U.S.A. would be if France could only take it over?"

It is a fair guess, I suspect, that the United States would react a good deal as Latin America is reacting.

There would be widespread anti-French agitation in the country, and practically no indications of "gratitude" toward the foreigners who were so busily at work conferring "benefits" on the national economy. There would be a rash of punitive taxes and laws hampering the alien corporations in their operations—if only to show them that the nation's political sovereignty took precedence over the rights of economic ownership. There would be a bumper crop of intensively nationalistic legislation, to keep the outlanders from extending their overlordship and from enlarging their executive and technical personnel to take over more key posts in finance and industry.

Wherever labor unions were given a chance to operate, their demands would be extreme, and, often, from the standpoint of persons interested in seeing a capitalist system survive without serious impairment of its functional mechanisms, highly unreasonable. For the unionists would have old scores to settle with the foreign paymasters and would not be much interested in seeing capitalism survive as a means to the economic ownership of a free, sovereign republic in any case.

A distinctly casual attitude toward debt and interest payments would grow up both on the part of the government and of private loan beneficiaries. Why should anyone bother whether this or that particular loan was paid, when the foreign coupon-clippers and shareholders were getting the cream off the top of the nation's economy already?

Finally, a horrid tendency would develop to take French property away from its owners more or less regardless of circumstances and with a minimum of compensation. Elaborate pretexts would be created in law for devious expropriation procedures and elaborate justifications rationalized for pursuing such conduct: most of the justifications revolving around the point that the successful economic enterprises of foreigners in the republic had already earned many times the original value of the investment, and therefore expropriation was no hardship.

Even to the most enlightened and considerate French overlords, that is to say, the Americans would make it pretty plain that they did not propose to live indefinitely on their theoretically free and independent soil in the status of share croppers.

☆   ☆   ☆

Now it is precisely by such short cuts and artifices that Latin America is trying today to extricate herself from semi-colonialism. Her struggles—including the errors and the "fast-corner" operations—need to be viewed in the light of the psychological atmosphere just described.

Naturally, the investment groups' apologists will insist that the conditions are not parallel; that "semi-colonialism" exists in Latin America because the twenty republics are not politically stable, or economically "sound" or technologically expert enough to manage their own resources, and that the imaginary semi-colonialism we have just conjured up for the United States was averted generations ago simply because we possessed all these virtues. But, though based on considerable factual truth, this is not, strictly speaking, a practical argument. It does not contain the kind of points that control actual political conduct.

Increasingly the Latin-American governments and politicians— including even some of the "farthest right" dictators—are coming to take the position that, however much they need the foreigners and however badly they manage their own affairs, at least they can manage them well enough to get more out of their resources than they do under the foreigners' ownership. They may be wrong in these conclusions—though not necessarily so wrong as the aggrieved foreign investors declare them to be—but political actions are inevitably determined, both in democracies and dictatorships, more by what the ruling circles think than by the realities or by perfect judgment.

Consequently, Latin America today presents a panorama of efforts to throw off the semi-colonial yoke. To indicate all that is going on in this direction would require an appendage of several volumes.

Mexico, for example, after tying knots in the operations of foreign-owned industries for years with heavy taxes and complicated labor regulations, has expropriated the railways and the foreign oil industry. Power and the mines may, or may not, follow, but their owners undoubtedly regard the current omens as unpropitious.

Nor is the Mexican action, as originally advertised by its victims, the single aberration of a leftist government. At another end of Latin America, in Bolivia, a government proclaiming fairly "rightist" principles also in 1937 expropriated American-owned oil properties, and the succeeding government of the late "totalitarian" Colonel Busch eagerly reaffirmed the action. Dictator Vargas in Brazil has "decreed" government ownership of oil resources even before any has been discovered, and has taken similar, if slightly less drastic, steps to secure Brazilian control of future discoveries of mining wealth.

One of the Ecuadorean presidents of 1938, General Alberto Enriquez, who ruled provisionally for several months under the interesting title of *Jefe Supremo,* horrified the foreign investment groups by defending his alterations of the terms of certain mining concessions with the declaration that "a concession is not a contract." What he meant, of course, was that Ecuador proposed to be, as far as she could get away with it, the arbitrary and final judge of the rights of foreign capital operating in the republic.

Similar programs are definitely in the offing elsewhere. Chile is openly debating the expropriation of copper mines and nitrate fields. In spite of the wealth it has paid into the treasury, there is a strong agitation for expropriating the oil industry in Venezuela, and conceivably it may play a significant part in the 1940 election issues. Even gentle Costa Rica has taken steps from time to time toward expropriating the San José power plant, although there are more indications here than in some other places that the former American owners might be paid in full.

Over an immensely wider field, where expropriations are not yet so definitely threatened, the foreigners' empire is being, as one North American entrepreneur somewhat melodramatically put it to me, "stabbed in the back with pinpricks."

A tangle of labor regulations or personnel-control restrictions—such as the nationalistic statutes of more than half the republics, limiting the number of technical and executive posts which can be held by foreigners; of financial auditing requirements; of safety and health regulations supervised by local bureaucracies; of exchange and customs restrictions and of pyramided taxes—these and a thousand other measures are applied to make the foreigners' business operations more costly and more difficult. Slowly the foreign overlords are being forced to relax their grip on the republics through a process of petty attritions.

There are, of course, certain "white spots." Guatemala is almost as friendly to foreign investors under Ubico, and for somewhat the same reasons, as Mexico was under Porfirio Diaz. The Guatemalan dictator would like to see a modern technical and physical plant built in his republic as quickly as possible and at the least possible expense to the body politic—though even Ubico can hardly give guarantees that the plant, when completed, will not be taken over by some more radical successor.

Besides the "white spots," moreover, there are numerous surprising crosscurrents. At the same time that his "decree laws" and restrictions on exploitation are making it more difficult for foreign capital to operate in Brazil, President Vargas is pleading for larger foreign investments. So, for that matter, are several republics in which "anti-foreign" agitations are stronger.

Rarely is it possible for even a visiting newspaperman to escape from a republic without having a cabinet minister or two, an "administration" newspaper publisher, and perhaps a confidential group of local financial Titans expatiate on the profits which would accrue to the United States if only the loans were forthcoming to attack its economic maladjustments at the root.

In Colombia, whose unserviced debts to the United States amount to considerably over $100,000,000, I was reminded that another hundred million advanced to the government's three-year plan for general economic renovation would restore the nation to solvency as a borrower and glowing prosperity as a customer. In El Salvador, a sternly anti-American cabinet subordinate spent an energetic dinner hour sketching me a prospectus of the openings for United States capital in small local industries. In Brazil, again, whose arrears dwarf Colombia's, President Vargas informed me that the ideal tonic for Brazilian-American friendship would be immense capital investments in Brazilian railways and industries, gold loans to straighten out the republic's foreign exchange entanglements—and a national campaign to raise the price of Brazilian coffee.

In such appeals and arguments all the stops are pulled. "Señor," they murmur in their best piteous inflections, "go about my country and look at our poverty. Then you will see what it would mean in practical advantages to the United States if these suffering people were raised to a standard where they could buy a few comforts and luxuries. And do you not realize, señor, that if their misery were cured, our people would know to whom they owe gratitude?"

The Yankee colonies, on the other hand, are cynical toward

[237]

these solicitations. "What they want," the colony philosophers instruct the visitor, "is for Uncle Sam to send his dollars down here to wet-nurse their industries and grub-stake their politicians to a lot of New Deal experiments. And the moment one of our investments begins paying real dividends, they'll turn on the heat of their latest fake Socialist statute and take it away from us."

These bilious accusations will be denied in all Latin-American official circles. Yet they are not quite devoid of shreds of plausibility. Latin America yearns for the development of her resources which can only come about through foreign investments, but is passionately unwilling to pay the price in the domination of her interests and economies which capital exacts when development occurs. For governments are not likely to look upon control of the internal economies of their peoples as an item that can be acquired with titles to real estate and majority blocks of voting stock, or bought and sold like groceries.

Thus rightly or wrongly—though for highly comprehensible reasons—Latin America has entered upon a program of freeing herself from the economic dominance of foreign capital. The foreign policies of the republics will therefore be increasingly controlled by their demands for economic freedom, while the play of their diplomatic coquetries as between the heavily investing nations and the so-called "have not" powers will be to a large extent determined by such objectives.

The Fascist penetration in Latin America today, as well as during the crucial prewar years of the 1930s, can best be viewed against the background of this economic struggle. The struggle is perhaps the most important key factor we must consider in charting a prognosis of the republics' attitude toward totalitarian world empire as the war of the 1940s approaches its climax.

CHAPTER XV

Menace, East and West

Wʜᴀᴛ ᴅᴏᴇꜱ ᴛʜᴇ ꜰᴀꜱᴄɪꜱᴛ ᴍᴇɴᴀᴄᴇ in Latin America amount to?
How many of the twenty republics are "anti-American" to the
point where they would rather submit to a German-Italian world
hegemony than to risk being partially controlled from Washington under the Monroe Doctrine? How many are in a position where
they may have to submit to Fascist economic or military pressure
regardless of their wishes? And how much may they have to
submit?

In sizing up these questions it helps to recapitulate what the
Fascists were up to below the Rio Grande down to the war's
outbreak in 1939:

1. Rome, Berlin—and then suddenly Madrid and Burgos—radio
broadcasts were hammering away day and night at the Latin-
American public with adroit or impassioned statements of the
case for Fascist institutions, ways of life, and the Fascist "cause"
in international controversies.

2. The Fascist propaganda bureaus were subsidizing Latin-
American newspapers and coloring the news in their favor through
free "mat" and virtually free wire report services; through huge
advertising "gifts" and occasional straight bribery of owners and
news staffs.

3. Germany and Italy, by strong-arm and high-pressure methods,
were forcing their nationals in Latin America into working for
Fascist economic and political programs everywhere, as well as
serving as missionaries of Fascist ideas in all Latin-American cul-

tural centers. This phase of the effort very much included "nationals" who have been naturalized in the various republics, and, as far as possible, descendants of families whose naturalization may date back several generations.

4. Fascist big business was using the "barter system" of foreign trade and trick foreign-exchange devices, like the famous German Aski-marks, to overcome its more orthodox competitors in Latin-American markets, with a view to eventual domination of the republics' economies.

5. Highly placed undercover representatives of the Fascist powers were intriguing in the domestic politics of the republics to foment Fascist movements and Fascist administrations; or, when this was not possible, at least to keep ruling groups friendly to the Fascist states, ready to give them aid and comfort behind the scenes.

6. Fascist agents were subtly stirring up all the social and political controversies involving the Roman Catholic Church in Latin America, and encouraging the conservative interests in the republics to demand the Franco solution of their internal adjustment problems.

7. Fascist transportation agencies—especially the German—were getting control of the commercial services of the republics with a view to "spying out the land," acquiring potential military air bases and locating air fleets in the Latin-American land mass which would serve as a nucleus for fighting squadrons, if, as, and when needed.

8. Latin America's armies were being indoctrinated with Fascist ideas through German-Italian military-instruction missions to the republics and generous provision of "study facilities" for Latin-American army offices in the Fascist countries themselves.

9. Fascist secret services were organizing a vast espionage network to checkmate in advance such plans as the United States and the twenty republics might have for the defense of the hemisphere.

Following the Berlin-Moscow agreement and the outbreak of war, these efforts were thrown into confusion. With a few exceptions, governments from the Rio Grande to Patagonia had pointed to

Soviet Communism as the last word in religious defilement and social destructiveness. Hence, until the full import of the Hitler-Stalin alliance had been digested, practically all Fascist or Nazi activities went under a cloud.

Latin leaders got an uneasy feeling that the new German policy might mean the end in Europe of all the values and conventions which they regarded as the mainstays of civilized society. After Europe, what new crusades for barbarism might not be let loose upon weaker republics overseas? For the time being, the Germans looked almost as dangerous to the ruling groups in Rio de Janeiro and Buenos Aires as a shipload of Russian "agitators"; or as American Marines marching on Managua would look to a club of Nicaraguan esthetes.

So through the 1939–40 winter, harsh laws and regulations hurtled down on Fascist activists everywhere, closing their schools, prohibiting propaganda, disbanding working staffs as well as social clubs. A number of Fascist military missions were replaced by instructors from the United States; the German airlines virtually went out of business.

Yet from present indications it was more a case of throwing the Fascists for a loss than of permanently blocking them. The prestige that comes with sweeping victory has attracted to their cause not only previously indifferent members of German and Italian racial groups but also Latin-American politicians on the make. Nazi salesmen, confidently predicting total victory, are already promising early delivery of goods in tempting future barter deals.

It is a question if—in spite of the handicaps—the totalitarian elements are not stronger in Latin America after *Blitzkrieg* than they were at the height of their open activities. Thus it becomes immensely important how many potential followers there are and where they are settled in numbers sufficient to be dangerous.

☆   ☆   ☆

The count begins with the Germans.

Close to 200,000 Germans have emigrated to Brazil in a little more than a century. Descendants who are more or less conscious of their German heritage are estimated at fully a million. There are probably close to 200,000 Germans of similar status in the Argentine and well above 50,000 in Chile. Through the Central American states, down the South American West Coast and around the southern Caribbean shore, Germans rate as powerful elements both in business and politics. Bolivia's dictator of recent mysterious suicide, Germán Busch, was the half-Bolivian son of a German immigrant.

Next to the Germans are other immigrant peoples who are much closer in temperament and blood to the populations of the twenty republics.

On the surface, this element is prodigious. Nearly a third of the population of Uruguay is of Italian extraction; perhaps between a fourth and a fifth of the population of the Argentine. Brazilians count their first- and second-generation Italian immigrant group at 2,000,000, and some experts insist that if all the Italian strains mixed with Brazilian blood were included the figure would run above 3,000,000.

If the Spaniards could be counted as universally susceptible to the Fascist propaganda, the figures would rise toward bankers' mathematics. All of the republics, including even Portuguese-speaking Brazil, have received a steady stream of Spanish immigration since the Wars of Liberation. Indeed, it was easier for Spaniards to come to the republics after independence was established than it was in the days of tight royal control over the subjects' movements when Latin America was colonial. So a population hardly less great than that of contemporary Spain itself has flowed overseas to the New World in the past dozen decades. Argentina owes her modern growth as much probably to Spanish immigration as to natural increase. Hundreds of thousands of Spaniards have come to Cuba since the war of 1898.

But this is not saying that an imposing majority of the Spaniards would be in the Hitler bag even in the most favorable circumstances. An overwhelming number of General Franco's nominal "nationals" have merged completely with the general population in the overseas republics and drifted out of range of Burgos' political appeal. Only the young men who have come over late enough to have seen the late civil war on the way are directly responsive to its issues; and many, if not the majority, of these are on the anti-Franco side.

The Italians merge hardly less rapidly. "In one year," a Brazilian newspaper editor, from a city where the Italian population is large, assured me, "a smart Italian boy is speaking fluent Portuguese with only a trace of accent. In two years he has changed his name to its Portuguese equivalent. The third year he marries a Brazilian girl. Often their children are only vaguely conscious that they have anything but direct Brazilian ancestry."

This represents, perhaps, a slight patriotic exaggeration of the assimilative process, but it conveys the truth that, without racial and religious barriers, and with a practically interchangeable language to assist them, Italians lose their national identity in a Latin-American environment simply through the normal play of its social forces. Furthermore, comparatively few of Latin America's Italians are Fascist in their convictions. The bulk of the immigration arrived between the 1870s and the first World War, when Italy was in a relatively liberal phase, politically speaking, and before the Fascist march on Rome was dreamed of. Actually, Italian skilled workmen, with some assistance from Italian farm laborers, have come close to being the backbone of labor and leftist movements in Uruguay and the Argentine.

Only in the top economic ranks of the Italian "colonies" are there groups which maintain close cultural and business relations with Italy. Many of their members find it expedient, or consider that it adds to their social prestige, to cultivate a constant and direct personal relationship with the Mussolini regime and do real spadework for the Fascist party. But counting even all the confidential employees and social hangers-on, and adding professional "patrioteers" created by the war, it is doubtful if more than 300,000 Italians in Latin America do much serious gospel spreading.

The German element, on the other hand, has been immensely active. Because of racial barriers, they have merged less completely with the native populations. Comparatively few of them belong to the laboring classes—except where they work for

German employers. The majority are merchants, planters or industrialists (or their employees) who maintain more or less direct business connections with Germany. Through these connections they can be reached by Nazi agents and the German consuls; and the consuls and agents, since the Third Reich arrived, have worked with a vengeance. By threats of boycotts, shutting off of commercial shipments, or retaliations on relatives in Germany, German "colonies" practically everywhere have been bludgeoned into giving noisy lip service to the Hitler regime, ostracizing Jews and organizing themselves to carry out the Führer's orders in furthering Germany's Latin-American programs. Individual liberal Germans found that to stand out against the stream requires great—sometimes dangerous—sacrifices, while the less conscientious and the indifferent have been whipped up into enthusiasm for the "cause" by the constant Third Reich victory propaganda and the persistent adroit arguments that their practical interests will be improved through realizing the Führer's objectives.

Despite the four generations of immigration which have helped to blend the Germans into the local racial scenery, and the fact that many oppressed into the lip service and shadow-boxing performances of the Nazis would no doubt still welcome a chance to be free of restrictions on social and business conduct, a sizable group of German-extracted citizens have been unreservedly corralled by Herr Hitler's Latin-American drill sergeants. Moreover the war, by strengthening the Fatherland's hold on old immigrant families has also tightened the Nazi control strings around the minds of still others who might otherwise remain indifferent to the pressure.

Latin America's 300,000-odd Japanese—in contrast with the Western members of the working "axis"—are, in the practical life of the republics, political ciphers. Their immigration is highly restricted, or prohibited, and as a rule they are ineligible to citizenship. Their trade is limited by discriminating tariffs in a number of countries. Their investments, except for land and fishing rights in a few strategic areas, are negligible. Although their diplomatic activities in favor of Fascism have been considerable, their usefulness to penetration efforts consists chiefly in espionage services—and the chance that some of the Japanese settlements might usefully be organized to attempt serious military operations, with Japan on the Hitler side in a war of two oceans.

☆   ☆   ☆

The gains in potential force, however, should not be taken as proof that totalitarian missionaries in Latin America are scheduled from now on for easy sailing. Even in the prewar stage, when their activities had a free field, they were constantly encountering subtle difficulties.

For half a dozen years prior to September 1939, for instance, Latin America's presses rolled forth their daily tonnage of praise for the Fascist regimes and the Fascist interpretations of world happenings, it is true. Nightly Latin America's radios blared forth more of the same. But the Latin-American public is, in some respects, even more cynical than the United States public about what it hears over the air and reads in its newspapers. Some fairly expensive dictators have taught it to be. So when someone is extravagantly praised or events are excessively interpreted, it is likely to wonder casually what the profit motive may be, and turn the page to the sporting section or the dial to the comedy programs. This sort of thing happens to much of the Fascist propaganda even in its victory celebrations.

Neither did "managed" Fascist trade with Latin America turn out to be a perfect bond of beautiful friendship with the republics. At first the proposals of the Germans, that the Reich's immense output of mechanical and luxury gadgetry would be available for payment in kind in tropical products without embarrassing suggestions of gold in the transaction, seemed the answer to the starving maiden's prayer. But various practical developments shortly made it clear that "barter systems" in international economics held quite as many causes for dissension in their exchange convolutions as some more strictly orthodox forms of trading.

The blocked German Aski-marks, through which the "mere bookkeeping" of the transactions was supposed to be conducted, developed unprofitable sinking phases, for example, as the markets of certain republics were overloaded with German gadgets. The Germans infuriated a number of governments by dumping stocks of coffee, cotton, sugar and other prime Latin-American commodities on world markets at ruinous prices. While they painfully shell-shocked the Latin-American price structure by these operations, the Nazis got from the final purchasers, in return for these dumping services, the dollars which Latin America would far rather have than gluts of German typewriters.

Brazil, as a result of this major grievance, cut off cotton trade for a while altogether with Germany in 1938, and resumed it in a curtailed form only after the stiffest of diplomatic bickers. Other countries were equally annoyed from time to time without feeling that they could permit themselves the luxury of diplomatic swear words.

Finally, as Germany throughout 1939 concentrated her industrial activity more and more on war-munitions output, her barter-trade collaborators in Latin America found it increasingly difficult to get deliveries on German goods at all. The war's outbreak, consequently, left them with barrels of Aski-marks, which were unnegotiable elsewhere and which suddenly became, in practice, unnegotiable even in Germany.

Worst of all, German trade lines, whether in Aski-marks, for cash or by normal exchange methods, snapped absolutely. The very distress of half a dozen or more republics at the stoppage— and the shortages produced by it—helped to bring them in line for sinisterly "democratic" old Uncle Sam's programs at the September 1939 conference in Panama.

On the other hand, none of these difficulties, even the war difficulties, is conclusive. Republics grumbled through ten months of the year at the Aski-marks' deficiencies, but when their crops came in and the usual obstacles presented themselves to floating the surplus on world markets through normal foreign-exchange transactions, the Aski-marks would again appear as a godsend. So the war found Nazi trade in most of the republics still gaining. If

Germany can once more return her production schedule to a peacetime basis, her chances of nudging the United States in its dominating position in Latin-American markets will be for the time being perilous if not decisive.

☆   ☆   ☆

In the line of direct political intrigue efforts the Fascist program began receiving a series of body blows long before the war. The organizations and practically all the open operations of the totalitarian pressure groups—including foreign-language schools for their children—were outlawed in Chile, Brazil and the Argentine during 1938. In a number of the smaller republics individual Germans were quietly deported for undue political activity with a minimum of publicity, and the process still goes on.

Side by side with admiration for totalitarian military success and a yearning to share in the commercial profits of totalitarian Weltmacht when established, most governing Latin groups felt a rising queasiness at the presence of such "dynamic" foreign forces in their somewhat languid patios. Beginning with Munich, the fates of so many of the weaker European nations which have permitted such penetration have hardly reassured them.

Not all of the counter-devices against Nazi intrigues are so easy to analyze, but the facts are generally clear that the Latin-American governments prefer to stand no nonsense. There was much excitement in the Argentine in the winter and spring of 1939, for instance, over an alleged German plot to seize Patagonia, ostensibly revealed in the correspondence of Nazi party members.

Government investigators, after laborious sifting of the evidence, eventually concluded that the documents may have been forged. Explanations were made to the German authorities; and the original informant spent a long time in jail awaiting trial for his inaccuracies. Conceivably, he may have played a rather clumsy *agent provocateur's* part in the proceedings. In any case it was significant that powerful interests in Argentina were sufficiently alarmed about the Nazi menace to put an *agent provocateur* to work on the intriguers. That the tightly conservative Argentine government should have felt that such drastic investigation of not too responsible charges was necessary is even more significant of Latin-American prewar suspicions of Fascist activities.

The case of Brazil offers a still more pointed illustration. Much adroit Italian organizing effort and hundreds of thousands of dollars of German money went into the Brazilian Integralista Fascist movement. When President Vargas effected his November 1937 coup and proposed a corporative constitution for the republic, the European Fascist capitals were jubilant. Brazil, their propaganda bureaus confidently predicted, would join the Anti-Comintern axis—it was very much alive then!—immediately, and from Brazil as an organizing focus Fascism would spread throughout Latin America.

There is some highly interesting internal evidence—deposited for future historians in certain archives—that Dictator Vargas did toy briefly with the idea of nominally joining the Axis. From his viewpoint on Brazilian domestic balances it would have been slick practical politics. He had just seized a kind of "totalitarian" control of the state with the support of the Integralistas, but he had no intention of employing any of their wordy and would-be domineering leaders very prominently in his government. So joining the Axis would be a sop to their disappointment. The gesture, as Vargas saw it, would flatter a powerful local faction a good deal as North American presidents titillate special groups on the home front from time to time by joining curious lodge brotherhoods. He and the Axis were both "against" Communism for the moment; so, since it was convenient, why not sign the roll call?

Largely, however, by strenuous reminders from his Washington ambassador, Oswaldo Aranha, as to what might happen to his good will in the United States and to his American coffee market, General Vargas was talked out of his jaunty maneuver. And then, according to the good old rule of Latin-American politics that when you have let down a friend, it is advisable to liquidate him as an enemy, things began to happen.

In December 1937 an executive decree disbanded the Integralistas, and after an extremist faction tried to overthrow the President in a palace-guard "putsch" on May 11, the government went as far as it dared toward charging directly that the German Embassy incited it. Releases were distributed through the Brazilian censors to foreign press correspondents announcing—without official "authorization," however—that the Germans were responsible for the "putsch." One Dr Von Kossel, who as "cultural attaché" of the embassy was in charge of Nazi activities within the republic, was asked to submit to a grilling from the national police on what he was alleged to know of the conspiracy. When the German ambassador, Karl Ritter, protested furiously against the treatment of Von Kossel, a quarrel was begun which finally led to his dismissal by the Brazilian government as *persona non grata*. All German nationalist activities in Brazil meanwhile had been outlawed, and even the four-generation-old German colonies in the southern states of Santa Catharina and Rio Grande do Sul lost their German-language schools.

Certain of General Vargas' seemingly pro-Fascist declarations after the defeat of France can still, not too unwisely, be read in the light of this record.

On the other hand, considering Fascism as a world movement, apart from the intimations of its Moscow ties, certain Fascist types of religious agitation against liberal and leftist governments continued to run powerfully after the war declarations, if not in a rising tide. In Mexico the domestic Fascist movement two years ago was composed of a handful of "Gold Shirt" eccentrics—mainly operating from the United States. By mid-1939, with the devotedly Catholic groups flocking to its corner, with the big landowners and the expropriation-fearing interests contributing to its war chest, and with the services of Nazi-trained propagandists to draw on, it appeared to be gathering headway as the most dangerous opposition to the Cárdenas regime. It still carries with it the most serious threat of revolutionary trouble which Mexico has faced in a decade.

In Chile the conservative opposition to the Aguirre Cerda government continues to make increasing efforts to persuade devout religionists that the "popular front" authorities—in league with the "godless" Moscow Comintern!—are plotting the expropriation of church property and the same suppression of religious activities that has occurred in Mexico. More recently they have circulated by hemisphere-wide whisper campaigns the legend that the "Holy War" against Aguirre Cerda is due in January 1941.

In Colombia, the more passionately conservative and pro-Catholic newspapers issued a steady stream of lurid warnings throughout 1938 and 1939 that the separation of Church and State accomplished by the recent Alfonso López administration must inevitably lead to the spread of "Communistic atheism" among the masses and condemn the republic to a civil war over religious issues as destructive as Spain's.

The victory of the Franco revolution enormously increased the strength of these forces. Many of the young men of well-to-do families in the universities felt that by joining the local "Falangist" organizations, parading the streets on holidays and beating up their less orthodox fellow students, they were acquiring the swank of an aristocracy defending its ancient privileges; showing their colors for religion and morality and associating themselves with the prestige of the Spanish victors. The effect, indeed, on collegiate circles was a good deal what might have been expected on "fraternity row" of the American campus if the Cromwellian wars were raging in England and socialite groups were being adroitly propagandized to take their stand for King Charles and the social security of really nice families.

All along the Latin-American trail, in result, the traveler from the United States is still challenged as to why American sentiment during the Spanish War was apparently pro-Loyalist. Indeed, it is advisable to devise a stock answer for it. Mine was that United States opinion didn't like the company General Franco kept.

"Neither do we," my Latin-American hosts almost invariably admitted. "But when its religion is in danger," they would go on, "a nation cannot always afford to be very selective about its allies."

Occasionally, when the atmosphere was favorable, I would go somewhat deeper into these matters. "We feel in the United States," I would say, "that when religion is strictly separated from the government and a few basic economic and political injustices have been corrected, the churches are in rather less danger than they are in some other countries."

Thereupon, almost without exception, I was treated to a flood of amazing dialectic. "But the conditions are not the same at all," the Latins would argue. "In the United States your people have the choice of many religions. In Spain and in our republics they have, in reality, only one choice—between Catholicism and atheism.

"The Protestant movement has no appeal to our peoples, and no standing. And the leftist leadership has no choice but to be atheistic. In order to get what it wants, it must incite our masses to reject the authority of the Church, and in order to drive simple people into rejecting the Church, it must first convert them to atheism.

"This has nothing to do," they would add, "with the fact that many of the aims of the leftists are excellent. The difficulty is that their movement, in order to reform a few very serious economic and political abuses, would destroy the only basis of social morals that we have. Is it strange, then, that a good many of us would be willing to accept help from any source where it is available before we would permit this destruction to happen?

"The legitimate reforms can be initiated in due season with the Church's aid and through the Church's Christianity. But giving control to the leftists means condemning our republics to long periods of bloodshed and godless anarchy, and we dare not risk it."

One hears this line of logic advanced too often in Latin America to dismiss it as the mere statement of an extremist viewpoint. Editors of successful newspapers use it—and in republics as strongly rooted in the liberal tradition as Colombia. Politicians with powerful followings use it. So do university professors with wide influence among the intellectuals; and moneyed men with the cash to back up their convictions with subsidies to rightist direct-action groups.

Yet precisely in proportion as these local brands of Fascism and pseudo-Fascism are religious in their prime motivations, they are alienated from the Nazi philosophy by its anti-religious overtones.

By its "national socialism," insofar as that term applies to the general leveling of classes and the economic subordination to the state, they are even driven toward the protecting aegis of the otherwise "godless"—in the sense of lacking a state religious establishment—democracy of the North.

Whether the local Fascist movements will go on in the ways they have started, or modify their appeals in the direction of democratic methods, depends, no doubt, on the war's final outcome, and who wins the Peace Conference.

☆   ☆   ☆

The remaining phases of Fascist activity can be dismissed somewhat more briefly. They are important, but not, for a program of conquest in the Western Hemisphere, crucial.

Unquestionably, the Fascist nations are kept fully informed as to the military secrets of the twenty republics through their widespread espionage service. Yet it is doubtful if this information is of much realistic value. If Herr Hitler's program aimed merely at military conquest and only the defensive forces of the republics were present to oppose them, the offensive strength of the Third Reich alone is so vastly superior that precise information could be largely dispensed with. As it is, the vital forces of hemisphere defense will have to be supplied by the United States. Hence the burden of the Fascist espionage problem consists in getting information on Washington's war plans.

Unquestionably, too, for what it was worth, the Germans entered the war with South America blanketed with their airlines. But so was it also blanketed by the Pan American Airways system, and down as far as Panama, American control of the potential air bases was—and still is—overwhelming. And with the war, the German transatlantic services were inevitably shut down, while, either through lack of subsidies or the recall of pilots home for military services, or Latin government opposition to civilian aviation by belligerents, the Nazi overland lines also folded. It left United States aviation not merely the outstanding factor in Latin America but the predominant factor. The danger here lies in how completely Herr Hitler will attempt to stock his South American airlines and bases with potential fighting planes when the war is over.

More specifically resultful has been the practice of penetration by Fascist military missions and the "student officer" hospitalities extended to promising Latin-American staff officers in the Fascist countries themselves. Deficiencies, to be sure, have cropped up in this method, for the authoritarian mannerisms of certain missions have not always proved charming to the more easygoing Latin-American military circles. Neither are young officers returned from their tours of foreign study always received as oracles of wisdom by superiors who did not happen to be invited.

The "student officer" system has achieved one result, however, which in its concrete potentialities makes up, to a degree, for its defects. By letting the Latin Americans see the immensity of the Nazi war machine and its efficiencies, the conviction was early spread abroad among professional military circles that the Fascist powers are unbeatable in world conflict; that in a military sense the democracies are finished. Thus most Latin-American armies are stocked with numerous powerfully placed personages who are certainly ready to jump as the cat jumps, the moment totalitarian conquest of Europe is completed.

The "indoctrinated" warriors, in other words, bring home a viewpoint more significant, perhaps, than their contributions to military science: the advice that Latin-American diplomatic cards should be played with a careful eye to the Fascist powers' good will; that, regardless of trade, political or sentimental ties with the democracies, the favor of "the winning side" should not lightly be tossed overboard.

☆　　　　☆　　　　☆

In a practical military and political sense, then, the Fascist menace of the immediate moment in Latin America boils down to this:

The Nazis are winning the war. If their winnings include the British Navy, Latin America, below the Caribbean, certainly, will lie open to limitless Fascist exploitation. If, with or without the aid of their allies and satellites, they choose to bring the war across the Atlantic, our present military strength might not suffice to prevent South America's military conquest. Having caught his flock of Gargantuan rabbits in Europe, Mr Hitler is in an improved strategic situation to catch others beyond his sunsets.

Yet it is questionable if Latin-American statesmen are as concerned over these perils as are the leaders at Washington. Despite enormously increased striking power, enormous physical obstacles still bar a Fascist invasion of the Western continents. And so long as the danger is not physically imminent, Latin politicos may find in it certain conveniences. The more the uproar over the menace from West and East, in fact, the more these astute personages see gains for themselves and their countries to be won from the traditionally dangerous power on their own land mass.

What, they keep asking each other, if the totalitarian forces from east and west, so alarmingly represented as threatening the borders and political integrity of the republics, could be played off against the northern forces which already have gained control of the republics' major economic resources?

As the republics' first statesmen see it, no matter how huge their investments the democratic powers cannot afford to antagonize Latin America while a struggle for existence is going on. On the contrary, up to the last limits of reasonableness and a little beyond, the democratic nations would be inclined to grant the Latin-American states whatever concessions they ask.

In fact, the mild partiality which many of these calculating gentlemen may have felt for the Fascist world movement as long as Herr Hitler let it remain a world movement, might teach the United States something.

Can the Fascist challenge be utilized, then, to free the republics from the yoke of "semi-colonialism"? Can the Axis menace be judiciously employed to remove the menace in the north?

Thus, provided they do not involve *Blitzkrieg* tomorrow morning, menaces east and west tend to be regarded by Latin-

American statesmen as convenient counters in an agreeable stratagem.

But to understand why they are welcomed as conveniences it is
necessary to look somewhat specifically into the viewpoint of the
twenty republics concerning the United States.

CHAPTER XVI

Menace North

LATIN AMERICA'S PRESENT ATTITUDE toward the United States has grown up since the war to "free" Cuba. We did not "free" it any too impressively.

We kept the island for nearly four years under a provisional governor who worked hard reforming its institutions and improving its sanitation while we debated its future. Finally, on the engaging principle that we were, in a sense, the new republic's sponsors in diplomatic baptism, and therefore would suffer acute embarrassments from its disorderly conduct and could be held responsible for its misdeeds, we turned it loose at the end of a rather short apron string.

We recognized Cuba's "independence" after requiring her to sign a treaty to the effect that the United States retained the right to intervene by military or political measures in situations of public disorder—this Magna Charta of guardianship having been framed in the United States Senate, where it was known as the Platt Amendment.

Meanwhile, under the military governorship, United States banks had been buying up control over Cuban finances, and other big business interests had been buying loan holds and actual proprietorship over Cuba's sugar and minor industries. Our degree of "ownership" when the island "acquired sovereignty" was actually larger in dollar valuations represented and quite as potent in its implications of economic mastery as any control which Spain had exercised during the island's later years as a colony.

[256]

And we did not "free" Puerto Rico or the Philippines at all.

When all this happened, the rest of the Latin-American republics were approximately seventy-five years old. For most of that three quarters of a century they had regarded the United States as a shadowy, if friendly, abstraction.

Very few of their citizens, and not a very large number of even their outstanding leaders, had ever been to the United States or known a North American. Years ago, at the very beginning of the period, the United States had issued some sort of a proclamation called the Monroe Doctrine, intimating, if not precisely promising, that it would defend the territorial integrity and the political independence of the Latin states against European aggressors, and in a mild way the republics were grateful for it.

True, the Monroe Doctrine had not always performed too efficaciously in the clinches. Great Britain had taken the Falkland Islands from Argentina in spite of it, and British Honduras from Guatemala. Nothing had been done to prevent Spain from reoccupying the Dominican Republic during the 1860s or from waging a number of mid-century wars against her former colonies which might have resulted in reannexations if Spain herself had not been defeated. And the United States through the Texas colonization and the war of 1846–47 had taken from Mexico more than half of the national territory.

Still, the Latin-American statesmen and publicists were not, as a class, inclined to nurse violent grudges over these lapses. The Falkland Islands and the British Honduras grievances were fairly minor squabbles. The Spanish wars had turned out satisfactorily, and produced a glorious crop of military heroes in several republics for exploitation in domestic politics.

After all, roars and sinister warnings from Washington had frightened the French out of Mexico after their brash experiment with empire and Maximilian of Hapsburg; and forced the British to back down on the high and mighty stand they had taken toward Venezuela in an 1895 boundary dispute.

The Monroe Doctrine had come through in the big emergencies. If it did not mean precisely what it seemed to say in all conceivable circumstances, the Latin-American statesmen were accustomed to dealing with—and *in*—fair professions which did not always live up to their face value. They protested indignantly from time to time, to keep records straight, but there was no passion of general hard feelings behind their cries of outrage.

As for our war with Mexico in the 1840s, that, too, was a faraway "boundary dispute" in the eyes of most of the republics. It did not concern their direct interests any more than the Alsace-Lorraine question—and was not half so dramatic. Also, the statesmen understood fully the temptations—and in some cases the practices—of imperialism. If sympathies lingered rather vaguely throughout Latin America on the Mexican side, the Texas-California conquest was seldom recalled—down to 1898—as a dangerous precedent.

Thus, few tangible developments occurred in inter-American relations to excite Latin statesmen one way or the other. Now and then there were disputes over the languid trade between northern and southern republics. Here and there United States sailors—or diplomats—offended against local codes of manners, and quarrels over injured heads or feelings had to be soothed by more or less colorful correspondence between foreign ministers. Revolutions with some frequently led to violations of the rights of rare North American expatriates in the republics or to expropriations of American shipping cargoes. But these items were seldom considered as crises except by the officials who handled them.

To be sure, for a decade or more before the Cuban war, a subtle but significant change was developing in this almost relationless relationship. American big business, with its job of conquering the frontiers and exploiting a continent more or less completed, began to look beyond United States borders for investments. North American capital began buying into the railways and the mines of Mexico; building power plants, setting up banking connections, establishing factories. Other North American money began buying its way into the Central American coffee and banana industries.

Yet Latin America as a whole scarcely knew that these processes were going on. The Mexican government—Porfirio Diaz was then president—registered no objections. On the contrary, rich foreigners' investments in Mexico's industrial development were just what the Diaz regime wanted. Diaz encouraged them, and his subordinates often went shopping for investors on Wall Street. The little Central American dictators thought of the banana and coffee entrepreneurs chiefly in terms of enlarged revenue sources.

To Buenos Aires, Rio de Janeiro and Valparaiso—weeks away by devious steamboat connections and having hardly more practical contacts with Mexico and the "banana republics" than with the Balkans—it was all very far off. To Lima and Caracas—to Bogotá, mountain-locked, three weeks away from the coast until the airplane age—it was not appreciably nearer. Neither Mexico nor the Central American states advertised the gringo penetration as a hardship. The leisurely young businessmen and exquisite politician-intellectuals in these remote fastnesses were considerably more interested in who was the best cancan dancer in Paris than in who owned Honduran banana groves.

Then the developments in Cuba and Puerto Rico occurred. The leisurely young men awakened to dangerous things that were going on; the tolerant indifference of the elder statesmen passed, and Latin America began to take stock of the United States as the great blond peril from the Northland. In the next thirty-five years their suspicions had plenty to feed on.

In 1903 the Theodore Roosevelt administration "took Panama." After the Canal was completed, the United States held a strategic control over the short routes of trade for the Pacific Coast republics and an advanced military outpost for quick potential action against all of the republics.

In 1906 the United States made its first "Platt Amendment" intervention in Cuba. The Marines and the regular army went in when revolutionary trouble threatened after the Cuban electorate and Congress had failed to choose a successor to the island's first president. For three years thereafter the republic was ruled by a Washington-appointed "provisional governor."

In 1909 the Marines were landed in Nicaragua to restore order during a revolution in which two Americans had been executed.

In 1912 they came again at the "request" of a subsequent government—to stay for thirteen years. And after being away not quite thirteen months, they were once more returned to cope with the Augusto Sandino revolution, to remain until deep in the 1930s. During part of this period the Marines were so much a part of the government organization that they directed the press censorships and supervised elections.

Between 1910 and 1930 Honduras suffered a number of brief Marine occupations, although no formal machinery of North American domination was set up.

In 1914 the United States Navy seized the Mexico port of Vera Cruz in retaliation for an "insult to the flag" delivered by the post comandante of Dictator Victoriano Huerta at Tampico. They held it for several months. In 1916 General John J. Pershing was sent hundreds of miles into Mexico with several thousand U.S. Regulars on the trail of the bandit-revolutionary, Francisco Villa, after he had attacked an American army border outpost at Columbus, New Mexico.

In 1915 the Marines "took over" Haiti. For more than fifteen years United States officers, with shadow presidents and congresses functioning in the background a good deal like Hindu maharajahs, administered the government. The real authority in the state was the general in charge of the Marine occupying forces, with the high-sounding title of "Ambassador and High Commissioner." The Haitians revolted against "Aryan" rule in 1918, and for two years the Marines saw warfare almost on the scale of the Filipino rebellion against annexation after the war of 1898. In Haiti the Marines controlled the press and political activities even more severely than in Nicaragua.

The Dominican Republic was 1916's victim. The Marines landed to quell a revolution and stayed eight years. During that time the regime was somewhat euphoniously entitled, "The Military Government of the United States in Santo Domingo." Editors were jailed by the American authorities and political critics exiled according to the best precedents of the Dominican Republic's home-grown dictators.

☆   ☆   ☆

Along with the occupations went certain other suggestive developments. All of the occupied republics as a matter of course accepted the services of financial advisers from the United States. In fact, this development spread beyond the occupation zone. Guatemala and El Salvador, on friendly advice from Washington, also found it advisable to acquire Yankee economic advisers. And while the labors of these technicians to straighten out the tangled budget and currency problems of the republics were generally honest and often prodigious, they inevitably assisted in increasing the fiscal dependence of the "serviced" governments on the United States. All of the states needed heavy loans to begin the "straightening out" process. The financial advisers steered the loans to the banking houses of New York.

The banking houses performed in character. Besides the basic government loans which they extended, they and the investment groups revolving around them went in heavily for credit and purchase operations where "the good old flag" was flying. The occupied republics, so their reasoning (and their prospectuses) ran, were "safe" for United States capital. The Marines' guns and bayonets would keep them safe. So there was more and still more of buying in of mines and coffee *fincas,* of sugar and banana and henequen plantations around the Caribbean littoral. Tidy little markets developed in various hitherto scorned brands of Caribbean republics' bonds.

Indeed, a kind of vicious circle developed. Originally, the Marines had gone into their various operations ostensibly to protect American lives from revolutionary desperadoes and to save the peoples of the Caribbean states from the horrors of public anarchy. But now that American interests had grown so enormously in the occupied republics, other plausible excuses for their presence could be cited. The Marines would have to stay indefinitely, if not forever, to protect honest and constructive investors in their property rights; to keep stabilized bond values permanently stabilized.

And this logic had further ramifications. Investors could not consider their properties safe, for example, if the republics did not pay their honest debts. So it became a subtle practice of the bank-

ing groups with wide Caribbean interests to encourage the somewhat easily persuaded nominal rulers of the republics to overload
themselves slightly with obligations. If the debts were not paid,
Marines would have to be kept on the job until perfect collection
services could be re-established.

Also, there was the question of civil order. Investments could
not be safe where there was the slightest prospect of revolutionary
disturbances. So, since there were always groups of exiles—some
of them Marine-exiled!—busily at work in the neighbor republics
plotting coups against the Yankee-supported regimes, it became
advantageous for the investment interests to maintain an efficient
espionage service among such chronic conspirators and to report
their machinations as horrid bedtime stories to Washington. Thus
the Marines, who had gone in to stop actual trouble, would have
to remain to head off potential trouble. And always on the
delirious fringes of Caribbean politics, potential troubles could
be sighted.

Back of all this logic, moreover, stood an imposing moral
rationalization. It was devised by Colonel Theodore Roosevelt and
his experts on foreign policies, and it concerned the Monroe
Doctrine. The Doctrine, the statesmen virtuously contended,
made us responsible for the political morals of the twenty republics. We had sworn to protect their territorial integrity and
their independence. If we forbade the European powers to violate
their territories and their political sovereignty when they ignored
their just debts or their revolutions endangered the lives and
property of European "nationals," we must "police" their fiscal
and political morals ourselves.

The Marine occupations, the provisional governments and the
tight financial controls over the republics were not, it thus appeared, designed merely to protect gringo investors. They were
necessary to save the republics from grave international dangers.
By taking over the administrations of their governments and
putting their natural resources in hock to United States capital,
we were really being extraordinarily tender and protective toward
their natural weaknesses.

During the Roosevelt and Taft administrations this charming

theory of Pan-American relationships was advertised by Washington's choicest spokesmen, including secretaries of state and presidents, with a naïve and noisy fulsomeness. And while the principle was verbally renounced under Woodrow Wilson and the
fulsomeness somewhat diminished when the guiding theory was
revived under Harding, Coolidge and Hoover, the practices continued. As Latin America saw it, the whole Caribbean area was
being reduced to a gringo political and economic colony, and the
"hypocritical" Monroe Doctrine was being used to justify it.

☆   ☆   ☆

In the course of a few years, in consequence, Latin America's
traditional friendly indifference toward the United States was
transformed into an attitude of passionate suspicion and poisonous
hatred.

The exiles from the Marine "dependencies" circulated through
the republics below Panama inciting governments to anti-
American policies, and private and public audiences to jitters,
with their horror tales of gringo atrocities. The poets, the writers,
the journalists, the intellectuals, whenever they turned their hands
to public questions, contributed to the literature of "Yanqui"
infamy.

The "Yanquis" were worse than the common or garden varieties
of open and dastardly enemies, ran the burden of these cries of
outrage. They came as friends and protectors—to steal away
weaker peoples' miserable birthrights. They came in the name of
democracy—to force free peoples under the yoke of cruel and alien
oppressions.

There was no estimating the eventual scope of their conquests
except to assume that it would ultimately have all-inclusive scope.
The gringos had the military might to seize the hemisphere down
to Cape Horn, and the Latin Americans recognized it. They had a
technique for conquest with a minimum of military effort—the
theory of "temporary occupation" for "protective" purposes—and
there were no practical means in the as yet unattacked republics
either for resisting it or guessing where it would end. So the

"rape" of Panama and the subsequent "rapes" of the other Marine-controlled republics were exploited in the Latin-American press and literature precisely as the successive 1938 and 1939 rapes of Czechoslovakia were treated in the press of the liberal democracies.

As North American capital began flowing into investments in the hitherto untouched South American republics after the Panama seizure, and especially when it began replacing European investments during the first World War, all these anxieties deepened. Were these titles to Venezuelan and Colombian oil properties, to Peruvian and Chilean mines, to Argentine and Brazilian branch factories to be read as announcements that the Marines would be along in due season?

"Remember," a Mexican friend once cautioned me, perhaps a little sententiously, "Nicaragua and Haiti and Cuba have given us reasons to believe that republics can be hanged with dollars."

Out of the suspicions and the anxieties grew a kind of Latin-American racial philosophy. Latin Americans of the nineteenth century had hardly been conscious enough of the United States to examine the differences between them. Now José Enrique Rodó in Uruguay wrote his graceful but poison-tipped little book, *Ariel,* asserting with almost a cultist's vehemence that the Latin and the North Americans were separated by the fundamental antagonisms of blood and spiritual inheritance. The form-loving temperament of the Latins, Rodó maintained, their quick emotional nature and passionate imagination proved that they belonged to a superior civilization. The materialism of the Northerners, the concentration on material values which gave them their vast technical competence, were the traits of a race of spiritually barbarous "Calibans."

Imitators danced to these self-titillating tunes in all the circles of Latin-American exquisites. Manuel Ugarte, the Argentine publicist, and Peru's Francisco García Calderón accompanied these metaphysical interpretations with devastating analyses of Washington's unholy aims in *Weltpolitik.* Rubén Darío, Nicaragua's, and Latin America's, greatest poet, wrote his blasting sonnet against Roosevelt. Distinguished novelists like Venezuela's Rufino

Blanco-Fombona made fiction the vehicle of passionate anti-gringo philippics.

Along with the intellectual outburst went a new technique in politics. Beating the Yanqui devil around the stump became the most profitable diversion of young men on the make for public notice, as well as of virtually all the established demagogues in the twenty republics. Frankly pro-United States leaders saw their careers endangered by whispers that they were in the pay of the gringo. Until the Panama grievance was allayed with an indemnity in 1923, competition in "anti-gringoism" was the prime issue between the parties in Colombia.

At the time of the 1914 World War strongly anti-American elements were in control of the governments in Chile and the Argentine. Anti-Americanism was the issue of the "outs" against the "ins" on every political front, and the "ins" had to prove their suspicion of Washington's policies by a grudging attitude even in the normal diplomatic courtesies.

The change in diplomatic orientations went, in fact, considerably beyond mere coolness. The Latin states in their foreign policies drew closer to Europe. Rodó and his followers were preaching with evangelical fervor that the republics' natural, spiritual and cultural kinships were with Europe—that the North Americans were as alien from the Latin-American scene as the Afghans or the Eskimos. Increasingly the republics offered their superior trade facilities and exploitations to Europe, confided their military and diplomatic secrets to European chancelleries. The game of playing off the remote—and seemingly less dangerous—European powers against the "Colossus of the North" had begun.

The advent of the first World War scarcely bettered matters. By high-pressure methods from Washington, war declarations against the Central powers were obtained from Cuba, Honduras, Guatemala, Panama, Haiti, Costa Rica and Nicaragua. Brazil, won by the example of the mother country, Portugal, declared war more definitely of her own accord.

But the high-pressure methods did not sit well in the remaining states. Mexico, raging from the recent Pershing expedition, geared its diplomatic policies as closely as it dared to German interests, and received draft dodgers and fleeing German espionage agents from the United States with applause. A proposal of the German Foreign Office, probably for propaganda rather than practical purposes, of an alliance with Mexico for the reconquest of California and Texas, while it caused a thrill of horror in the United States and was a crucial factor in bringing out President Wilson's war declaration, was hailed in President Carranza's intimate circle as a gesture of poetic justice. It could not be accepted, naturally, in view of Mexico's military weakness. But Mexico gave all the aid she was capable of to the German plans both before and after the United States' declaration, and forced the General Staff in Washington to maintain a maximum guard force along the border for the duration of the war.

In Central America, El Salvador was so infuriated at the war declarations wrung from the more dependent republics that her government adopted a virtually official pro-German policy. Washington, alarmed at the menace of a potential German saboteurs' nest so near the Panama Canal, retaliated by blockading the Salvadorean coast. Honduras, in spite of her nominal status as a belligerent, refused to enforce the laws curtailing German espionage activities and German trade rights.

At the other end of the Latin land mass, Hipólito Irigoyen, Argentina's able Radical president, calmly pocketed a warlike resolution of his Congress after official orders had been issued by the German Admiralty to sink "without trace" Argentine ships which were engaged in supply-carrying traffic for the Entente powers. Chile, rolling in the wealth produced by Allied orders from her nitrate fields and copper mines, nevertheless sulked in cold indifference to the Allies' pleas for active co-operation and political sympathies. After all, the gringos and the British were collecting the vast copper and nitrate dividends. Why should Chile waste emotions and effort on "sister democracies" who were already using her economic resources and paying themselves handsomely for it?

Colombia was of a more divided mind. The propaganda of the British and French appealed to her relatively liberal ruling classes, but the still rankling grudge over Panama dried up these emotional predilections. Whatever the issues in world events, no Colombian practical *politico* could expect to stay in office and indorse the gringo's side. So Colombia maintained cordial formal relations with the Central powers and was another pleasant haven for German agents. In Venezuela the gloomy tyrant, Gómez, extended even more enthusiastic hospitalities. A philosophically consistent despot, Gómez liked autocracies and made no bones about it.

☆   ☆   ☆

With the war and its aftermath, too, came another anxiety for the republics—the speeding up of the gringo economic invasion. German commerce with Latin America sank to zero from the moment the German merchant fleets disappeared from the seas in August 1914. British and French and Italian exports to the republics shrank year by year, despite their vast food and raw-materials orders, as the Allied nations concentrated their production efforts in the munitions industries. Investors in both the Allied and Central powers dumped on the world markets their Latin-American securities and to some extent their physical holdings in the republics to clear their fiscal portfolios for the war effort.

The gringos snapped up these opportunities. By 1915 they were masters in the Latin-American import field. With the republics' own war booms to feed it, the volume of their foreign trade rose toward staggering and unprecedented totals of more than three billions. The bonds and the industrial securities of the republics were transferred in billions from London, Berlin and Paris to New York.

When the United States itself entered the war in 1917, the gringo "scout" for munitions raw-material sources became a lively figure on the Latin-American landscapes; and when he dickered for mines, plantations and concessions, price was seldom the object. Nor in the postwar boom of the 1920s, when the great North American money masters were combing the world for investment openings, did his ministrations slacken.

In result, Latin America was—or seemed to be—overrun with

gringos. The sales managers and their subordinates swarmed in the capitals and the minor metropolises from Chihuahua to Punta Arenas. North American executive managers with their staffs moved into the mines, the factories and the mansions of the plantations and haciendas. Branch banks and credit agencies—and their personnel—bloomed in the larger cities as abundantly as orchids at the coming of the rainy season.

The effects were not universally happy. The gringo hordes were less prodigious than they seemed, but they made up for lack of numbers by conspicuousness, and by conduct which their Latin hosts found sometimes merely vaguely disturbing and at other times definitely offensive.

They were not quiet young men like the Germans who came out to take minor clerkships in the export-import houses and the industries at the prevailing local wages, and who submissively accommodated themselves to the local lesser-bourgeoisie living standards while working themselves up to positions of affluence. They were certainly not like the Italians who accepted the lot of the Latin-American day laborers and asked nothing better than to merge themselves in the local economic scene; nor like the British who obscured their economic overlordship by unostentatiously retiring to their estates as soon as business was over and pursuing their sports in studied privacy.

The young North Americans came with New York-scaled salaries, and with the obvious conviction, often more or less expressed publicly, that while confined for the good of their future business careers in primitive and remote surroundings, they proposed to live the life of Riley. And in the bars and clubs of the Latin cities, and the rounds of perpetual country-club and cocktail-party festivities which they maintained in the swanky apartment houses and the mansions they rented from the local first families, they flamboyantly led it. On hosts already worried over the question of who "owned" their republics, the effect of these constant revels of the "new *conquistadores*"—coupled, often, with more alcoholic intake than the temperate Latins approved of—was highly disturbing.

Moreover, the gringos were not *simpáticos*. Most of them spoke

Spanish with cheerful indifference to accent and syntax, and their wives' conversation was frequently limited to the few phrases and ideas necessary to assist sign language in their communications with the maids in the kitchens. Their group interests, too, left something to be desired in the way of international amenities.

Partly because of their weakness in Spanish, the cultural activities and the historical backgrounds of the new environments left them cold. Their spritely conversationalists, when they dealt with Latin-American subjects at all, preferred to discuss how amusing the local customs were, how stupid the servants, how inefficient were the local business methods, and how gaudy the statues. They appeared to value their Latin-American acquaintances on the score of their charm as golfing and drinking companions, the expediencies suggested by their business connections, and their ability to take "a little honest-to-God American kidding."

Along with these deficiencies went an irritatingly patronizing attitude—and most of the patronage was naïve. It appeared that the highest compliment the outlanders could pay the artistic taste of local aristocracies was to say, "Why, the new houses these people are building are just like American houses." The highest praise they could give a local magnate or statesman was to say, "He does business just like an American." When they wished to make a guest flush with pleasure, they would merrily announce to the assembled company, "You can say anything you please before Don Arturo. He gets how we feel about things down here just like a gringo."

Gentlemen who had direct financial interests in the good will of the gringo "colonies" often accepted these fondling comparisons blandly but were not always internally pleased. Frequently they brought back reports of the latest gringo "insults" to circles less personally concerned for the Pan-American brotherhood, and the legend of the peculiar offensiveness of the "new *conquistadores*" was by so much fostered. There may be an interesting corollary to this reaction in the fact that the building boom which came to a large number of Latin-American cities during the late 1920s and early 1930s was marked by a considerable rash of dwellings and apartments built on the latest German and Italian models. Latin

Americans possibly did not care to be complimented on more than the necessary minimum of imitations.

Nor were all the rifts between "invaders" and local populations produced by these relatively frivolous incompatibilities. There were—and still are—genuine jams over the vital issue of national customs.

The gringos carped at the exclusiveness of Latin-American family life—at the slow and formal processes by which "recognition" of worthy outsiders by ruling local social groups must be sought and obtained. "If they won't ask us after buying 'em drinks and playing golf with them and scratching their backs and being good fellows, the hell with 'em"—became a kind of dominant attitude in the "colonies."

The Latins, on their side, fretted with scandalized emotions at American social freedoms. American women—including ostensible *virgines intactae*—drove their cars alone along country roads and into the shopping districts, went on the streets at night unescorted, visited cocktail bars and even night clubs until shocking hours unchaperoned except by their young men friends; and sometimes, especially during the harum-scarum '20s, got noticeably squiffed in public places and on formal and even official occasions.

The young men of this race of barbarians insulted the daughters of the authentic local gentry by inviting them to unchaperoned dances and immoral dinner and theater engagements; or, if they bowed reluctantly to the duenna system, crudely presumed to monopolize the time of eligible debutantes—to the extent of pursuing them for weekly or semiweekly engagements—without summoning their parents south to begin negotiations for honorable marriage.

Could a race abandoned to such obvious erotic indiscretions be composed of anything but congenital harlots and seducers? The Latin-American conservative families accepted the worst interpretation—the gringos' lack of psychological adaptability on other points encouraged them—and closed their social lines the tighter.

Neither was the gringo's charity broadened by his own experiences. Young girls in the North American "colonies" who, after proper introduction, made the experiment of granting appealing young sprigs of the local best families the same privileges of unchaperoned companionship which they were accustomed to granting the boy friends back home, found, to their horror, that they had extended invitations to be treated as trollops. American elders replied with prejudices in kind.

"Our girls can't trust these fellows down here as far as you can spin a nickel," an irate American father in a Latin metropolis as big as Buffalo informed me. "They're twice as well mannered as our boys when they meet them at formal gatherings, but if a girl goes so far as to have a cup of tea with one of them without a chaperone, he assumes it's for all night. Then if she walks out on him she comes home with a flock of Latin-American pretty sayings ringing in her ears that would make ordinary conversation in one of our red-light districts sound prissy."

Even apart from the sexual plane, international relations were difficult. The representative of an important New York financial corporation in one of the larger tropical republics told me a solemn story to illustrate certain barriers.

"When I first came here," he related, "I had some negotiations that made it necessary for me to get next to the city politicians in the capital. So being young and foolish, I invited them up to my house for a party. . . . All that happened was that they smashed the furniture, drank up the last drop in my cellar, wrecked the piano, tried to rape the maids, and one of them committed a nuisance against the reception-room wall!"

I suggested to him that the furniture and the amenities were not invariably preserved when parties were given for small-time politicians in Hollywood.

"The hell with 'em," he exclaimed in tones of permanent outrage. "Down at the office I can be a good fellow for what there's in it. But not a single one of the God-damned breed, high or low, has been in my house since that incident. And I haven't been in theirs. And by God, you find out, when you've stayed in these countries long enough, that if you keep away from 'em socially, they'll respect you for it."

Business relations tend to be soured by kindred incompatibilities. There is, for instance, the constant state of fury most gringos are in on the subject of delayed—or broken—appointments.

It is not according to protocol in Latin-American manners for a gentleman of business or political eminence to say "No" when an appointment is requested. Consequently, in the office of a man of affairs, appointments may have been made for 3 P.M. on a given day to anywhere up to two hundred visitors. Yet after they have waited until the end of a long Latin business day, around 7:30, anywhere from half to three fourths of the group may be informed with exquisite courtesy that the great man is sorry, but will they please come back tomorrow. And this may go on for days.

Many of the gringos in the republics live in a state of constant passionate neurosis over these disrupted schedules. Occasionally, in outer offices, they blow up with violent anger. But protests as a rule merely arouse the ire of the sensitive Latin bigwig that his courtesy has been impugned. After all, has he not more than reasonably flattered this gringo's self-importance by inviting him to return tomorrow? Was not that far better manners than telling him curtly—as might happen in a New York banker's office—that the date books were full until next Tuesday?

Or consider the more rancorous item of bill collection. As far as is emotionally possible, business arrangements in Latin America are supposed to be on a basis of personal friendship. So when Señor Sotomayer finds it inconvenient to keep up installment payments on his latest motorcar, he is likely to look up his friend, the American automobile agent who sold it to him, in his favorite club bar or at the President's reception, and murmur affectionately that he would appreciate being given a moratorium until next August.

Gringos are indignant—and sometimes express themselves torridly—when matters of this delicate character are brought up in places where arguments about money are outlawed and the law's collection agencies cannot be invoked. But Señor Sotomayer believes with hurt resentment that his North American creditor should feel conscious of a debt of gratitude because he has approached him as a social equal rather than as a mere bill collector.

There is humor in many of these discords, of course, although the gay aspect is not always apparent to the Latin Americans. And in the final reaction of the "Americans on the ground" to all discords, there is definitely, from the Latin-American viewpoint, no humor at all.

Nowhere in one's Latin-American travels is it seemingly possible to visit a sizable American colony without being instructed in an apparently general theory: Be decent to these people and they'll think you are afraid of them. Coddle them, and they'll insult you. Be generous to them, and they'll gyp you out of all you have. The only language they understand is *force*.

☆   ☆   ☆

To gauge the "menace from the North," then, as it appears to the Latin Americans, we must first strip and inspect ourselves as the Latin Americans see us.

The results of such intimate stock-taking are not altogether pretty. To "the neighbors" the conquest of Latin America by the nations of Europe has been, until recently, merely an implausible horror story. Conquest by the United States, on the other hand, is a familiar and realistic danger. Even after cordial agreement on concrete mutual interests, it is a danger they dismiss reluctantly and return to with alacrity on the least provocation.

In fact, as many Latin Americans see the realities, throughout the Caribbean area the economic phase of the conquest has been substantially completed. Below Panama it has been proceeding more rapidly than any other form of alien seizure.

The present hemisphere crisis may logically be expected to deepen the poisons of suspicion in the international atmosphere. For the United States has a long history of political, economic and military aggressions in its relations with the twenty republics, and an elaborate set of rationalizations for more of the same. The first World War immensely speeded up the conquering processes. To many Latin-American minds, President Roosevelt's leasing of British naval bases in the Caribbean has suggested that the second World War is not likely to slow it down.

If such conquest should come, it would be, to Latin judgment, a peculiarly disagreeable if not the most detestable of all possible conquests. For of all foreign peoples with which the Latin American has had experience, the gringo, as literal street neighbor, is the most openly contemptuous of his national pride and personal dignity, the most scornful of his cultural and moral values.

It is a simple matter, no doubt, to rebut these spectacular fears and convictions.

We can urge, for instance, that if the United States had been seriously bent on military and political conquest, American fleets and armies could have taken any of or all the republics in any decade since the Civil War. We can ask, with considerable pertinence, what would have been the fate of the republics if they had had Germany, or Great Britain, or France, or any of the imperialistic countries of Europe, instead of Washington, for a neighbor.

Latin America only knows that it has so far met none of the processes of military or political conquest from the European powers, but that the treatment the nearer republics have received from the United States offers occasion for permanent suspicion and vigilance.

We can plead that American finance's "colonial empire" in the republics, in so far as it exists, has brought about a development of the countries' economic resources otherwise impossible; that its somewhat spectacular "paper" earnings should be balanced, in any true accounting picture, by the billions of losses it has sustained in defaulted bonds and investments wrecked by political turmoils.

Latin America is only conscious that when its rare periods of prosperity arrive, most of the profits flow away into the foreign bank balances of the owners of the republics' resources.

We can point to the Good Neighbor policy. But national behavior in crucial periods such as this is seldom noticeably influenced by neighborly emotions. Even in peacetime, Latin America had frank doubts of the policy's permanence. "Why should it outlast Roosevelt?" they ask with pardonable cynicism, when the business elements which demand "force" as the solvent of the "colonial empire's" problems are precisely the elements which control the Republican party?

An "eternal Good Neighbor policy," the Bogotá liberal newspaper, *La Razón,* warned its readers recently, "is a delusion . . . The Republican still dreams of pursuing imperialistic policies . . . and would favor the end of the Rooseveltian program of treating our nations as equals."

We are hardly dealing here with points of dispute which can be answered with logical arguments or the rules of polite debating societies. We are dealing with what, in practice, amount to folk beliefs.

The deep-rooted folk belief of Latin America has been that the menace at the North is more constantly perilous than any menace from East or West. It would take a tremendous upheaval to dislodge this opinion. Meanwhile, from this psychological basis, fortified by all the prejudices and traditions and folkways of their environment, the republics continue the business of watching their ramparts.

CHAPTER XVII

Ramparts *They* Watch

For NATIONS ADRIFT in a world of forces immeasurably stronger than theirs, and definitely needing the help of some of the more dangerous of these forces to develop their own self-protective mechanism, the watching of ramparts demands an acute sense of power balances rather than military-defense paraphernalia.

Mr Chamberlain and M. Daladier might have met their problem before September, 1939—painfully and expensively but with fair practical results—simply by building their ramparts somewhat higher than Herr Hitler's. In the event of a Fascist conquest of Europe and Asia, the United States—at enormous sacrifice to the general welfare and provided it got started early enough—conceivably could assemble fleets and armies and air forces sufficient to defend the Western Hemisphere. Fundamentally, in such cases, it is a question of how much cash and material resources the beleaguered societies care to spend on armaments.

With their present munitions-manufacturing facilities, however, by no pooling of their credits and revenues, man power or raw materials, could the twenty republics put themselves in a state to stand off an attack by any one of the world's major powers. Individually, assuming that the problem of troop transport from abroad could be solved, it is doubtful if more than the three or four largest republics could successfully defend themselves from invasion by one of the more militant and better-organized prewar Balkan nations.

The military statistics, while hardly decisive as to ultimate defense possibilities, suggest the basic factors in the problem with reasonable accuracy. The total of all standing armies and nominal trained reserves in the twenty republics is probably under 2,000,000 —less even than Poland's before *Blitzkrieg*.

The normal defense quotas for the chief Balkan powers ran until recently close to a million of reserves and regulars combined. The largest standing army in Latin America is Brazil's—now estimated at 100,000. Even counting all her reserves and "state" armies as trained and equipped for field service, no Brazilian mobilization under present conditions could bring together as many as half a million men under arms.

The Argentine reserves are officially calculated at 500,000, but to leaven this lump of relatively considerable military inexperience there is a standing army of only 40,000. Chile, on paper again, could put slightly better than 200,000 men in the field, and Mexico somewhat over 300,000. In the rest of Latin America there is not a standing army above 11,000 or a nominal reserve corps above 50,000. None of the Central American regular establishments exceeds 5,000.

The air fleets of the republics are topped by Argentina's with 250 war planes, followed by Brazil with 200. The navies make a distinctly less favorable showing. Argentina, Brazil and Chile have eight cruisers among them, and thirty-six destroyers. There are five battleships divided among the ABC powers, but the youngest of these—Chile's—is twenty-seven years old. The two apiece of Brazil and the Argentine were built more than thirty years ago.

Worse still, there are no great accumulations of guns or supplies, no stocks of artillery or motorized apparatus sufficient for war under modern technical conditions—and only the most elementary facilities for arms manufacturing. Few republics could successfully attempt to arm their nominal reserve forces even with nineteenth-century weapons. For mass defensive operations it is doubtful if any republic, with the possible exception of the Argentine, possesses the necessary railways and road communications to supply large armies with food.

If forced to meet mechanized warfare on the modern grand scale, even the largest of the republics would have to figure on importing nearly all its technical fighting equipment, its ammunition and —again except in the case of Argentina—a considerable share of its troop rations. If the United States is considered as the attacking force in any of the Latin-American general-staff problems, the danger has to be faced that—like weak European states in their enforced dependence on Germany—the attacked nation would have to accumulate arms for the conflict chiefly through the generosity (or profit motive) of its enemy.

Quite obviously, then, Latin America must guard its ramparts with diplomacy—and sometimes a little duplicity—rather than with machine-gun nests; and sometimes admit potential enemies within the ramparts because it cannot prepare even its defenses without their aid.

☆   ☆   ☆

The situation gives to many Latin-American government policies and diplomatic wiles a curiously feminine quality. Women, under various social dispensations, have protected themselves in a world of boisterous forces—inclined toward ravishment—by capricious emotional conduct, by playing on the jealousies of rival suitors, by making a fetish of virginal innocence, or by an appealing public spectacle of their pity for themselves. So, it appears, may republics.

Mexico, for example, schooled by her losses in the war of 1847, wears a kind of territorial chastity belt in the form of a constitutional provision prohibiting her presidents from disposing to a foreign government, by sale or cession, of a single foot of the national soil. Even though a foreign power seized Vera Cruz and held it indefinitely, no Mexican president could officially recognize the changed status without being technically subject to impeachment.

Actually, the restriction has certain practical disadvantages. For two generations a dispute has existed over the ownership of a tract of land near the banks of the Rio Grande in El Paso, Texas, known as the Chamizal zone. The title hinges on the question of whether the river, some seventy-five years ago, changed its course by gradual erosion or by an instantaneous shift of the stream bed known as evulsion. So far no arbitration board has been able to answer this question to the satisfaction of both governments. Meanwhile, for at least a generation it has been known to the Mexican government that the United States Treasury would be willing to pay rather more than the negotiable value of the tract for an outright treaty cession that would clear all titles. But no Mexican president could constitutionally "sell" the Chamizal without risking prosecution for "high crimes and misdemeanors."

Along with this somewhat exaggerated consciousness of the physical territorial proprieties goes a passionate sense of national dignity. Latin-American governments, on the average, are easier to "insult" officially than any other powers in the world, hardly excluding Herr Hitler. Indeed, prior to the economic expansion era practically all of our difficulties with "the neighbors" have been in one way or another complicated by diplomatic sensitiveness.

A United States minister to Brazil in the 1840s, for instance, once spoke his mind to certain Rio de Janeiro gendarmes who had beaten up a crew of U.S. "gobs," seized by the local authorities while they were being taken to ship by their own navy police after a drunken shore brawl. In return he was informed that the United States had insulted Brazilian sovereignty. Although the minister himself was anxious to make personal explanations to the Foreign Office and the sovereign, the Emperor Dom Pedro II refused to have any diplomatic communication whatever with the United States until his demand had been met with an official apology from the State Department in Washington. After several months this particular impasse was relieved by the appointment of another minister. But there have been plenty of similar impasses.

Yet, diplomatic dignity notwithstanding, the traveler—or diplomat—from one of the stronger nations seldom gets far in Latin America without being reminded by his official mentors of the allowances he should make for local deficiencies on the score of the republics' poverty.

"We are a poor country, señor," it was said to me (often several times daily) in a kind of chorus of funereal meekness. "We cannot always meet our obligations promptly, or keep perfect order in our houses, as a rich country like the United States does. We cannot teach our ignorant classes to respect the rights of others like nations which can afford to educate the entire population. You must judge us, señor, by our strength, not by yours."

Poverty, indeed, is so often used to excuse all abuses on the Latin-American scene, from debt defaults to revolutions, from banditry to petty pilfering by servants, that one is sometimes driven to wonder if several of the republics would not be seriously embarrassed without it.

Nor can all the difficulties of foreigners be laid to the strictly ingenious reactions of the desperately poor to their hardships. In Mexico City a thriving practice has developed of tapping the wires of the American-owned electric-light company for household power. A group of competent technicians make a prosperous living by selling the gadgets and making the installations by which these pint-sized "expropriations" are accomplished. "Mexicans are poor and American power companies are rich," my Mexican friends defend the system. "Think of the profits they have taken out of the country in the past, and are still taking. Surely they can afford to be generous with people who would pay them if they could." It is an interesting commentary on the practice that the Mexican law makes it practically impossible to prosecute for theft in cases of the "borrowing" of power from private utilities corporations.

Or, to consider a somewhat more emotional phase of the use of ultrafeminine technique one day, in 1938, when I was in Rio de Janeiro, a distinguished Brazilian diplomat invited me to his office. What, he demanded to know when the coffee-sipping civilities were over, did the United States mean by sending a military aviation mission to the Argentine?

I happened to know from my conversations in half a dozen Latin-American capitals that United States diplomats and the American "colonies" generally regarded the invitation to the mission as a symptom of improving relations with the somewhat standoffish Argentines. They were pleased with it as a small diplomatic success which might help to increase our prestige in all the republics. I said something of the sort.

But my Brazilian friend was indignant. "Do you realize what you are doing?" he scolded me. "You are strengthening the military power of the one nation in South America which has always hated the United States, will always detest you, and will turn against you the first chance she has to give aid or comfort to your most dangerous international enemies.

"And more. You are forsaking the Brazilians, your best friends in Latin America, who have stood shoulder to shoulder with you in the World War and in all your Pan-American policies, and training our natural enemies in Buenos Aires to bomb our cities."

I took the perhaps irritatingly moral position that Washington was playing no favorites. Brazil already had a naval mission and a coast-artillery mission, I insisted. No doubt she could easily arrange for an aviation mission if she wanted one. Why shouldn't Argentina, too, have the services of gringo flight instructors if she wanted them?

The Brazilian sank into a mild coma of injured dejection. "It does not matter, perhaps," he sighed in the dead-pan tone of a lady wounded by wanton unkindness. "If the United States does not care for its hundred years of loyal Brazilian friendship, I suppose the explanation is that it finds untrustworthy friends more attractive and feels that it no longer needs us.

"You and I need not disagree over this horrible mistake personally," he went on with somewhat more energy. "But I hope that you will make it clear to your people that if they are finished with Brazil's friendship, our government will have to look for friends"—and his glance gave these words a sound of sinister significance—"elsewhere. I cannot say now where we will turn, but I am sure we shall find them."

I left him with a slightly sharpened consciousness of the gringo's naïveté in these delicate international courtships. "Do you remember when you were so young," one of my friends had said to me just before I left for Latin America, "that you thought, when you liked two girls, you ought to bring them together so they could like each other?" In their cheerful expectations of the effects of the Argentine mission on Latin-American opinion generally, the diplomats and the good-will seekers in the "colonies" had been behaving just like that.

☆　　　　☆　　　　☆

Such attitudes and tactics of Latin America, both in their studied and unstudied phases, are all counters in the major strategy of fending off stronger forces and powers. Because they are met in almost every phase of the foreigner's practical, day-by-day relations with Latin governments and individuals, the out-lander is forced to indulge in a more or less perpetual struggle to extricate himself from the position of being "in the wrong" in all his controversies. Indeed, he begins most of his negotiations, for good or evil ends, at a more or less acute moral disadvantage.

If he wishes to buy concessions or property titles, the question must be gravely looked into as to how far he is infringing upon the national sovereignty. If he is firm—or possibly a little bumptious—in standing up for his rights, he is insulting the national dignity and the constituted political authorities. If he insists on full payment of his debts and full protection for his investments, he is grinding down the poor and taking advantage of his host republic's economic weakness. If he comes bearing favors and more or less free benefits, he can usually be accused of having, for the lowest of motives, shown even greater generosities to rival republics.

To the considerable psychological extent implied in these viewpoints, all foreign "penetration efforts" in the twenty republics must "climb out of a doghouse" before they even begin business.

Moreover, fending off and shaking off stronger forces and powers is also a matter of legal strategy as well as providing an unfavorable emotional climate. Hence, throughout most, if not all, of Latin America today new principles of property rights and of the diplomatic standing of alien economic interests are arising.

That the economic front should be considered the major line of defense is easily understandable. In practically every case where a republic has lost control over its natural resources or has seen its political freedom threatened or curtailed, the situation has been brought about historically by permitting the unrestricted spread of alien ownership. And behind the ancient laissez-faire principle of pre-power-age international law—that every man's railway or oil well was his castle wherever he built or drilled it—stand the inferences of military intervention and political subjugation.

So, beginning approximately at the century's turn, there has been a distinct tendency throughout the republics toward deflating or wholly eliminating these menacing concepts. To cover all of its manifestations would require a separate volume. But in general terms the major developments can be summarized substantially as follows:

1. Foreign purchases of real property and incorporations of aliens for industrial exploitations or development have been placed increasingly, by most of the republics, on a footing of special contracts with the state. The result has been to render foreign investment interests subject to extraordinary restrictions on their activities—to say nothing of sudden changes of restrictions—imposed by the republics' governments.

2. In a number of the more "imperialism-conscious" republics—Mexico and Chile, for instance—these special contract obligations require foreign purchasers and incorporators to agree not to demand diplomatic support from their home governments in the difficulties they may encounter with the authorities in countries where their economic activities are pursued. This disposes—for whatever a technical agreement of this sort may be worth—of the danger of "intervention" whenever an investor's fingers are pinched by the economic policies of a host republic.

3. Guided by the difficulties the older laissez-faire democracies have had in regulating exploitation of their natural resources, the majority of the governments have in one way or another asserted "national ownership" of the subsoil wealth of the nations. The practice was initiated by Mexico in her famous 1917 constitution, and its net effect has been to reduce the foreign raw-material industries in several important world-supply zones to a status roughly equivalent to that of tenants on sufferance.

4. The republics have made strenuous and fairly successful efforts to bring about acceptance into international law of the

principle of the so-called Calvo and Drago doctrines: namely, that force may not be used as a means of collecting either the public or private debts of nations, or of securing reparations for damages attributable to public disorders.

5. The governments have immensely enlarged their powers of expropriation; and wonderfully and fearfully, from the standpoint of orthodox property concepts in several instances, piled up new precedents for expropriative action. Where, originally, few of the legal systems of the republics contemplated the seizure of private property except for essential public-construction activities, today, in many of the "rightist" as well as in all the "leftist" countries, virtually any phase of social need can be cited either in constitutional law or in common judicial practice to justify the necessary Latin equivalents for "eminent domain" proceedings.

Lands can be taken, for instance, to relieve the propertyless state of the agrarian proletariat. Oil and mineral properties can be made to "revert" to the nation's "natural" proprietorship of its subsoil resources. Factories can be seized to enable governments to solve wage and distribution problems. Or property rights may be voided in consequence of the failure of foreign owners to live up to their complicated obligations with governments, or to obey the complex regulations imposed by authorities on their operating methods.

These ultimate powers have been invoked, it is true, in fairly rare instances. But the effect of their presence in the background is to put foreign business continually on the defensive. It must meet its pyramided tax obligations and conform to a bewildering array of petty regulations and red-tape restrictions of its internal conduct and management, or its legal rights of operation may be revoked or embarrassingly curtailed. It must keep on a friendly footing with the ruling political groups—perhaps with a succession of highly diverse ruling groups—or risk the chance that domestic social and economic problems will be used to justify expropriation of its properties and eventual banishment. And if it induces its home government to demand redress for its hardships through diplomatic channels, it automatically forfeits whatever may be left of its legal rights and contract standing for having incited diplomatic protests.

Naturally, this is a rather too unqualified picture of the situation; for within the convolutions of Latin America's rising economic ramparts, a great many of the potential disasters just noted may be warded off through quiet understandings and intimate personal arrangements.

Where government services are corrupt, inspectors do not always see violations of elaborate codes and red-tape requirements with a strictly impartial vision; nor are courts and legal functionaries always keenly awake to violations of contract obligations. Dictators can be persuaded by tact and flattery—not to mention more solid inducements—to overlook social problems as cause for expropriations. Diplomats have been able to secure advantageous settlements of disputes involving the rights of their nationals in discreet talks which sedulously avoided the technical color of "formal protests."

Nevertheless, the republics on the whole have put themselves in a position to check further advances of alien "colonial empires" where the dangers are sufficiently apparent and the will exists. Nor is the future prognosis for "empire" growth altogether favorable even in republics where foreign investment interests are enjoying at present a relative field day. In Peru, for example, the current dictatorship barely holds the upper hand over the determined Aprista movement, which—over and above ideas for the social and economic reorganization of Latin America—passionately maintains that all basic resources should be restored to native or national ownership.

For that matter, the foreign investors can hardly look forward with confidence to improving their prospects, regardless of political changes. For wherever a new regime comes to power, it usually is conscious that the surest practical political method of promoting its popularity is to turn the screws a little harder on the foreign interests. More than one rightist "savior of order" in Latin-American presidencies has found, after a few months' experience with office, that expropriation threats against foreign investments help his popularity and his budget problems quite as much as they do in the case of wicked "radical" presidents.

☆   ☆   ☆

On the whole, too, in this continentally diffused self-defense movement the North American investment interests, as compared with foreign interests in general, have tended to get the worst of it. There are many reasons for this, not all of them rooted in abstract justice.

The American "colonies"—for reasons sufficiently discussed elsewhere—are not "liked" in the Latin republics generally. Hence, when measures to restrict foreign economic privileges are ripe for enforcement, it is a pleasure (and to some extent sound politics) for Latin-American officials to bear down hardest on the foreigners who are least ingratiating. The gringos also tend more than the other alien elements to lack effective intercessors with the government authorities within their own groups.

German and Italian "colonies"—quite apart from Fascist factors —can usually count on the help of racial kinsmen whose naturalization and prominence in the affairs of the republics date back several generations. North Americans seldom spend even their entire business careers below the Rio Grande, and the overwhelming majority of the members of most of the "colonies" are merely "away" on foreign assignments of a few years between jobs at the New York or Detroit main offices.

Naturalized former gringos are as scarce as arctic moss in the republics, and as a rule are definitely unprepossessing specimens of the beachcombing genus when found. Something is suggested on this point by the fact that the only gringo family of four generations' Latin-American residence I met on my travels still maintains its American citizenship and its uncontaminated gringo bloodstream after seventy-five years. Its members expressed their disrelish for all phases of Latin-American life and politics with more scatological vehemence than I encountered anywhere. Even more surprisingly, the founding great-grandparents had come to Mexico with a Tampico "Confederate colony" in 1865 to escape the "Yankee conquest."

Most appealing of all the motives for dealing harshly with North American investment interests is the fact, however, as the Latin Americans see it, that the gringo brand of imperialism has long been the most subtle and dangerous. After all, during the past generation, it has been the gringo trade and the gringo bond and capital investment holdings which have most rapidly expanded. It is Washington, not Berlin or Rome, which, in defense of the flag and of North American dollars, has conducted most of the disciplinary actions and violations of sovereignty of which the republics have been conscious during the non-ideological years of the twentieth century.

If gringos could be kept from extending their "empire" too rapidly for the next few decades and put in their places as tolerated "merchant adventurers" rather than masters, Latin America's control over her own natural wealth might yet be held. Interesting precedents could deal with other brands of imperialistic efforts upon the actual appearance of the emergency.

For, in the Latin view, the economic resources of the republics are their first ramparts. And the foreigner is not customarily permitted to dictate—or sabotage—national defense measures merely because he holds a mortgage on the guns or the ground the fortifications stand on.

"We are happening to find it necessary," a young Peruvian Aprista exile in Chile sardonically told me, "to fight a war of independence without the usual accompaniments of military action. And I have not gathered from my studies of history that in wars of independence the international laws of property rights are ever particularly binding."

☆   ☆   ☆

It by no means disposes of the situation, however, to say that Latin America is undertaking certain measures to make economic invasion difficult. In a practical sense the republics regard themselves as invaded already. Hence a highly conscious strategy has developed of trying to bring about a kind of stalemate between the invading forces by playing them off against each other.

For obvious reasons it is a strategy which, at least until the war's outbreak, ran strongly in favor of invaders from Europe. To synthesize the Latin view of these necessities not too elaborately, the points for "pro-European"—including pro-Fascist—economic and political policies appeared about as follows:

1. The European economic "colonies" were more interwoven with the life of the republics than were the gringo penetration groups. Their leaders were more effective as negotiators. They were more agreeable to do business with, and many special concessions and favors went to them simply because of their control of the "inside lines."

2. European economic expansion, whatever may be said of its ultimate implications, was less immediately dangerous to the republics than the gringo menace. Furthermore, if European expansion could be used to check United States expansion the risks involved might be justified.

3. Mildly punitive discriminations were warranted against the United States because of its long history of aggressions against the republics in defense of its "imperialistic" interests—a type of offense significantly lacking in the record of the European powers since the turn of the century. (On this point perhaps it should be incidentally suggested that the Theodore Roosevelt policy of "policing" the Latin-American states against failures to perform their international obligations has developed a distinctly "hairshirt" side. If Washington had continued its former policy of standing as a kind of buffer between Old World creditors and New World debtors, the United States might enjoy considerable kudos today as the protector of the republics against *European* aggressions.)

4. In any final showdown with an aggressive European imperialism the republics can count, anyway, on the aid of the United States and the Monroe Doctrine in resisting Old World invaders. But there are few conceivable circumstances, as world power balances exist today, in which the republics could count on the help of the European nations in resisting gringo imperialism. This critical analysis of the forces in the situation may seem an ungrateful response to some of the idealistic oratory with which North American statesmen occasionally hold forth on the Monroe

[288]

Doctrine's merits, but it can hardly be objected to as sound international practical politics.

With all these considerations in the background the difficulties which efforts to increase United States influence ordinarily meet in many Latin-American sectors become somewhat more understandable.

Washington, for example, would like to make the twenty republics dependent principally upon the United States for military supplies, and in a quiet way has been seeking, ever since the World War crisis became tangible, to set up a kind of collaborative understanding on plans for hemisphere defense. Naturally the plans would involve increasing the number of United States military instruction missions in the Latin-American armies.

Yet Peru and Ecuador and Bolivia, Chile, the Argentine and Uruguay, not to mention the truculently anti-American El Salvador, maintained, at least down to the war's actual outbreak, close military ties with the Fascist powers. The armies of these countries were drilled by German or Italian instructors and in most cases still are. Increasingly, as a result, Fascist principles have been introduced into their methods of organization and discipline.

Such military toeholds as Uncle Sam has on these republics have been mainly in side-show departments. There is a U.S. naval mission in Peru, but the Italian-taught Peruvian army, not the navy, could, in a world emergency, be Peru's only significant contribution to hemisphere defense operations. Argentina's acceptance of an American aviation mission was a flattering compliment to the expertness of American bombing-squad officers. But whatever new skills the Argentine fliers may learn from them are likely to be co-ordinated neatly into the republic's German-planned army system—to the considerable advantage, perhaps, of the Nazi espionage service.

Moreover, the republics' munitions business went, as a rule, down to the war, with the military missions. Instruction officers from Italy and Germany not only insisted, as far as possible, on working with the types of equipment with which they are already familiar, but their official instructions required them to act as salesmen for the products of the armament factories in the homelands.

When I met Colonel Negroni, head of the Italian army mission to Ecuador in Quito, he was so steeped in these promotion operations that most of his conversation with me consisted in a sales talk for the performances of Caproni planes in the Andes.

In result, up to September 1939 the dependence of the "Fascist serviced" block of nations for munitions was predominantly, and in some cases almost entirely, on the Fascist powers. Caproni planes, German and Italian heavy artillery, German machine guns, Italian tanks and armored cars were almost as much the normal trade stock of these relatively large Latin-American armies as they were of the armies in the "Axis-controlled" nations of Spain and Hungary.

Along with the sales talks, the Fascist powers made armament purchases easy with barter trade arrangements. Peru was enabled to stock its army with all the German and Italian war gadgets it could use, for instance, in return for simple shipments of cotton. Dictator Martinez of El Salvador could—and still can, to a degree —accumulate enough planes to stand off any conceivable combination of revolutions by simply pledging to Italy a moderate fraction of his coffee crop. And with the barter conveniences went certain other attractive perquisites. The Fascist governments, until war gave them other employment, were always willing to send new instruction officers, free of charge with all sizable orders, to teach Latin-American soldiers how to use the new technical equipment. They would "entertain" officers from the republics at the armament factories back home and "invite" them to participate in the technical instruction courses given to their own armies.

Charmed by such inducements, republics ostensibly beyond reach of the "military mission" system tended to increase their armament orders at the Fascist factories. In spite of its close ties with the United States and the navy and coast-defense missions, considerably more than half of Brazil's present military equipment comes from Fascist sources. Little Nicaragua, though only recently released from Marine chaperonage and considered as being definitely in Washington's influence orbit, bought her 1938 consignment of artillery and ammunition from Italy. Colombia and Venezuela found that their quick-trick needs for technical equipment could be met more speedily, and at less outlay, by the barter system. Mexico got under the wire by trading a considerable proportion of the oil expropriated from United States and British interests for German artillery.

From the Latin point of view, all this was sensible arranging. In addition to more favorable purchase terms, the dependence of the governments on the United States for their physical defense needs was lessened, and the perilous "Yanquis" could be kept guessing as to where their closest military friendships lay.

Again, take the question of commercial airplane concessions. The gringos were first in the field with the Pan American Airways development of "round-the-hemisphere" passenger and air freight transport, and there is little question in most of the republics that the Pan American personnel has solved the problem of adaptations to the Latin-American scene with an almost all-time gringo record for tact and consideration of the republics' internal needs. Yet throughout South America the republics saw to it that the competing German interests received equal or better treatment than the flight pioneers.

Every air-mail contract the Pan American holds was matched, it seemed, by a favorable contract offered the German Lufthansa services. Special inducements were given the Germans to fly over necessarily unprofitable, but strategically important, routes—such as the flight from the eastern Brazilian coast across the jungles to Bolivia and Lima. Announcements of airport concessions to the North American interests were followed almost invariably by announcements of similar concessions to the German competitors. Grants of landing fields to the Pan American system in obvious strategic areas were often followed within a few days or weeks by adjacent grants to the Germans.

German transatlantic services were suspended with the war, inevitably, and most of the German overland interior flights blew up with the Aski-marks. Very slowly, as the European war advanced, subsurface efforts were launched toward reviving some of the more commercially profitable lines—as contrasted with the mere strategically interesting ones—under native auspices, with North Americans entitled to investment privileges and contract rights to direct technical management. But the going was not easy. The efforts, being concerned with franchises, necessarily involved politics, and in a general way the statesmen of the republics concerned seemed to prefer letting the lines lie fallow for a while to aiding a program which not too unplausibly could result in gringo air-transport monopoly.

German competition, to be sure, has been present only in South America below the Caribbean area. Down to Panama the Americans are top dogs in the aviation field. But down to the war there were plenty of undersurface indications that the Central American states and Mexico would give a hearty welcome to competing German or Italian flying interests if conditions for inaugurating rival services should become propitious. After all, it would show the "Yanqui" what the South American powers have already showed him—that he cannot build up a preponderating influence in Latin America through air dominance of the land mass.

To trace the discrimination strategy all through the tangled field of trade and political relations would require an endless inspection of such convolutions.

Now and then one of my Latin mentors—including a statesman or two—put the situation to me frankly, with no holds barred. "You Norte Americanos are richer than your European rivals and have a special interest in our countries," the arguments ran in general. "Is it unfair, then, that we should expect you to pay a little more for concessions to exploit those resources, and sometimes place slightly greater restrictions on your operations than we do in the case of nations which have less practical motives for desiring to control us? Is it unreasonable that we should not wish to increase our dependence on North American markets?

"It is not that we fear your conscious imperialism," the gentlemen would smile politely. "But you are powerful and very near. Your competitors are powerful, also, but still far off. We must oppose the logic of certain physical factors in the hemisphere which tend to place the weaker republics at a disadvantage in dealing with you, whether you seriously wish to control our destinies or not."

So, as the picture has developed, wherever in the republics the foreign-exchange regulations can be juggled against one nation's trade and in favor of others, the United States, as in the case of the Argentine's denial of "free exchange" market privileges to United States shippers in January 1939, has had to bear the brunt of the severest restrictions. Even in Brazil, which has a reciprocal trade treaty and an enormous coffee commerce with the United States, exchange transactions are made more of a red-tape nightmare for the American import-export interests than for the British or Fascist nationals.

Whether concessions for oil and mineral and other subsoil and raw-material exploitations have come higher to the Yankees than to other breeds of outlanders is more difficult to trace in view of the secrecy surrounding the majority of concessions contracts. But the fact that members of the American "colonies" all but unanimously insist that they have, and that responsible Latin Americans have been known to defend the process, speaks strongly for the plausibility of the legend.

Moreover, in all prewar deals favorable, or ostensibly favorable, to the Axis powers, the Latin-American governments were decidedly not chary of publicity. Contracts for military equipment might be kept fairly secret, for the Latin Americans had learned through considerable experience that the gringo mind found a shuddery glamor in these matters when the mysteries were preserved. But German acquisition of a huge air base on the Amazon headwaters at Trinidad, Bolivia, was covertly exploited by the Bolivian authorities themselves in the early summer of 1939 as a step in the Nazi drive for *Weltmacht*. And Argentine arrangements for piping oil from the northern provinces, and eventually from Paraguay and Bolivia, into the holds of German tankers have been interpreted—not without "off record" official assistance in Buenos Aires—as symptoms of Nazi control in the Plate river system.

While President Cárdenas doubtless meant his original March 1938 declaration that he proposed not to sell Mexico's expropriated oil to the "anti-democratic" powers, subsequent disclosures of the extent of Mexican oil sales to Italy and Germany manifestly gave Mexican officialdom acute pleasure. For gringo alarm at a smart

Fascist bargain helps to pay off the score for the virtual United States boycott on expropriated oil products. Nor were these consolations decreased by the prominent part which certain North American promoters have played in the German negotiations.

To keep the gringos conscious that their economic empire is far from secure, even in the face of a mutual overseas threat, is, in any event, the object of more than one subtle policy; governs the twist of many a publicity release in the twenty republics.

☆   ☆   ☆

Less obviously, but with hardly less diligence, the republics watch their ramparts against excessive gringo cultural influences. There are, to be sure, not the same official barriers that are encountered in our efforts at economic penetration.

North American books are read in the twenty republics. (For the few that run afoul of censors, scores are pirated by the translation publishers.) Gringo artists have their appreciators and imitators in the more sophisticated centers. Our professors and lecturers are ostensibly welcome in the Latin universities. Gringo manners, customs and fashions spread slowly through Latin America on the wings of the evangelistic labors of the motion pictures.

Yet in powerful circles these influences are subtly deprecated as strange and discordantly alien, when not specifically pernicious. European cultural influences, on the other hand, are hailed by these ranking pundits and conservative moralists as harmonious and beneficial—"the natural complements," as a Peruvian journalist expressed it to me, "of our own cultural deficiencies. . . . If we tried to build our cultures on North American models," he added, "we should first have to destroy all that we have."

Somewhat less extravagantly, a similar point was made by Dr José Maria Cantilo, recent Argentine Foreign Minister, in a written answer to a question I put to him on the prospects of closer cultural relations with North America:

"With respect to the Argentine Republic there is no doubt that our cultural affinities with Europe are greater than they are with the United States," Dr Cantilo wrote. "We receive our spiritual life from Spain, primarily, and then from France. From Italy we have felt a constant artistic influence. In the same way Germany, with its philosophy, has affected the modes of thinking in our universities. All these factors represent a great deal for us, without depreciating, however, the importance which North American precedents have in the Constitution and the constitutional jurisprudence of Argentina. . . .

"Even [the democratic professions made by North American statesmen like President Roosevelt and Secretary of State Hull] will not be enough to change our intellectual and esthetic orientations, which, on the other hand, are undergoing a certain degree of rectification due to the new ideologies of the totalitarian states and of Communist Russia.

"All of these developments render, in one way or another, a greater acquaintance with the Anglo-Saxon cultures desirable—the British as well as the North American. This closer acquaintance has of course been facilitated of late years by a wider diffusion of English-language teaching in the republic. It is a pity that the majority who study it do so for merely practical reasons. There are genuine treasures in English and United States literature which deserve to be better known to us, just as certain profundities of the great thinkers of our countries deserve to be better known abroad.

"No matter how much this acquaintance is cultivated, however, it will never become instinctive—as our responses are instinctive to the problems of the mother country and to the appeal of our ancestral Latin culture."

Rather oddly, not only the Europeans but the Japanese as well often are viewed as within the scope of these acknowledged affinities. "We and the Japanese respect dignity and value prestige," I was told more than once in my conversations with Latin intellectuals. "Both peoples cultivate etiquette and exquisite manners as a virtue. Both admire grace and form in the arts. In spite of all that we admire in your civilization, we are closer to the Japanese in these essential traits than we are to you North Americans. There are, after all, spiritual kinships which transcend even racial differences."

Again, although the efficiency of North American educational processes is generally recognized, the net results of life on American university campuses are seriously questioned. "Our young men come back from their studies in Europe broadened by their contacts with the older cultures, but basically unchanged," a Brazilian physician with a number of European degrees on his office wall once told me. "Their social habits and viewpoints have not been radically disturbed, and they resume their places in our society without a struggle.

"But when our young men come back from the United States, although they often have much that is valuable to teach us, they do not seem to belong to us. They are unhappy without your 'jazz life' and your social freedoms. Often they are, frankly, a disturbing influence. They spend their energies, not on improving our scientific or our business methods, but on trying to wean our young people away from the old customs. . . . Sometimes," he added more caustically, "they are so dissatisfied with the prospect of returning to a society where an honorable formality governs the relations of the sexes, that they prefer not to come home at all."

And all Chile shuddered not quite mildly a year or two ago at the story of a brilliant young woman university student who answered the question, "Why would you like to study in the United States?" on her application for an international exchange-student fellowship, with—"To enjoy the freedom of the American campus."

Nor is this disapproval of too close cultural intimacies with the gringo entirely a matter of private opinion. In the less liberal republics overt actions are not infrequently taken to check "indoctrination" efforts from the North which the authorities, in their wisdom, consider dangerous. American professors lecturing in Latin universities have had the experience of being watched with uncomfortable vigilance by the local censors. The International Rotary Clubs, when they have not been actually disbanded by the more suspicious dictators, have received fairly clear intimations that both their serious programs and their most innocent frivolities are recorded in the files of the government secret services.

International gatherings at which gringo viewpoints bulk large on the programs have increasingly in recent years met with a series of polite discouragements. The International Congress of American Democracies in Montevideo early in 1939 was prevented from discussing most of the points on its agenda by a government ruling that no subjects relating to political questions in friendly nations could be mentioned.

A Pan-American Conference on Indian affairs was called off in La Paz, Bolivia, in August on the plea that the late Dictator Busch's housing reconstruction program for the metropolis would deprive the conference of accommodations.

An international educational group, bound for Rio de Janeiro in 1939 for a "good will" gathering with Brazilian colleagues, was notified that, while the government would be delighted to extend its social hospitalities, all business sessions were banned. Somewhat surprisingly to the Brazilians, the utilitarian pedagogues accepted the hospitalities and held their sessions in transit on shipboard.

Throughout most of the ruling conservative circles, too, runs a vaguely hostile suspicion of American movies. "How can you expect to win our friendship," I was challenged in at least half a dozen republics, "when the only art form that you send us in quantity belittles the dignity of your men and the chastity of your women, and is looked upon by our own respectable people as the chief unsettling influence in the lives of our younger generation?"

These protests, it is true, often lack something on the score of consistency. The movies are the chief night delight of the populace in all the republics. Even the protesting "respectables" are frequently present at the local "premieres." Although films with a definitely leftist or pronounced democratic "message," like *Emile Zola,* are occasionally censored or prohibited, no government has felt itself strong enough to deprive its subjects of Hollywood entertainment in mass, or even in significant fractions.

Nevertheless, the spirit of opposition is there and most deeply entrenched in the circles where it can make itself most effective.

☆ ☆ ☆

At this point in the discussion the question necessarily insinuates itself—what have the republics done about watching their ramparts against Fascism at all?

The answer is considerably more encouraging than some of the points just under discussion would indicate. Even as the Fascist menace rolled up there was considerable difference between "stringing along" with the Axis to embarrass the imperialistic expansion of a nearer and one-time more dangerous neighbor, and accepting the Fascist ideologies as state religion, or lining up as underling members of any Fascist system of alliances.

Neither the precedents to date nor the balances of the instinctive temperamental and subconscious forces in Latin-American politics suggest that the republics are inclined to tighten their bonds with totalitarian seducers beyond the needs of their own "balance of power" problem in the Western Hemisphere.

Some of the precedents have been considered in previous chapters. Wherever foreign Fascist elements large enough to be dangerous have sought directly to influence domestic politics, they have been promptly and painfully stepped on. Brazil, Argentina and Chile have proscribed Fascist organizations as well as activities of the foreign-language school systems. Not all of these regulations may have been enforced to the letter, but the totalitarians even on their strongest Latin-American fronts found themselves at the disadvantage of operating against the law and public policy for nearly a year before their war embarrassments arose.

Brazil, catching the scent of dangerous foreign entanglements in the ostensibly home-grown Integralista movement, has outlawed even native Fascist movements. Argentine police, when mobs of bright young local *falangistas* have run riot in the Buenos Aires parks and on the grounds of the University of Córdoba, have used their clubs as diligently as they would upon any other brand of revolutionary disturbers.

With all their continuous outcry over discriminations, the North American "colonies" have seldom encountered anywhere in the twenty republics even a minor fraction of these disciplinary restraints. It is true that the republics where the foreign Fascist elements are small and less troublesome in internal politics are, on the whole, more tolerant. But the governments below the Rio Grande are distinctly more vigorously on guard against serious totalitarian "political penetration" than they are even against gringo economic penetration.

Neither do the precedents suggest that the prewar methods of Fascist agitators on the Latin-American front possessed all the serpentine wiles that suspicious rumor sometimes attributed to them. On the contrary, Fascist influence in the republics was fairly constantly being thrown for losses because of bumptiousness or ineptitude on the part of the Fascist home governments.

Nazi Ambassador Karl Ritter in Rio de Janeiro, for instance, adopted, in his clash with the Brazilian government over the alleged part played by embassy attachés in the 1938 "putsch" proceedings, approximately the same manners that Hitler field marshals used in September 1939 in commandeering Slovakia's military services. Brazil declared him *persona non grata* for his pains, and for several months Berlin and Rio hovered on the brink of a complete diplomatic breach. For presuming to invite Germans naturalized in Guatemala to vote in the plebiscite on the Austrian *Anschluss,* the German minister to Central America received a tongue-lashing from Dictator Ubico which would have burnt the ears of an Indian labor agitator on his way to the firing squad.

The indiscretions of the Spanish Fascist regime, while it was a Hitler appendage, sat no better. When some of General Franco's favorite editors began talking loosely in the summer of 1939 about restoring the Spanish colonial empire, the press, both rightest and leftist, throughout Latin America screamed its indignations in the same key that the United States press would use if a spokesman from the government benches in the British Parliament recommended reconquest of the thirteen colonies.

Official indignation rose to an even higher pitch—Chile finally broke relations over it—when the Franco government attempted to prevent the Latin-American legations in Spain from using their time-honored privilege of giving asylum to political refugees from the regime's vengeance. Asylum rights are an integral part of the diplomatic and political favor-trading systems in the more revolution-stricken republics, and, besides having emotional standing as attributes of sovereignty, have been useful on occasion in meeting embassy and legation board bills.

In the Nazi racial theories, also, is an element of offense to peoples somewhat nervously concerned for their color-line status. Berlin restrictions on mixed marriages between expatriate Nazis and Latin-American "nationals" have had an especially corrosive effect on sentimental approaches from Nazi political wooing squads. President Somoza, for instance, expelled from his country a German forced by Nuremberg racial statutes to jilt a Nicaraguan fiancée.

"I am conscious of the valor and pride of my people," the dictator defended Latin America's romantic ramparts, "and as Chief Executive of the nation will not permit insults to our women and violation of the sanctity of the home."

☆   ☆   ☆

Beyond these reactions to specific offenses are the intangible resisting forces. This much is in our favor.

Life in Latin America does not move at totalitarian tempos. The dictators observe the totalitarian methods of political organization and social discipline with interest and professional admiration, no doubt, but also with a wary eye to their practical deficiencies. After all, it is not agreeable to share the mastery of the state with a complicated party organization, presumably full of the internal dissensions and personal rivalries which congenitally bedevil so many of Latin America's organizing efforts. It is difficult to think of inflicting the "goose step" psychology on Andean mountain villages and negroid settlements about the coastal sugar patches. To think of ruling such people through a rigid ideology is not even intelligent.

"Innumerable dictators may call themselves Fascist before the end of the century if the word catches on," an analytical Mexican friend once summed up this aspect of the problem for my benefit. "What it means is that the palace guards will wear colored shirts instead of tunics. But behind the new stage properties they will still be the same old one-man dictators."

[300]

What the people know, instinctively, is that nations which roar aloud about their racial superiority are more dangerous to Latin-American pride than even the gringos. What the people know, without saying it even to themselves, is that dictators who for a century and a quarter have left them comparatively free in their private lives and amusements, and who today rarely succeed in forcing them to obey the simplest and most rational traffic regulations, are the kind of dictators they are used to—and the kind they prefer.

Latin America's most formidable rampart against Fascism, in brief, lies in the fact that her hundred and twenty millions can be dictated to but not regimented.

At the same time, it should not be forgotten that the Fascist bandwagon has already taken aboard a fantastically assorted group of fellow travelers and that even the strongest mental resistance can hardly stop swarms of Stukka bombers.

CHAPTER XVIII

Dilemma with Three Horns

U PON THE somewhat appalling array of facts and factors which we have been piling up through so many pages rests the central question of this discourse: Come war, come the peace of Hitler, what can the United States do about a practical Latin-American policy? Can we even defend enough of Latin America to have a policy for?

A great many of our policies in the past have been made in a dream world of smugness and wishful thinking.

We have imagined, for instance, that the Latin Americans were a people very much like ourselves, or that it would take only a little persuasion—or compulsion—to make them so. Whereas, as we have seen, practically everything in their historical experience, economic situation, cultural inheritance, political methods, and their scale of social values tends to make them irreconcilably different from us.

We have imagined that our interests are the same as theirs, which, in the long view and a remote idealistic sense, is doubtless true. But this does not prevent millions of Latin Americans from seeing that most of our concrete, immediate interests in the republics conflict with theirs, and that the immediate profits from many of our activities on the Latin-American scene are their equally positive losses.

We have imagined that Latin Americans look on us as their mentors in the arts of civilized progress and their protectors and defenders against a world of ravening enemies. Actually, the Latin

Americans believe that it is we who stand in need of cultural and moral education; and—for not entirely fallacious reasons—that the most dangerous aggressors against their rights and properties are ourselves.

Moreover, almost in exact proportion as we are unconscious of these differences and conflicts, we seem, to the "neighbors," either incredibly stupid or artfully hypocritical. Latin America is conscious of them with a profound and cynical realism: the same sort of realism with which we would be conscious of certain clashing purposes if Brazilians and Colombians—instead of being occasional polite guests at our intellectual and business conferences—ran our banks and our industries, kept huge war fleets within striking distance of our shores, and now and then issued communications suspiciously like orders to our presidents.

Finally, we have imagined that the republics have the same stakes in world power balances that we have. To the extent that they would not relish seeing the power of the United States to protect them utterly destroyed, the Latin statesmen no doubt would more or less freely—as at Panama and Havana conferences—concede this. But their idea of a perfect power balance is one in which the gringo aspirations toward dominance in the hemisphere are checked by strong opposing forces, and in which the gringo himself must pursue his quest for influence in the twenty republics as a suppliant among rivals.

A practical Latin-American policy in Washington would recognize these differentiations and antipathies, these conflicts of aims and interests as, in the main, genuine; and as basic factors in its problem, whether genuine or not. But simply recognizing them does not bring the problem around a dramatic corner to clear and easy solutions.

Meanwhile, the question of what to do about major discords with 120,000,000 neighbors remains, and increasingly involves itself with the defense problem. Can we let Latin America stew in its juice even if Hitler grabs it? Should we "defend" the twenty republics by grabbing them first? Or should we win their co-operation in defense and in economic life by programs of just "appeasement"?

The war, in short, snaps us out of dream-world concepts of Latin-American relations to sit on a dilemma with three horns.

☆   ☆   ☆

Before the crisis sharpened, there was something to be said for a policy of consistent indifference. Until recently, a good deal more has been said, perhaps, than the general public, or even some of our sharper news commentators, may have realized.

It cropped out in congressional debates, for example, over loans and reciprocal trade treaties, in newspaper editorials and ordinary people's "bull sessions" on hemisphere politics and the future of the Monroe Doctrine, in the predominating popular attitude toward the status of our investing interests in the republics.

This view of the future of Latin-American relationships would fit into a nutshell about as follows:

Trying to be "helpful" to the twenty republics costs more money than it is worth and involves us in a lot of unnecessary diplomatic headaches. Why not "forget it" and let the republics find their own way out of their troubles as we once did? Or, if they are not up to finding the way out, sink in their troubles. What difference would it make?

There is no sense in loaning vast funds to these republics for their rehabilitation experiments, since there is a considerable chance, as a matter of historical experience, that we shall not get our money back. There is no sense in granting them special favors to increase our trade with them. No rational expectation exists that Latin America's capacity to buy United States exports will ever exceed $2,000,000,000. The development of one new domestic industry, like motorcars, would be worth two or three times that. There is no sense, either, in permitting Latin-American trade commodities—Argentine canned beef, for instance—to compete in our own markets with home-grown products. Countries thus favored would probably go on throwing their best accounts to the European powers in any case.

There is no object in trying to influence the governments down there in favor of our political ideas or our foreign policies. It cannot be done effectively without stirring up their natural anti-American prejudices and leading us, at times, into rather expensive interferences in their internal affairs. Below Panama, at least, there is not even any practical advantage in a policy which pledges us to protect them from European conquest. After all, a Nazi regime in Brazil or Argentina would still be farther away from us than the Third Reich is at Le Havre. So long as we keep a hold on the major Canal defenses, what happens to the political sovereignty and territorial integrity of the rest of the hemisphere is the Latin nations' own funeral.

As for our investors, they know, when they go into these unstable foreign environments, the risks they take. If they lose their stakes, or run into trouble with the authorities, it isn't up to Uncle Sam to reform foreign governments—by expensive military operations—in order to balance their budgets.

If the twenty republics wish to be good friends and customers with us on these terms, excellent. But let *them* make the advances. . . .

Such a program should not be dismissed too lightly merely because few of our own ranking policy molders have ventured to put it forward specifically and *in toto* or in these bald terms. The congressional debates on Latin-American loans and reciprocal trade arrangements as a rule have centered on the immediate issues and have paid lip service, at least, to our Monroe Doctrine commitments. But the principle of withdrawal from the Latin-American front is implicit in all the current popular philosophies of "isolationism." Indeed it might fairly be described as the Western division of the isolation thesis. A consistent "minding our own business" policy, say the same statesmen professionally hottest against "foreign entanglements," begins, not at Cape Horn, but at the authentic national borders.

Under certain circumstances we may hear more of this thesis. Totalitarian conquest in Europe already is forcing us to face the question of whether to arm, or not to arm, for the protection of Brazil. Increasingly, certain puissant statesmen think it less important to protect Brazil than to get along with Hitler.

The disadvantages of setting Latin America adrift, however,

are fairly obvious. It would mean throwing open the hemisphere to European spheres of influence and systems of power balances, and running almost certain risks that the struggle of the European nations for raw materials and supremacy will be carried eventually to our own doorsteps. In its ultimate developments it will logically require us to arm to the teeth in the best European "crisis" fashion, to protect ourselves against hostile forces on our own land mass. In essence it must mean abandoning a reasonably "practical" hemisphere isolation policy for a doctrinaire isolation which invites the world's most consistent troublemakers to come and do their fighting in our own back yard.

☆   ☆   ☆

Before the war, among the gringo colonies South, I frequently heard the case for a more vigorous control of the neighbor republics' destinies put in the chaste aphorism: "A sixteen-inch gun is the best Goddamned salesman in Christ's world."

By the time Mr Hitler had won his triumph in France, and threatened shortly to have sea power and sixteen-inch guns of his own, this simple Gordian-knot-knifing prescription was being widely defended by the rationalizations of some of our best patriots and technicians.

Generals and admirals were saying publicly and not without persuasiveness in Washington that to defend the hemisphere we must have naval and air bases, and arrange for, if not execute, troop landings at least as far south as Uruguay. And adding not too privately in their nominally "off-record" discourses that, since there might not be time enough to deal about these delicate matters with skittish alien governments, the thing to do was to seize the strategic points first and arrange agreements with the beneficiaries of Uncle Sam's emergency protection when leisure returned.

Nor were the generals and admirals speaking merely for the martial spirit. A part of the word-of-mouth campaign for an outstanding aspirant for the Republican Presidential nomination at the 1940 National Convention in Philadelphia, was the assurance given by his managers that he would deal with Latin America with hard-boiled realism. Hard-boiled realism, they explained, meant he would seize strategic spots, garrison them, and see that the republics had governments "friendly" to American interests.

Similar counsels were offered on the floors of Congress. In intimate New Deal circles, until Mr Roosevelt and his foreign-affairs advisers stopped them, bright young experts in government, during the early 1940 summer, suggested that the army needed a "practice game" with Mexico, for which their mid-summer election troubles might offer the opening. The fever attacked even some of the country's isolationist war horses. As conscious of "manifest destiny" as Stephen A. Douglas and apparently craving safety as much as Mr Hitler, the late Senator Lundeen of Minnesota argued for planting the flag from "Greenland to Cape Horn."

Obviously, each rise in the nation's fear temperature due to the debacle of the former allies strengthened the cause of hemisphere imperialism. Obviously, too, the threat of invasion from east and west placed Latin America, by 1940's early summer, in greater danger of conquest from the north than at any time in history.

There are, of course, military exigencies in the interests of reasonable self-protection which all except the doctrinaire brand of liberals and leftists will have to recognize. One doesn't need to know the secrets of hemisphere defense to realize that no military bases of conceivable offensive value below the Rio Grande could be left open to an enemy; that no Latin-American government could be permitted to ally itself with powers hostile to Washington. The difficulty, however, would be to confine the situation, after war, to strictly military implications. For there would undoubtedly be an impressive effort by the imperialist-minded to retain the focal points. Countries which had opposed seizure might be represented as seething with public disorders and in need of further discipline for the hemisphere's future safety. In countries which had accepted occupation passively, "friendly" administrations could be induced, through behind-the-scenes pressure, to "invite" us to stay.

Final arrangements, begun in the light of the martial spirit, could be completed in the full glare of a demobilization economic crisis. Shrewd propaganda could make it seem almost virtuous to repay ourselves for all our patriotic sacrifices by grabbing something in Latin America. And the masses could be won by the bait that "sharing" with the Latin-American brothers the privileges of developing their resources would solve their demobilization unemployment emergency.

Even without war involvements or peace deflation emergencies, the imperialist program might be rationalized out of simple hemisphere "necessity." The thesis that economic troubles of modern societies are due to the passing of frontiers could be invoked to popularize a mass demand for bigger and better economic penetrations. Latin America has "frontiers," the case could be put by the imperialists with tenderhearted reasonableness. Why should not North America's jobless millions be employed in developing them—to Latin America's bonanza profit? What if—to make the vast humanitarian transplanation possible—a few governments had to be smashed and a few decrepit fortresses occupied? Human need knows no international-law fustiness.

In a sense, a demand for a share in the Latin-American "frontiers" would amount to flavoring the favorite cliché of the gringo colonies south—"My God, what a wonderful country this would be if the United States could take it over"—with mass appeal. On the surface it may look like evidence of shortsightedness that such demands have not been put forward already.

Here, too, however, the problem is complicated with other self-interests. Anything like a mass emigration of the unemployed gringo to Latin America would mean demands for higher wages in the industries of the republics and the beginnings of union agitation, North American style, among the imported labor groups. The gringo colonies would rather pass up the remote potential assistance of mass emigration toward "taking over" the republics, and keep the low-wage scales and the unionless Edens they have. Ownership of a permanent international sweatshop is their prime economic objective, not colonization.

In any case, the imperialist recipe for meeting the issue by direct action would be no bed of roses. The occupation of mere strategic control points and the bullying of the weaker governments into accepting Uncle Sam as a kind of Hitler to their Czechoslovakia would hardly be difficult, but this would be only a preliminary operation.

The Latin Americans perhaps have more instinctive skill in passive sabotage against unpopular employers and masters than any other people in the world. The rank and file in the hinterlands, from their long revolutionary traditions, know things about guerrilla warfare which North Americans have forgotten since Quantrell and the Marines have never learned. With all his twenty thousand men, Pershing never caught Pancho Villa in the Mexican Sierras. The Marines, in spite of several years of nominal contact between their fronts in the Nicaraguan jungle, never caught Augusto Sandino. Our little "side show" war to subjugate Haiti went on for more than two years and left few of the participants under the delusion that it was less dangerous than war on the grand scale.

It may be true, as apologists for our military prowess often venture, that Pershing was handicapped by secret Washington orders to avoid extensive occupation of Mexican territory; that, to save ourselves the embarrassments of "martyrizing" Sandino, the Marines were under instructions not to capture him. The facts remain that disciplining whole populations even in the weaker and less settled republics is a serious and dangerous military operation; that permanent discipline could hardly be maintained without outright and total conquest.

To say nothing of the fact that reducing 120,000,000 people— or any considerable fraction of them—to hating and vengeful political subordination for indefinite generations hardly seems an intelligent way of removing discords.

☆   ☆   ☆

There is nothing new, of course, about the third and final prescription for the Latin-American Problem. Indeed, we have built up considerable experience, in periods of both calm and stress, trying to smooth away discords by neighborly co-operation. In a sense, every administration since the Spanish-American War has registered ingratiating announcements of its special brand of Good Neighbor policies.

President Theodore Roosevelt unquestionably meant his declarations about "policing" the hemisphere as a neighborly gesture. Down to his time it had been customary for European powers in serious debt trouble with the Latin republics to do their collecting at the point of their warships' gun muzzles. As late as 1902 a German war fleet was checked in one of these enterprises off the Venezuelan coast only by a stern warning to the Kaiser. If our "policing" activities merely kept these emergencies from arising, as the Colonel's "hit the line hard" philosophy saw it, the republics would be spared much unnecessary humiliation and violence, and presumably in time would learn to feel grateful for it.

Neither did his somewhat single-track conscience discover any just cause for grievance in the Panama Canal difficulty. Gaining possession of a great geographic obstacle and building a half-billion-dollar ditch through it at our own expense to the benefit of the neighboring nations' trade interests seemed, after all, an almost unprecedented deed of practical community service. Colonel Roosevelt apparently went to his grave with the conviction that he had shown a more neighborly consideration for Latin America's true development than any president since Monroe.

The Taft administration promoted the operations of "dollar diplomacy" in the republics in the same benevolent spirit. Every time a new exploitation or trade concession was wrung from a Caribbean government by masterly legation negotiators or friendly Marine commandants, the Taft policy makers were stirred with authentic emotions. Think how Pennsylvania and Iowa had blossomed like the rose under the dew of our best banking circles' saved dollars! It would be the same way with Honduras.

By the time Woodrow Wilson arrived in 1913, however, the more glaring abuses of "dollar diplomacy" were becoming self-evident. So he began the "good neighborly" policy of his regime with an address to the Pan-American Commercial Conference in Mobile announcing that as a controlling factor in our Latin-

American relations the profit motive was out. From now on we were not going to support regimes in the twenty republics on the basis of how generous they were toward our investors. On the contrary, we were going to make the Latin world happier and more *simpático* in respect to its gringo big brother by shedding our special favors on governments that were authentically democratic.

Mr Wilson, in short, saw his neighborly duty in the light of a clear call to transform Latin-American politics as nearly as possible into a replica of Indiana politics. And in pursuing his aim of suppressing dictators and high-pressuring democracies into existence, he achieved more armed interventions than any of his predecessors or successors.

Hence the Harding and Coolidge administrations were in a position to speak fair words about making amends to offended republics for Mr Wilson's "aggressions." Actually Mr Coolidge did withdraw the Marines from Nicaragua for a few months and from the Dominican Republic permanently. And appointed Mr Dwight Morrow on his celebrated embassy to adjust the long list of controversies with Mexico.

Mr Hoover was rather more dramatic about it. As a prelude to his inauguration, he made a "good will" speaking tour of South America and encouraged his Commerce Department to strengthen the ties with the neighbors by helping to whoop up the sales of Latin-American bonds. He met the "imperialist" grievance by sending down a commission to study the advisability of removing the Marines from Haiti. But the speeches said more about the good that would come to Latin America through sound gringo trade connections than about respect for political sovereignty; and the Marines stayed on.

Regrettably, it appeared, one president after another was being led into further aggressions or embarrassments—the sale of the Hoover era's quickly defaulted Peruvian bonds, for instance— in order to make *his* particular brand of Good Neighbor policy work. We were getting deeper and deeper into misunderstandings with the Latin states through our efforts to promote "understanding." We were creating new resentments along "Hemisphere Street" with each fresh effort to be of neighborly service.

Could it be, then, that there was something wrong with our system? Did we fancy, perhaps, that making "the neighbors" like and admire us and feel sympathy with our motives and confidence in our aims was a matter of a few simple gestures? Were we imagining, perhaps, that the neighbors would recognize it as a rare privilege when we condescendingly attempted to make them over in our own image?

Were we expecting them to be grateful to us for coming in, often on slight, or no, invitation, and assuming the direction of their industries and a trusteeship over their financial affairs? Was it our idea of being friendly and helpful to supervise their lives, their tastes, their morals and their amusements; to instruct them each time we set foot on their premises how we expected them to keep their back yards?

We had overlooked, quite obviously, the fact that the primary basis for a successful neighborly relationship is respect for the neighbor's rights rather than concern for the state of his soul and his bank account.

If the "helpful" approach was to get us anywhere, the time was ripe for a change in the direction of policy; and the change came.

The change was crucial. Without it, it is questionable if Washington could have faced a hemisphere defense crisis without finding nearly every government below the Rio Grande secretly or overtly aligned with the enemy. With it, far better than by isolation or advance military occupation of strategic defense bases, some national hope has been preserved of enlisting the neighbor people with us against the new imperialist economies and their conquering armies.

With all its loose ends and fine sentiments unrealized, the Roosevelt version of the good neighbor policy came in time to build us block houses along our most exposed frontiers.

CHAPTER XIX

Neighbors, or Else—

THERE WAS NO unprecedented ardor, however, in the declarations with which, in December 1933, the Franklin Roosevelt brand of Good Neighbor policy was announced. Mr Roosevelt, indeed, could hardly have improved upon the sheer lyrical quality of several previous definitions of perfect Pan-American relationship.

As Theodore Roosevelt's Secretary of State in 1906, Mr Elihu Root had assured the Third Pan-American Congress at Rio de Janeiro that the United States—

neither claim nor desire any rights or privileges or powers that we do not freely concede to every American republic.

We wish to increase our prosperity, to expand our trade, to grow in wisdom and in spirit, but our conception of the true way to accomplish this is not to pull down others and profit by their ruin, but to help all friends to a common prosperity and a common growth, that we may all become greater and stronger together.

President Wilson had put the case for gringo disinterestedness in even more polished rhetoric. He told the Pan-American Scientific Congress in Washington nine years later:

All the governments of America stand, so far as we are concerned, upon a footing of genuine equality and unquestioned independence. The states of America are not hostile rivals but co-operating friends . . . in a very true and deep sense a unit in world affairs, spiritual partners standing together, quick with common sympathies and common ideals. . . .

[*313*]

And Mr Wilson appealed to the Latin states to join with us "in guaranteeing to each other absolute political independence and territorial integrity."

Mr Roosevelt, when he rose to speak at the Woodrow Wilson Foundation dinner in Washington in December 1933, did not attempt to outrange these flights of comprehensive idealism. Mr Roosevelt contented himself with defining more concrete relationships.

He began by quoting President Wilson's pledge that "the government of the United States will never again seek one additional foot of territory by conquest." Immediately afterward, however, he accomplished something which the rhetoric of his predecessors had never tried. He put himself in Latin America's shoes. Said Mr Roosevelt:

As the citizen of some other republic, I might have found it hard to approve of the occupation of territory even as a temporary measure.

The maintenance of constitutional government in other nations is not a sacred obligation devolving upon the United States alone. The maintenance of law and of the orderly processes of government in this hemisphere is the concern of each independent nation within its own borders first of all.

And when individual governments patently fail to provide the elementary conditions of public security, he concluded this phase of the discussion, the situation "becomes the concern of the whole continent in which we are all neighbors."

Earlier in the month Secretary of State Hull had already assured the Montevideo Pan-American Congress that—

no government need fear intervention while the United States is under the Roosevelt administration.

Every observing person must thoroughly understand that the United States government is opposed as much as any other to interference with the freedom, sovereignty or other internal affairs or processes of the governments of other nations.

Mr Roosevelt's Good Neighbor policy thus differed from the Good Neighbor policies of his predecessors in several important particulars.

It was put in specific terms. There were to be no interventions whatever while Mr Roosevelt was President. There were to be no interferences whatever in the internal affairs of the republics except in cases of clear necessity and through joint agreement with the other hemisphere powers.

There were no weasel words. Secretary Root had spoken seductively about helping weaker neighbors toward progress and prosperity, but there were no pledges implicit in his language against providing such assistance through the Marines. President Wilson had rejoiced in common ideals and "co-operative" friendships, but had said nothing against enforcing co-operation with his personal ideals and policies upon reluctant republics at the point of bayonet.

Moreover, Mr Roosevelt's declarations called for specific actions and restraints upon action. And what was called for followed. Within a few months after the President's Woodrow Wilson Foundation speech, the last Marines were withdrawn from Haiti. The offensive Platt Amendment convention guaranteeing intervention rights in Cuba was repealed. Instead of making the defaulted debts of the Latin republics an occasion for pressing them for further commitments and economic concessions, a practical moratorium was granted in Washington for the duration of the world depression. Instead of enlisting his diplomatic corps to serve as the advance agent for extensions of the American capital front in the republics, Mr Hull began the toilsome business of arranging reciprocal trade treaties.

Finally, the Roosevelt Good Neighbor declaration was magnificently timed. The fair words were not spoken because fear had driven Washington to sudden repentance. It was effectively timed precisely because, at the moment of pronouncement, World War loomed less than usual on the international horizons. Fairly manifestly, Mr Roosevelt spoke without military axes to grind. In that specific 1933 moment our rivals for both political and economic influence in the twenty republics were curiously impotent.

Great Britain, impoverished by her efforts to steer her unwieldy empire through the world depression, was having difficulties in holding on even to such of her Latin-American investments as were still paying profits. Incredible as it now seems, Germany was helpless. The depression, on top of her back-breaking World War indemnities, had paralyzed her industries, killed her credit, left her with neither the means to seek capital investments overseas nor the energy to seek customers. Still disarmed by the Versailles Treaty, the Reich, as a military menace to the Western Hemisphere, seemed scarcely more dangerous than Rumania.

Italy was negligible as an economic factor on the Latin-American scene, and her political troublemaking activities were as yet confined to the Mediterranean. Spain's then two-year-old new republic was running into economic foul weather and showing symptoms of grave, if not incurable, internal political tensions. For a good many decades, there were apparently sound reasons to believe, Spain's political and cultural influence over the daughter republics would be less than under the monarchy.

Patently, the Roosevelt administration had not made its concessions merely to win a temporary advantage over competitors. Even in their chronic suspicion of gringo gestures, the Latin-American statesmen and leaders of opinion could see that here positive action had been taken to heal old sores and for better "understanding's" sake.

So, for a few brief years, the newest Good Neighbor declaration ushered in the hemisphere's first and only international love feast.

☆   ☆   ☆

Through the sheer drama of its contrasts with what had gone before, the new Good Neighbor policy had an immense sentimental success. In Latin America's reactions, indeed, there was an emotional atmosphere not unlike that of a reconciliation between quarreling lovers. Not only must Uncle Sam be praised for his reformation and the beauties of character hitherto unrevealed in his international manners. All the harsh jibes that had been hurled for his sins and deficiencies must be made up for in tender endearments. Since the old gentleman was not the predacious and hypocritical ogre he was supposed to be, he must be hailed as a beloved fellow idealist.

For months the statesmen and newspapers and literary personages of the various republics vied with each other in paying the lately detested gringo handsome compliments. New salvos of applause broke out with each fresh action by which Washington's sincerity in the new role was certified.

When the Marines left Haiti, it meant the end of an old bad era. When the Platt Amendment was repealed, Latin America greeted it as the final Magna Charta of Western liberties. As the new reciprocal trade treaties were one by one achieved, their Latin beneficiaries exulted that, with co-operation and selflessness, suspicion and prejudice could be banished and all human blessings attained. On his journey to Buenos Aires for a special Pan-American Conference late in 1936, Mr Roosevelt—besides being publicly embraced in Brazil by President Vargas—was lyrically cheered as the moral folk hero of two continents.

The joy of the republics was greater, perhaps, than the mere rectification of a few specific grievances warranted. There were even elements of coquetry in it. The swelling—and, as we have seen, not strictly unfeminine—Latin-American ego was flattered that the great power of the North felt itself constrained at last to make its conduct and its manners pleasing to the "neighbors." Mingled with the practical satisfactions of receiving overdue justice was a distinct consciousness of racial triumph.

The epithet "sentimental" should not be applied to the new policy's results, however, in a belittling sense. These were important results in the sense that "sentiments" are often curiously determining factors even in the most hard-boiled of human negotiations. And "sentimental" is a word with considerably deeper meanings below the Rio Grande than in Chicago.

The "Roosevelt Doctrine," as some of the Latin publicists gratefully christened it, cleared the emotional atmosphere in the twenty republics. No longer was gringo baiting the most productive sport of the Latin-American practical politicians. Other and more practical politicians now could shush the "agitators" by mentioning that

—through their personal prowess, as they frequently insinuated— the gringo menace had been removed. As the totalitarian agents, too, got under way in the republics after 1934, they lacked the stock-in-trade of the World War generation of German propagandists—"Yanqui" military and political atrocities to be cited as motives for closer bonds between Latin America and the "antidemocratic" powers. All the more because the dangers from the Axis front were not apparent when it was initiated, the Good Neighbor policy scored an indispensable victory as a vast forestalling maneuver in the battle for Latin America's sentimental attachments.

This is saying, however, that the problem of Latin-American relations in the shadow of the *Blitzkrieg* has been smoothed rather than solved. To hold to our side the twenty republics continuously exposed to the economic seductions and military scare threats of Fascism, requires something more than fair promises, pleasant official compliments and the performance of a few of the elementary duties of neighborliness. The Good Neighbor record was excellent moral armor for Uncle Sam to wear under his coat to a Pan-American conference of September, 1939. For the tests of a sterner future it needs to be tighter and heavier.

To bind Latin Americans to us through the years of our trouble, there must not only be a good neighbor policy, but the people and leaders of the twenty republics must believe in it: find it both "good" and "neighborly." They will hardly trust their economic interests or even their defense to us on any other terms.

Washington's problem of winning—and keeping—friends for the hemisphere's critical period thus reduces itself to a paradox:

In the face of a situation painfully lacking in most of the facilities for neighborly contacts—how to implement neighborliness with reality?

☆   ☆   ☆

Both the obstacles and the need of implementing facilities can best be viewed from the Latin-American scene.

Gringo colonies in the republics, for instance, are wholly unconscious of serving as fifth columnists against Uncle Sam's defense program, yet most of them are perpetually in a surly state toward the whole idea of neighborliness.

The Latins, you are told, believe that we pulled our troops out of the Caribbean and abandoned intervention as a diplomatic method because we were afraid of them. In so far as we were moved by nobler motives than cowardice, they believe that we are trying to buy our way into their affections. So they propose to make the price as high as Uncle Sam's reputed status as a multibillionaire among nations will permit; and henceforth to conduct their "persecutions" of American business enterprise in the republics on the assumption that Washington will be too "yellow" to do anything about it.

It is a pity, the "colony" philosophers enlighten the visitor, that we ever abandoned force as the primary instrument of our Latin-American policies. Eventually we shall have to come back to it, with or without defense needs, because the advantages the Latins will take of "neighborliness" will drive us to it. When we *do* return to force, we shall look more than ever like double-crossing hypocrites to the Latin Americans, because Mr Roosevelt, in his folly, promised never again to use it.

Then your advisers on "practical" Latin-American relations proceed to ask you for the latest delicacy in the Roosevelt-family dirty-story saga, and are done with the subject.

The quite obvious effect of these tirades on Latin-American opinion—which by no means is unconscious of the vehemence behind them—is to spread abroad a rapidly growing impression that the United States as a whole does not "mean" the Good Neighbor policy; that it cannot be expected to outlast a war emergency or the presidency of Mr Roosevelt.

Nor does this discontent of the "colonists" with Washington's official attitude tend to sweeten the concord between gringo and Latin in the communities where the "colonies" are actually located. Since Uncle Sam will not support them with force, the more truculent of our "ambassadors of initiative" in the republics feel it essential in their dealings with Latin Americans to be a little more "forceful" than usual. Since Washington is officially practicing "neighborliness," the "colonies" may "keep face" for the "superior race" by drawing in their lines and being, if possible, less neighborly than before.

At the same time, the policy is almost equally handicapped by the fact that few Latin Americans have more than the shadowiest ideas of what a North American means by "neighborliness."

To be sure, "neighbor" translates literally and correctly into the Spanish word *vecino*. But *vecino* connotes a mere physical propinquity rather than the grocery and book-borrowing status and the back-fence psychological intimacies of the Smiths and Joneses on Maple Avenue.

In Latin America when people of more or less equal social and economic standing are *vecinos,* they live in their tight-walled, sidewalk-fronting houses about darkly secluded patios. For sugar-loaning and gossip-trading negotiations there are no front yards or back fences. The Herreras and the De la Torres bow to each other, undoubtedly, with an impeccable formality when they meet coming out of their fortresslike doorways. But, partly because of their concern for the proper seclusion of the Latin sacred family life, the formality is perhaps a little stiffer with *vecinos* than it is in the case of acquaintances who live at a safer distance. On the other hand, if families who happen to be closely allied through other connections dwell by coincidence in adjacent fortresses, Maple Avenue's subtle barriers to cloying intimacies are often so removed that the two households may be practically merged in a single impassioned family friendship.

In general, however, in numerous typical residential environments, Latin Americans are not inclined to think of their social and economic equals in terms of "neighborliness" at all. Actually there are often more human contacts between households when the *vecinos* belong to different social levels. The neighbors of Don Bartolomé Gutierrez y de la Vega, for example, are the lowly and impecunious Jesús Garcías. When a Gutierrez y de la Vega wants an errand run or a little extra help in the kitchen or with the laundry, a butler or someone in the permanent service establishment of the household steps to the side of the mansion nearest the Garcías' hovel and gives a series of handclaps or makes the same long, low sibilant "P-ssss!" sound with which Latin

Americans universally summon waiters. Enough Garcías of all ages come running to take care of any emergency.

In return for this, the Garcías are eligible to choice leftovers from the Gutierrez y de la Vega kitchen, serviceable cast-off clothing from the Gutierrez y de la Vega wardrobes, loafing privileges in the mansion doorway, siesta rights in the less decorous corners of the patio—and occasional slight but appreciated cash gratuities. In addition, Don Bartolomé Gutierrez y de la Vega's political influence is available when Garcías are in jail.

Loans (hardly expected to be repaid) and strengthening food snacks are at hand when unusual hardships, or severe sickness, come to the Garcías. There are certain to be gifts, both alcoholic and monetary, when new García babies are christened. In proportion as Don Bartolomé is generous in these matters, he is known to the Garcías—and to all their social circle—as *buen vecino,* or "good neighbor."

This is a familiar relationship throughout Latin America ("a palace with no poor at the door is no palace," runs an old Spanish proverb). And, although Latins may deny it with proper emotional fervor, it conditions—to a degree—the psychological response to Mr Roosevelt's Good Neighbor pronouncements. Uncle Sam is a fantastically rich neighbor. If he wishes to be the "good neighbor" also, let him fling his wealth around a good deal as would be expected of Don Bartolomé if there were a García christening every morning.

So the republics—and their leading citizens—simmer more or less constantly in expectation of immediate pragmatic benefits. All the "sales talks" I heard for further loans and extraordinary credit considerations were hitched one way or another to the Good Neighbor policy.

"But, señor," gentlemen in the confidence of a dozen or more governments put it to me, "neighborliness is a co-operative way of meeting each other's needs, is it not? It is through your wealth that you can meet our most vital needs most quickly. We can serve your needs best with our loyalty, with our support for your idealism in world affairs, with the trade which will be created by your wealth. . . . Or is it too much, señor, to say that we weaker nations can strengthen you simply through our gratitude?"

The greater our defense needs, the greater grow the importunities. None of the suggested favors, seemingly, are regarded as beyond the strong "good neighbor's" powers of arrangement. In countries with relatively huge debt defaults, I was showered with elaborate prescriptions for gigantic refunding operations—often coupled with admonitions that the "neighborly way" was to support the delinquencies of debtors until better times came.

"We have not wished to buy from these Germans," I was told in various intimate *causeries* on trade problems. "You are our real friends, and we like your products better. . . . Ah, señor, it would be such an easy thing for a rich nation like the United States to reduce the price on your exports to us so that we would not have to sell our crops for those detestable Aski-marks."

But when I suggested the practical difficulties of putting costly export subsidy programs through a somewhat "home-front"-minded Congress, they were sorrowfully incredulous. "Surely if the true situation down here were explained," they would shake their heads, "your congressmen would realize that trade ties can be built up only by consistent practical measures."

Furthermore, when pragmatic benefits are not fairly promptly forthcoming, the republics are hurt. The Argentines cannot understand how nearly three years have gone by without a suggestion of action in Congress since President Roosevelt came to Buenos Aires and publicly pledged a speedy repeal of sanitary restrictions excluding Argentine beef from U.S. markets on the grounds of remotely possible contamination with foot-and-mouth disease. Explanations of the difficulties which confront Mr Roosevelt, in the response of our foremost "cow state" lawmakers to agreeable international gestures, leave Latin America's "deep Southerners" cold.

The net effect has been to render the statesmen of many republics highly skeptical of whether Mr Roosevelt or his successor can really jam through our undisciplined Congress ambitious cartel plans for hemisphere economic protection.

A somewhat similar attitude is to be found in Brazil concerning

President Vargas' widely popular prescription for having the United States raise the price of coffee. When I explained that statutory prices for coffee would be doubtfully constitutional, my Brazilian friends waved such mere technical objections aside.

"But this is an emergency," they argued—"an emergency for you as well as for ourselves. A difference of two cents a pound in the price of coffee would mean the difference between a Brazil which cannot pay its debts today and a Brazil which could buy as many of your products as Canada or Great Britain. Surely you cannot say that you have not practiced price control to meet your domestic emergencies. Look at your NRA and your agricultural stabilization measures. Look at your war regulations."

And the little Central American republics murmured, before the war, about armaments: "Why can you not trade us guns for our coffee the same as Italy does? Surely you have better reasons for seeing that our armies are supplied than Il Duce has."

Again, there is a widespread impression that "good neighborliness" implies a large tolerance even for programs hampering or definitely injurious to North American interests. Reasonable and unreasonable alike, all the petty red-tape restrictions on the operations of United States trade and industry within the republics, all the nationalistic statutes governing the choice of personnel in technical and executive posts, are defended against gringo protests on the ground that the United States no longer desires a "selfish" solution of the problems even of internal management of business.

Indeed, in an inverted sense, the nearest neighbor of all has adopted the Good Neighbor policy almost as a banner in her resistance to settlement processes in the oil-expropriations controversy. The mere fact that the policy was protested and compensation to the oil companies asked at all was cited by Mexico at the outset of the dispute as a serious breach in our new Latin-American ethic. Each subsequent downward adjustment of Washington's artificial silver prices has been hailed as further proof of Uncle Sam's incurable hypocrisy.

In the summer of 1939, when Undersecretary of State Welles made a somewhat peremptory demand that a compromise settlement of the oil companies' claims be worked out, his attitude was advertised in the pro-government press of Mexico City as indicating that the Good Neighbor policy has been abandoned and traditional coercive methods toward Latin America resumed.

Mexico, not impossibly, is developing a technique for getting what she wants under the Good Neighbor policy with which—in our more deep-seated disagreements with Latin-American powers—diplomats long after Mr Welles and defense emergencies may still have to cope: the technique of standing on the borders and shouting, "We dare you to go back on it!"

☆   ☆   ☆

Over all such psychological barriers to understanding, in peace or war, stands the sheer physical obstacle of distance. However desperate the need, it is hard for us to get on practical speaking terms with the people in the rest of the hemisphere because of the difficulties—and costs—of ever meeting each other.

Virtually all Latin America below Panama is farther away from the major United States ports than western Europe. The deep-south metropolises, Buenos Aires, Montevideo, Valparaiso, Santiago, are farther than Moscow. For sea voyages to these remote places two to three weeks must be allowed both going and coming. So an ocean voyage to South America which allows any time for contacts with the people at all must last three months or more.

The Pan American Airways, to be sure, takes you to Buenos Aires or Santiago in less than five days. But necessarily neither its fare tariffs nor those of the steamship lines can be accommodated to the type of casual trippers who "do Europe" every non-war summer on a few hundred dollars. Sailing and flying distances of more than five thousand miles inevitably "run into money," and the cost element drives away the volume of tourist traffic which might otherwise make moderate fare reductions possible.

For Latin Americans traveling north, such problems are further complicated by currency-exchange difficulties. Guatemalan, Cuban, Venezuelan and Dominican currencies are usually close to par with the dollar, but even in these republics income levels of average American middle-class travelers are approached only by the economic aristocracy. Visitors from the less favored republics find their funds melting away with each pocketful of dimes bought at North American exchange rates.

For instance, one night in Quito, in Ecuador's most pretentious night club, I cocktailed, wined, dined and liqueured four guests more or less lavishly at a total cost, including tips, of not quite five American dollars. An Ecuadorean entertaining four friends on a similar scale in New York would find his bill running well over a thousand *sucres*. If it is discouragingly expensive for most North Americans to travel in Latin America, it is prohibitive for all but the wealthiest Latins to come to the United States at all. In Europe in peace years exchange rates are easier and living costs cheaper.

Besides these obstacles are those of transport facilities. Below Panama, Latin America in normal times is literally on more neighborly terms with Europe than with the United States because shipping lanes run that way. It is largely a question of cargoes. South America's bulk products—grains, cotton, lumber, meats, livestock, nitrates, sugar—go chiefly to Europe. Frequent sailings and low passenger rates follow the bulky cargoes. So, while in Buenos Aires or Rio de Janeiro you could get boats several times a week with passable accommodations leaving for Europe, you had to wait anywhere from one to two weeks to pick up a vessel for New York.

Add to these serious—and not easily remedied—intercommunication difficulties the fact that there are less than one hundred thousand Americans living in all of the twenty republics; that, apart from Cubans and Mexicans largely in the unskilled labor groups, hardly more than fifty thousand Latin Americans are living in the United States.

In all of these aspects the Good Neighbor policy takes off from a fallacy—the fallacy that neighborly conditions are already established. A good many changes in the travel habits of the hemisphere need to be made and a good many barriers to travel removed before, with most of the peoples of our land mass, we can get even on a footing of bare acquaintance.

"We have heard rather vaguely that you are a virtuous people of amazing abilities," a Colombian acquaintance once put it. "But we neither know what you like to laugh at nor the things that make you angry. We neither know your tastes in cooking nor what you consider scandalous. Until we have a little further information on these fundamentals, is it not a little daring for either to offer ourselves to the other in utterly confiding friendship?"

☆   ☆   ☆

So the "good neighbor" relationship comes down to something immensely more complicated than the simple preachment that twenty-one republics may cleave to each other in the same friendly bonds that unite the Smiths and the Joneses on Maple Avenue. They might, if they tried with angelic persistence and had an Aristotelian millennium in which to work out the necessary adjustments. But meanwhile, against an almost continuous storm of disappointments, misunderstandings and exacerbations of sensitive points, they must work at it. Especially, as father and wet nurse of the "neighborliness" project and the hemisphere's chief exemplar of the Maple Avenue type of neighborliness, Uncle Sam must work at it.

And none of the work is easy.

The simplest obstacle to overcome is, no doubt, the distance hazard. Subsidize the Latin-American steamship and air lines to make travel cheaper, say the ready prescriptioneers. Devise a "tourist dollar"—with U.S. Treasury support—to ease the Latin's exchange tragedies.

All this might be arranged under the proposed 1940 cartel system, but would a Congress support it, when each member knows what opponents will say if he spends Uncle Sam's money on anything but the direct needs of the home-front population and new Federal buildings in Oshkosh?

And if increased travel back and forth between the republics were fostered, would the immediate effects be altogether happy? Latin America is full of prominent citizens—including not a few ruling statesmen—whose antipathies to the United States date back to occasions during their visits when they were mistaken for South European immigrants, or made to feel—often without biological warrant—the pressure of our exquisite color-line discriminations. Or to student days when the glamorous "fraternity row" of some freshwater university cheerily ostracized them as "greasers."

Again, it would be possible to organize Federal travelers' and students' aid services in gringo-land, to welcome each Latin-American tourist and visiting scholar at his landing port and guarantee him a reasonably good time free from unnecessary insults and painful experiences. But would "good times" be possible to travelers of swarthy aspect until we learned, as a people, to modify our attitude of complacent indifference to foreigners "unassimilated" to our conventions and to divest ourselves of our cherished race prejudices?

Thus, even such fantastically idealistic solutions of the mere physical problems of neighborly visiting present other and equally baffling problems of practical relations, equally rooted in the realities of different values and manners.

Nor would more and cheaper intrahemisphere travel necessarily increase affection for us among the Latin Americans who stayed at home. A row of "Sloppy Joes" from Tampico to Valparaiso, full of close-harmonizing male and female good-will apostles, might benefit the local beverage trade each time the biweekly boat came in from the North, but would scarcely draw "the neighbors" closer together in cultural or political sympathies. A few more delicately unofficial international "incidents" such as the occasion in the mid-1920s when a delegation of American businessmen, out of healthy animal spirits, wrecked the premises of the Buenos Aires Jockey Club, might cause more doors to be closed against us in Latin America than if we stayed at home. The Jockey Club has not been open to visiting firemen in mob formation since.

Neither are the omens altogether propitious when we consider the gringo "colonies," south, as channels for neighborly approaches. In a sense, perhaps, I have been unfair to the "colonies." In nearly every one of the expatriate settlements you find a handful—sometimes several dozens—of individuals who make it a practice to mingle in the cultural and social life of the Latin community, to cultivate its manners, abide by its conventions and win its friendship. There was even one United States oil corporation with considerable holdings in Mexico which managed to live up to the labor codes of the republic with so much tact and cooperative spirit that its properties have not yet been expropriated.

In this field, then, could not North American business, or at least the larger corporations dominant in the Latin field, pick men for these curious gifts of adaptation rather than simply on their "go-getting" prognoses?

Yet this facile remedy, too, is unfortunately shot through with dismal perplexities. For the average representative of American business in Latin America is inevitably—owing to the psychological structure of executive establishments—picked by a captain of industry who has little more native capacity to recognize adaptability in promising young salesmen or branch managers than to decide the points of *odium theologicum* in a Holy Roller heresy trial. It was, after all, on the pay roll of a corporation with a vast foreign-service organization and an elaborate "personnel check" system for selecting its foreign representatives that I found the gentleman who had never permitted a Latin American to cross his door after someone defiled the wallpaper at his debut party. The more gringo penetration is spurred by defense and cartel activities, the more his tribe is likely to increase.

Moreover, if all the personnel-picking processes of gringo business could be imagined as revolutionized, the new consignments of "adaptable" neophytes would still have to run the gauntlet of the old "all-colony" ban on "that sort of nonsense." For, with few exceptions, the ruling elements in the "colonies" are united in an unconscious conspiracy to brand "adaptation" as almost as dirty a word as Nazism.

"When you've been here as long as I have," the "old Latin-America hands" instruct newcomers suspected of undue fraternizing tendencies, "you'll find that these people will respect you more if you stick to your own ways and keep your distance." . . . "When you've been here as long as I have . . ." is, in fact, the usual beginning and ending of each "colony's" wisdom. More or less naturally, in young men whose standing in the "colonies"—to say nothing, often, of their chances of promotion and pay—depends for several years on "yessing" such social philosophers, the adaptive impulse tends to wither.

To check the "colonies'" habit of offending Latin sensitiveness, however, gringo business needs to revise the basic concept of its stakes in the twenty republics. There would be less talk about the merits of "force" and the benefits of "taking over" sovereign nations, for profits and our safety's sake, if our "economic ambassadors" were commissioned to build up purchasing power in the republics rather than to exploit them for cheap labor costs and quick dividends. Young men sent south to "grow up with the country" and carve out careers for themselves as experts in Latin business psychology, rather than to compete with each other for monthly sales and production records, might find that adopting an aloof and superior air with the "natives" rated, as a business device, a little below not paying poker debts.

Fundamentally, in fact, the problem of the winsomeness of gringo business as the agent of better intrahemisphere relationships reduces itself to a question of long-pull practicality. Will business see that its stake in the republics is in a permanent, and necessarily subordinate, partnership in the development of their resources? Or will it continue to act on the "theory" that the function of an entrepreneur in his foreign adventures is to milk cows dry and let "the natives" live on the carcasses?

On the answer to this question depends not only a great deal that is pertinent to the future of friendly official relations with Latin America but the future of our legitimate business holdings in Latin America and our chances of having neighbors and friends on our side in world crises instead of good haters in league with our enemies.

☆   ☆   ☆

In the field of government policies there are equally subtle adjustments to be made when, and if,. there is time. The Latin republics will hardly be bound to us in an enduring friendship by the Good Neighbor policy's sentimental and economic charms alone.

No matter what perils of invasion or military emergency they may not safely be forced into a permanent system of hemisphere alliances, formal or implied, in which Uncle Sam is to be rider and they the horses.

In general, the Good Neighbor policy needs to be transformed from a verbal declaration of amiable intentions into a consistent practice of concrete mutual helpfulness. In almost every conceivable direction it needs to be implemented with specific realities which will make it clear to the republics that the stronger neighbor prefers co-operation to coercion, cherishes their advantages, economic, social and military, along with his own.

Thus, the sooner the better, machinery should be set up for the arbitration of all disputes between the republics, including especially disputes of the United States with the Latin republics. New definitions should be written into our treaty relations and our diplomatic practices, both of the rights of investment capital in Latin-American territory and of the obligations of exploiting capital to share its earnings with the peoples from whose land its profits are taken.

New principles may have to be inserted into the international law of the hemisphere, both of the rights of nations to full economic sovereignty over their possessions, and of limitations of the rights of private ownership. Nor are these readjustments to be simply attained. For each separate revision faces baffling difficulties in the highly diverse social needs and political systems of the republics. The perfect "oil policy" for Colombia may by no means turn out to be the satisfactory "banana policy" for Honduras or an adequate form chart of the rights and privileges of foreign banking corporations in Brazil.

Yet "neighborliness" in its economic phase must go even further. It must find practical ways of spreading the wealth won by gringo exploitations among the republics; must assist in raising wage levels and living standards, in maintaining the solvency and the service efficiency of the Latin governments—or cease to be accepted as "neighborly." For "neighborliness" used as a cloak for further imperialism, or dollar diplomacy disguised as a lightning-rod against Blitzkrieg, will not take in the chronic Latin suspicion of all gringo enterprises for one superfluous second.

Neither is it possible to build successful neighborly relations, either on a street or in a hemisphere, without learning first what the neighbors "are like," in their incompatibilities and differences as well as in our points of congeniality and resemblance.

It is true that long exposure to the Latin-American scene is necessary to the building up of this knowledge in an authoritative form. The public schools and the universities of the United States could hardly be expected to turn out future generations of graduates who were pundits in Latin-American history and literature, experts in Latin-American economics and qualified psychoanalysts of the Latin-American temperament.

Here, perhaps, we can trust something to the new curiosity concerning the neighbors which the hemisphere's peril has awakened. Schools may go further from now on because of the emergency, toward dispersing the dense clouds of ignorance with which United States public opinion has faced its "Latin-American problem" so far. Latin-American history can be taught in our high schools and universities as comprehensively and realistically as Western European history is taught. The several million Americans studying Spanish in the secondary schools and colleges can read the classics—and some of the vernacular prose—of Latin-American literature rather than concentrating on the more exotic masterpieces and literary backgrounds of authentic Castilian.

Shocking as this procedure might be to certain pedagogues who discover preciously superior cultural values and glamorous pedantry in Castilian literary forms and accent, it would have the advantage of offering our students an acquaintance with the only Spanish diction which most of them practically need.

More quickly than might be supposed, these innovations in instruction might sweep away the widespread notions that Latin Americans are either democratic and "republican" peoples like ourselves, or armies of chronically revolutionary bandits. More effectively perhaps than any other immediately practicable procedure, there could be built up by these means a sector of reasonably informed public opinion in the United States on which intelligent Latin-American policy makers and permanent alliance seekers in Washington might depend.

Prescribing, however, is one of the wishful arts, and none of these remedies can be made effective simply by mentioning it. Both our university and our secondary education are organized on the theory that only United States and European history, only North American and European cultural and economic problems, are of "practical" importance to the student; that courses dealing with Latin America cannot possibly have an appeal except to groups of esthetically exotic or highly specialized interests. The emotional effects of asking a city school board or a university faculty's committee on curriculum to put Latin-American history on an equality with English and Western European history are not difficult to imagine.

Most pedagogical circles, in fact, can be thrown into acute melancholia by merely suggesting that Spanish be taught without the authentic Castilian accent. In at least one case at the University of Minnesota a distinguished South American scholar felt constrained to resign his position in the Spanish faculty because his accent was criticized. It was a good deal as if an exchange professor from Minnesota were forced out of the Sorbonne for not knowing how to pronounce the Oxford "haw!"

A vast inertia must be overcome, in other words, before the twenty-one republics can even begin making each other's cultural acquaintance. Thus, even if a program to push Latin-American studies in secondary and university education could be agreed upon, it would take several cycles of Ph.D. output to train the teachers needed in the larger field of effort. And it is a suggestive corollary to the educational situation that all of the twenty-seven Latin-American literary works translated in the United States within the past few years, including novels, have been commercial losses to the publishers.

Nor is the inertia wholly on the gringos' side. For Latin Americans not a single standard one-volume work on United States history is available in either Spanish or Portuguese. In the Brazilian intellectual center of São Paulo when a survey was made early in

1939, just ten works on United States history—all of them in English—were found in a search of the state, municipal and university libraries.

Gringo general literature, to be sure, goes somewhat better in the twenty republics than the twenty-seven Latin-American classics fared in the North. Indeed, a few of the novels highly critical of the United States scene during the 1920s were moderately popular. But here again neighborly enterprise is confronted by a distressing combination of distribution obstacles. Books published at normal New York prices of from two dollars up are not only beyond range of the average Latin-American intellectual's pocketbook, but far more expensive than the paper-backed volumes he is accustomed to buying from the European or the Chilean or Buenos Aires presses. Worse still, for distribution purposes, New York publishes only in English. Yet North American authors in general discourage the translation of their works into Spanish for the Latin-American trade because until recently the publishers below the Rio Grande have snapped their fingers at international copyright conventions and paid no royalties. As late as the summer of 1939, in fact, an inter-American cultural congress in Montevideo declined to recommend the adoption of international copyright laws by the southern republics on the ground that the expense of paying royalties would hamper "the diffusion of culture" in the poorer nations.

Thus the mere matter of a meeting of minds between the republics runs up against barriers akin to those imposed upon international trade by a network of tariff walls.

In result, many of the efforts at cultural approach between Latin and Anglo-Saxon Americans necessarily are marked by a somewhat self-conscious synthetic quality. In Lima, Buenos Aires, São Paulo, Rio de Janeiro and half a dozen slightly smaller centers, little Inter-American Cultural Institutes struggle effectively but on insufficient funds to bring about exchanges of art exhibits, books, ideas, educational motion pictures and lecturers. In Washington the newly created Division of Cultural Relations in the State Department has drafted an ambitious but commendably realistic program for serving as a clearinghouse for almost the entire range of cultural-contact problems.

Yet, where the Germans and Italians have spent and in spite of the war are still spending millions on Latin-American propaganda, the Cultural Relations Division's initial budget request for actual field work in the republics was only $66,000. Congress is inclined to spend more money keeping Argentine beef out of Chicago than getting American ideas into Buenos Aires.

In fields where a certain degree of cultural contact is already normally established, the outlook is somewhat more promising. United States news reporting in Latin America has been improving since the 1914 World War both in volume and competence. The special correspondence services maintained by the leading Latin-American journals—notably those of Bogotá, Buenos Aires and Santiago—from the United States are far more objective and less biased than in the pre-"good neighbor" era.

Spurred on by the threat of government competition, the United States radio interests in 1938 conducted an interesting, if superficial, survey under the direction of Mr Linton Wells on the kind of news and entertainment programs the Latin Americans want from the northern neighbor's broadcasting stations.

The longer the war goes on, the greater the need becomes for revising our studies of Latin America's radio as well as movie responsiveness with our best psychological acumen. More effectively, perhaps, than any other agency, Hollywood has it in its power to create a vogue for the Latin-American scene in the United States. The recent success of the film *Juarez* in the republics went a long way to impress Latin Americans with a new consciousness of North America's appreciation of the best in their record.

Yet all these enterprises require, along with infinite tact and understanding, almost infinite bank accounts. True cultural *rapprochement,* Mr Hubert Herring felt forced to declare, after a survey of the physical and psychological difficulties of neighborly intercourse, in the September 1939 *Harper's,* needs a Cecil Rhodes. But even with a dozen Rhodes-sized fortunes and foundations to help us steep ourselves in each other's literatures and cultural backgrounds, even with the military perils of a narrow world to drive us toward understanding, certain temperamental discords, raw and basic, would still remain.

For any rational survey of the "hemisphere problem" is, in fact, and inevitably, largely a survey of obstacles. Because the obstacles must be faced—and overcome—before we can get anywhere toward solutions, or perhaps even toward saving ourselves, some portions of this book may have made, at any rate for wishful thinkers, "prescriptioneers" and "simplificationists," somewhat dreary reading. When critical integrity is applied, so many of the remedies of the "prescriptioneers" ooze away, to the communal sorrow, out of smashed bottles.

All this is a police complaint, however, against easy-minded and simple and too lighthearted solutions rather than against solutions *per se*. Possibly it makes sense to consider broad solutions from a more hopeful angle. Unless international power-age society itself is too complex for the human intellect to handle, Latin-American relations are not too complex for *us* to handle.

Indeed, we can find a partial analogy for the solution of a "difficult relations" problem in the long and complicated process by which the peace of friendship, rather than the mere technical peace of the cessation of battles, was made between North and South in the United States after the Civil War. The "simplificationists" and the "prescriptioneers" were early in the field. Force the races on an equal footing, shouted the "prescriptioneers" from the North, and all will be well. Terrorize the Negroes with the Ku Klux Klan and horsewhips, urged the ex-Confederate "simplificationists," and the future will be almost as romantically glamorous as the past.

Yet both their houses merely contributed to two generations of acrimony and misunderstanding. Peace came at last when economic ties had grown up between two once quarreling sections—ties so lithe, so vital, so matter-of-course that they seemed more important and more real than differences of opinion about the status of races or old, warmed-over rancors. Peace came as the warring generation, gingerly itself, and less gingerly, the second and third and fourth generations, discovered that they could laugh a little together at the violence of their own prejudices: a laughter which said, inferentially at least, that the humor we share is more alive and better worth living for than ancient romantic animosities.

Something like these bonds of mutual economic advantage and mutual understanding of each other's inner minds and psychic inheritances can yet—given time, good will and self-knowledge on both sides—unite the Americas. Certain programs, for instance, are now being "thought towards" in certain strategic departments of the Washington government: plans for repatriating Latin America's hundreds of millions of capital investments in foreign securities and for enlisting that capital in an "even break," not a "conquistadores'" and "semi-colonials'" partnership in the development of such Latin-American resources as our markets could buy. If such programs can be put into effect through the Roosevelt Administration's enormous cartel program or otherwise, and become matters of course in our relations with all the republics, a kind of economic life conceivably might spring up within the hemisphere like that which has united North and South within our own republic. If our cultural interchanges would deal less with the "masterpieces" of our separate arts and literatures and place more emphasis on informing us, as neighbors to neighbors, what we find human and endearing and even ridiculous in ourselves, we should doubtless make more progress toward the not impossible delights of understanding intimacy.

But these things cannot be set down in organization charts and graphs of progress any more than human courtships can be mapped in advance by cartographers. These greater aims of the human spirit—like all casually and cheerfully magnificent objectives—must be felt for as friends explore each other's minds and dispositions for wider reaches into the gaiety and beauty, the utility and the sheer liveliness of life. They alone are worth defending life for—and hemispheres.

☆   ☆   ☆

So this book leaves immediate prescriptions for action in the hemisphere's emergency to those who must act upon the basis of each day's barbarically earth-shaking news. It offers no final answers; for final answers are inevitably simplifications, and about Latin America nothing is simple whatever.

A concert of friendly nations can be built up in the Western Hemisphere only by reconciling the incompatibilities of races differentiated in values, in customs, in their ways of looking at life by almost every factor of economic circumstance and of historic and racial inheritance.

The war calls on us for certain deeds and decisions of immediate practicality—chiefly actions holding the prospect of a better life together and a better friendship. The creation of this larger Western World after we have saved ourselves is a task for time and the patient testing of methods by trial and error. But in a profoundly pragmatic sense there are no acceptable alternatives. In a world of risingly ferocious acquisitive forces, we must either enslave Latin America or see others enslave it; or preserve its freedom with ours by winning its immeasurably difficult friendship.

We shall be lucky if there is time to achieve this either in peace or in war, and under an economic organization of society that is recognizable to us. We shall be luckier still if we find the brains and the sympathies to achieve it in all the time there is.

INDEX

Aguirre Cerda, Pedro, President of Chile, 196, 249–250

Air lines, 13, 87, 291, 324; German, 252, 291

Alessandri, Arturo, 195, 196

Almazan, Juan, 177

American "colonies" in Latin America, 60, 81, 230, 268–73, 286, 318–19, 327, 328, 329

Annexation, 7, 130, 132, 159

Anti-Americanism, its expression in Latin America, 263–67

Aprista movement, 207, 285

Aranha, Oswaldo, 191, 248

Araucanians, 156, 200

Arbitration of disputes, 330

Arce, Manuel José, 164

Architecture, 35, 63, 69–70, 269

Argentina, 9, 21, 24, 25, 39, 53, 56, 58, 92, 95, 122, 127, 157, 159, 162, 163, 166, 200, 221, 293–294; at the Lima Conference, 123–25; despotism in, 182; democracy in, 193, 194; and the first World War, 7, 266; defenses of, 277; U.S. military aviation mission to, 280–81, 289

Armies, in Latin America, 114–16, 240, 253, 289; standing armies and reserves, 277

Art, 68, 72

Artigas, Ismael Enrique, 133

Aski-marks, 10, 240, 245, 246, 322

Atheism, 10, 217, 241, 250

Audiencias, 163

Baldomir, Alfredo, President of Uruguay, 195

Bananas, 14, 16, 218

Banks, 221; U.S. branch banks, 268

Barley, 20

Barrios, Rufino J., 71, 165, 183

Barter, export-import system, 10, 61, 240, 245, 246, 290

Batista, Col. Fulgencio, 178, 203

Beals, Carleton, 3, 4

Beans, 18

Beef, 122, 123

Benavides, Oscar, General, 187, 188

Blanco-Fombona, Rufino, 264–65

Blitzkrieg, 2, 26, 254, 318, 331

Bogotá, 19, 20, 33, 69, 73

Bolívar, Simón, 38, 70, 71, 158, 161

Bolivia, 155, 157, 158, 159, 161, 167, 168, 169, 179, 188–89, 235, 293

Brandão, Pimentel, 191

Brazil, 7, 16, 22, 25, 26, 38, 41, 59, 116, 127, 157, 159, 160, 166, 167; dictatorship in, 189–92; "corporative constitution," 190–91, 248; Italians in, 190, 242; Germans in, 241–42; Spaniards in, 242; Fascist activities in, 248–49; defenses of, 277

Buenos Aires, 24, 29, 34, 39, 69, 73, 162, 163, 322

Bull fights, 80

Bungé, Alejandro E., 221

Bureaucracy, 36, 39, 40, 143, 145, 146, 147, 150, 191

Busch, Germán, 188, 189, 235, 242

Cabrera, Estrada, 183

Cali, 19, 33

Calles, Plutarco Elías, 174

Calvo doctrine, 284

Camacho, Manuel Avila, 177

Canal Zone, 10–11, 132

Cano, Sanín, 54

Cantilo, Dr José Maria, 123, 294

Cárdenas, Lázaro, President of Mexico, 146, 174, 175, 176, 177, 212, 249, 293

Carias Andino, Tiburcio, President of Honduras, 180, 181

[339]

INDEX

Carranza, Venustiano, 135, 136, 144, 203

Carrera, Rafael, 165, 183

Cartel system, 10–11, 211, 322, 326, 328, 336

Castro, Cipriano, 183

Cattle, 22, 53, 56, 218

Caudillos, 40, 71, 131, 179

Caxias, Duque de, 71

Censorship, 178, 184, 188, 190, 191, 260

Central America, 156, 157, 158, 159, 161, 163, 165, 167

Central American Court of Justice, 165

Central American Union Treaty of 1907, 130

Chaco war, 167, 168

Chase, Stuart, 60

Chile, 20, 21, 39, 41, 92, 156, 157, 166, 167, 193, 200, 201, 236, 249, 296; democracy in, 195–96; and the first World War, 7, 266; defenses of, 277

Church, *see* Roman Catholic Church

Civil liberties, 190

Civil War, U.S., adjustments after, 335

Coca, 154

Cochineal, 48

Cocoa, 20, 53, 59

Coffee, 14, 22, 53, 59, 218, 222

Colombia, 15, 19–20, 34, 80, 81, 87, 92, 114, 131, 132, 157, 159, 167, 193, 201, 237, 250; democracy in, 197; and the first World War, 266–67

Colonial economy, 47–8, 50

Colonial period, in Latin America, 26, 29, 32–9, 46, 47, 50, 51, 156, 161; in United States, 28, 31, 35, 45

Color-line status, 300

"Colossus of the North," 159, 265

Communism, 178, 184, 185, 190

Concessions, economic, 236, 291, 293

Conservatism, 194, 197

Contract obligations with Latin-American governments, 283, 285

Coolidge, Calvin, 311

Copper, 55, 59, 195, 236

Corn, 17, 18, 22, 218

Costa Rica, 14, 92, 114, 156, 158, 164, 193, 236; democracy in, 197–98, 200

Cotton, 16, 19, 59, 218

Courts, 113, 175, 176, 190

Credit, 221, 224

Cuba, 71, 91, 158; dictatorship in, 178–79; intervention by United States in, 202; military governorship of, 256, 259

Cultural relations, 8, 211, 294–95, 331–34, 336

Cultural Relations Division of U.S. State Department, 333–34

Culture, Latin-American, 64–78

Currencies, 221, 224, 324

Custom, sacredness of, 93–4

Darío, Rubén, 70, 264

Debts, 8, 192; to United States, 237

Democracy, 42, 193–212

Deserts, 20

Despotism, 38, 39, 42, 182, 184, 185, 187, 188, 198

Diaz, Porfirio, 41, 42, 182, 258

Dictators, 8, 38, 39, 40, 42, 71, 161, 162, 163, 166, 169, 170–92, 193, 202, 204, 205, 208–11, 300, 301

Diplomatic asylum, 299

"Dollar diplomacy," 129, 135, 211, 229, 310

Dominican Republic, 157, 158, 159; despotism in, 188; Marines in, 260

Drago doctrine, 284

Dreiser, Theodore, 76

Economic advisers in Central America, 261

Economic co-operation, 9, 10, 211, 330, 336

Economic penetration, foreign, 8, 54–55, 57, 61, 218–24, 231; resistance to, 232–36, 282–87

Economic penetration, U.S., 267–68, 273, 307–8

Ecuador, 20, 21, 24, 63–4, 72, 137, 157, 158, 161, 166, 167, 179, 180, 183, 236, 290

Education, 296, 331

Ejidos, 146, 147, 149

Elections, 43, 92, 175, 179, 187, 189, 194, 195, 196, 197, 199, 202, 203, 260

El Salvador, 14, 104, 152, 164, 165, 237, 261, 266; despotism in, 187

Enriquez, Alberto, 236

Espionage, Fascist, 252

INDEX

INDEX

INDEX

INDEX